THE
TABLETS
of LIGHT

"Danielle's inspired scribing and deep personal relationship with the ascended master Thoth allow for the emergence of ancient wisdom for modern times to assist humanity in activating the hidden keys of quantum consciousness. The true key is to remember unity consciousness at all times and for each of us to begin to develop our own direct connection to this great master of multidimensional consciousness and the Councils of Light."

LINDA STAR WOLF, PH.D., AUTHOR OF *SHAMANIC BREATHWORK* AND COAUTHOR OF *SHAMANIC MYSTERIES OF EGYPT*

"Danielle's capacity to bring the transmission of Thoth to enliven consciousness and awaken oracular vision is profound. The increase in vibration you'll receive reading this book activates a new level of soul purpose and a deeper level of unity consciousness within."

LISA MICHAELS, AUTHOR OF *NATURAL RHYTHMS*

"This book will raise your vibration just by reading it! It's filled with specific exercises to awaken the universal Divine design codes and to apply the wisdom of Thoth, in order to create in unity consciousness instead of from the energies of separation."

EUGENIA OGANOVA, AUTHOR OF *THE SECRET OF SEKHMET*, *AWAKENING THE HARMONY WITHIN*, AND *MISSION ALPHA*

"Danielle Rama Hoffman has done it again! *The Tablets of Light* is a crystal clear transmission that outshines the many titles covering a similar theme. Why? Because it is evident that she is truly scribing this wisdom. It's dripping with truths that soothe, inspire, activate, and heal. Thank you, Danielle, for continuing the journey with us."

"Danielle has put on paper a hypnotic and rhythmic message that can open and advance each reader. Anyone seeking life's fulfillment and enlightenment can throw themselves wholeheartedly into the flow of this river and allow themselves to become this river, experiencing its entirety—from source to wherever it is meant to take you."

"Danielle Hoffman's new book is inspirational. It is a potent source of wisdom that encourages us to wake up to our true identity. If also offers sustenance as we choose to live from our true authentic divine self and live out of our own divine design. I love this book!"

THE
TABLETS
of LIGHT

The Teachings of Thoth
on Unity Consciousness

DANIELLE RAMA HOFFMAN

Bear & Company
Rochester, Vermont • Toronto, Canada

Bear & Company
One Park Street
Rochester, Vermont 05767
www.BearandCompanyBooks.com

Bear & Company is a division of Inner Traditions International

Library of Congress Cataloging-in-Publication Data

Names: Hoffman, Danielle Rama, author.
Title: The tablets of light : the teachings of Thoth on unity consciousness /
    Danielle Rama Hoffman.
Description: Rochester, VT : Bear & Company, 2017. | Includes index.
Identifiers: LCCN 2016041982 (print) | LCCN 2016056051 (e-book) |
    ISBN 9781591432814 (pbk.) | ISBN 9781591432821 (e-book)
Subjects: LCSH: Thoth (Egyptian deity) | Consciousness—Miscellanea. |
    Spirituality. | Energy medicine.
Classification: LCC BL2450.T5 H64 2017 (print) | LCC BL2450.T5 (e-book) |
    DDC 299/.31—dc23
LC record available at https://lccn.loc.gov/2016041982

Printed and bound in the United States

10 9 8 7 6 5 4 3 2

Text design by Virginia Scott Bowman and layout by Priscilla Baker
This book was typeset in Garamond Premier Pro with Jenson, Bodoni, Helvetica
Neue, Gill Sans, and Legacy Sans used as display typefaces

Cover images courtesy of iStock

To send correspondence to the author of this book, mail a first-class letter to the
author c/o Inner Traditions • Bear & Company, One Park Street, Rochester, VT
05767, and we will forward the communication, or contact the author directly at
www.divinetransmissions.com.

To Thoth

Contents

PART ONE
The Divine Awakened
*Your Evolution into Unity Consciousness
Resides Within*

Acknowledgments

This wave of appreciation, acknowledgment, and thanksgiving is an ode to Source: the Source consciousness that resides within me, within you, and within all that are named and not named below. This scribed text has been brought into form direct with Source to Source with a plethora of midwives along the way. For that co-creation I am eternally grateful.

Each week, my beloved husband, Friedemann, and I have an appreciation dinner where we appreciate all that we've experienced during that week. This tradition is one that we savor and hold in high esteem, for it acknowledges our accomplishments and blessings, and expands the energy of appreciation into a contagious tidal wave, which we complete with a high five and a scrumptious meal. This practice opens our hearts and supports us in integrating and anchoring all that has occurred. It is my wish that these acknowledgments do the same for you if you choose.

To you the reader, I extend great gratitude for your asking and calling this consciousness into being and for your devotion to your journey in the evolution in consciousness. I am inspired by you daily. Thank you scribes, and all of you who have journeyed to France with me (in these bodies or previous light bodies), for bringing the keys, codes, and access points for me to unpack these tablets. A heartfelt thanks and oodles of appreciation to all those that have participated in Divine Transmissions offerings and all those to come. It is a joy to partner and co-create with you and to support you in bringing your Divine light mission into the world.

A special thanks to Denise Maroney and Libby Provost for your conscious transcription of these tablets and midwifing them from the oral realm into written form. To everyone at Bear & Company: Jon Graham, Manzanita Carpenter Sanz, Jennie Marx, Jeanie Levitan, Anne Dillon, and all of you "behind the scenes," I am sending you an energetic care package of the Joy Ray and the Venus Ray of opulent bliss. I love our collaboration and greatly appreciate having your support in bringing these bodies of work and scribed texts to the larger audience who is asking for them.

Thanks to my friends and family, two legged and four legged, for your love and support. A special wave of gratitude and appreciation to my beloved Friedemann: I appreciate you for your kind heart, unwavering belief in me, and for the beautiful life we have co-created. I feel very blessed and honored for the deep connection we share.

Thank you, family of light: Thoth, The Council of Light, Isis, Sanat Kumara, Venus Beings of Light, and all the Light Beings I have the blessing of multidimensionally communicating with. I adore our Divine partnering and am enriched and enlivened by every interaction we have. It is a delight to scribe, divinely transmit, and co-create with you. It is to you that I dedicate this book as an acknowledgment of your contribution to my life, the Earth star, and our mission to come together to co-midwife a stellar evolution in consciousness.

In completion I am extending an intergalactic wave of appreciation and unity consciousness high five to all the beings who have contributed to midwifing and giving birth to *The Tablets of Light,* including you, the reader. Happy birthday, *Tablets of Light:* I am grateful to welcome you into being and to introduce you to those who are called to interact with you.

And now that our hearts are opened and expanded from the energy of appreciation, let's enter into the halls of this Temple of Light with delight, celebration, and a readiness to embody light, frequency, and consciousness.

Keys to Enter This Light-Conceived, Scribed Text

A LETTER FROM THOTH: ACCESS CODES FOR YOUR JOURNEY

Hello Dear One,

It is I, Thoth, that is moving more into the forefront of this divine transmission, the subject of which is *The Tablets of Light*. These tablets of light are explored in the scribed text that follows. This letter to you from me, Thoth, is a transmission that includes keys, codes, and frequencies to support your system in accessing all that you choose to access from this text.

To begin I would reintroduce myself to you, for it is through our connection that the tablets are accessible in this form. I, Thoth, am most known in Egyptian form as the god of infinite knowledge, with an ibis head and masculine body. In this form I have ascended mastery in several areas of infinite knowledge. As keeper of the Akashic Records every molecule of consciousness is accessible. As scribe each of these molecules can be translated from vibration into word with the full spectrum of consciousness being imbued in each individual word. I am also known for serving the goddess in a lunar masculine way, as well as being the creator of Tarot or divination—the capacity to intuit consciousness and decode symbols. There is more that I could share about what I am associated with or what other forms I have taken; however at times to overidentify what someone or something is actually limits what is possible through connecting with that someone or something.

This leads us to the lineage of Thoth, which has various prongs of infinite knowledge as a part of it, including Akashic Records, scribe, merchant priestesshood, magic, divination, sacred architecture, Divine Transmissions, and alignment (healing). There are more prongs of knowledge within the lineage of Thoth, yet these are being mentioned for they are the areas of ascended mastery that your Divine transmitter and scribe, Danielle, is adept within, and therefore are the most utilized within the pages of this scribed text.

We, a wider band of consciousness, are now moving into the forefront to introduce ourselves, for we are also accessible within the lineage of Thoth and within the pages of *The Tablets of Light.* This is Isis, the Council of Light, Sekhmet, Ptah, and Anubis that are coming forward first. Now this is the Emerald Tablets and the Tablets of Light Councils of Light that are moving more into the forefront of this Divine Transmission. We, the wider band of consciousness, which still includes Thoth, have come forward to share with you specifically about the magic of being within *The Tablets of Light,* which are also stored in the Akashic Records, within the Emerald Tablets section.

These tablets of light have not been accessible for eons and were not predetermined to be accessible now. However, your conscious choice and free will has brought them forward at this time as a tool and contribution to your evolution in consciousness. As such, the tablets were scribed by your scribe Thoth through his partnership with Danielle.

In order to share the full spectrum of multidimensional consciousness of each tablet, they were divinely transmitted—brought forth orally and captured through audio recording and then transcribed and compiled into this sacred text. This has imbued the chapters that follow with multidimensional wholeness. Therefore, as you proceed it is recommended that you enter into the temple of *The Tablets of Light* from the vantage point of your multidimensional wholeness, your totality. This will assist you in decoding and accessing what you've left for yourself to find in these tablets.

You may be wondering at this point how you enter this temple from your multidimensional wholeness. Some ways that could assist you in making this slight adjustment in how it is that you are with this sacred consciousness is to imagine that you are walking into each tablet. That each tablet opens up multidimensionally as you engage with the material in that tablet. Just like a pop-up book would go from two-dimensional to three-dimensional as you open it, each segment creates a sacred architecture that forms a hologram that you can be within. This scribed text is an environment. This environment has treasures, keys, codes, and frequencies that serve to unlock that which resides within you that is currently dormant that you are choosing to activate at this time.

You can think of each tablet being like a room in a temple, with hieroglyphs and light language on the walls. Certain elements in the chamber of the tablet are accessible the longer you are in the consciousness, for some are grown into. When you walk into a chamber in a temple you don't enter into it with the expectation that you are going to instantly understand each sacred symbol or hieroglyph. You enter into it with openness, with a sort of osmosis energy that you can absorb the high vibrational energies that are in the chamber. This is one example of how you can enter into this sacred text with your divine wholeness.

You could also look at the scribed material that follows being like entering into a Tarot deck: each segment is a Tarot card that comes alive, and you are in the card. Some of the elements of the tablets or in this example of the Tarot card are shared symbolically; they are shared through analogies and similes and at times parables and at others through direct transmission of the energy and consciousness of the material. Therefore, if you enter into this Tarot card with an openness and a curiosity then the meaning of it will come to you; it will be revealed. If you enter into it with your intellect and the idea that it is something that you will instantaneously understand then you may become frustrated. This material contains energies and frequencies that are beyond your current understanding, and require being spiraled into as the tablets are being unlocked and will continue to be unlocked by you for the first time in eons.

Another way to think about entering into this material is as if it is a ceremony or a session. When you enter into a ceremony or a session you enter into it holistically. With all of your sensations, your body, mind, emotions are present, and also your intuition, your soul, your heart, your Divine self, your totality are present as well. To experience this material multidimensionally would be our suggestion, rather than to try to only understand it.

The way that scribed consciousness is accessed is as scribed consciousness. You are scribed consciousness, meaning you have come into form in this incarnation with access to your wholeness. Everything exists within you. You are invited to engage with this material from the awareness that you are choosing all along the way to reveal more of your wholeness to yourself.

We would add one more component before we complete, and that is equanimity. These tablets of light are being placed on the altar of the heart, and it is up to you to choose to pick them up and integrate them according to your free will and conscious choice, as an equal. We are connecting with you from the absolute knowingness that we, as Beings of Light, are communicating with you as a Being of Light, eye-to-eye, peer-to-peer, Divine-to-Divine. We are extending our appreciation to you for your contribution to this material and the larger evolution in consciousness. We look forward to being within the tablets of light with you in the pages that follow.

ALL IS LIGHT AND YOU ARE ALL,
THOTH AND THE TABLETS OF LIGHT COUNCIL OF LIGHT

A DIVINE PARTNERSHIP WITH THOTH:
A MESSAGE FROM YOUR
DIVINE TRANSMITTER, DANIELLE

This book is not only a journey in consciousness, it is also an invitation to enter into a Divine partnership with Source consciousness. This partnership may take the form of being in direct connection with Thoth or a wider Council of Light, or directly with Source consciousness. It is not about the particular facet of Divine consciousness that is important per se; it is about you expanding your vibrational territory to be in a space of multidimensional Source consciousness.

For me, Danielle, Thoth is my friend, mentor, business partner, and access point to Source consciousness. I am in a sacred, committed, Divine partnership with him. The level of connection we have is one that touches every area of life; he is me and I am he. This lifetime isn't the first time we have come together and it won't be the last. Like any partnership, our connection is always evolving, dynamic, and expanding. Through my connection with Thoth and the Council of Light I experience Divine Union. This has called me to evolve, to move beyond my fears, and to engage fully. Our partnership is interactive; it is a give-and-take, and it varies. There have been moments where I have dedicated my life to the work we have to bring forth together and there have been moments where I have doubted whether he exists and "fired" him or took a break.

Yet our connection has only blossomed from this full range of expression. At times Thoth steps back and the Council of Light steps forward, depending on what evolutionary stage I am in. I have a deep connection with other Beings of Light as well, such as Isis, Metatron, Melchizadeck, Archangel Michael, Infinite Oneness, Mary Magdalene, and others.

The Tablets of Light has been brought forth through Thoth and yet it taps into a larger bandwidth of consciousness and panel of Light Beings. Therefore, most times when Thoth is speaking he refers to himself as we. My understanding of this *we* is that it includes a multidimensional consciousness that can simultaneously be laserlike, specific, and vast. My experience as I am divinely transmitting is one of great bliss. I am conscious, present, a part of the larger panel, yet not in my regular state of consciousness. I am off to the side, in the role of the highly engaged conduit, with a strong sense of identity and signature energy yet plugged into something wider. I don't know the words that are coming before they are spoken and there is a flow to the speech that is quite different from my normal speech patterns. As conduit, sacred architect, midwife, scribe, Divine transmitter, and partner with the Divine at this level, I am matched. I am enlivened; I am living on my edge of brilliance.

Getting to where I am now with Thoth and the adeptness with which I scribe and divinely transmit has been a process, one in which I am aware of the highly refined energies that are accessed and transmitted in a vibrational state of multidimensionality. I know that embedded within them is all that there is. I know that it isn't the words that hold the power; it is that they have been scribed from wholeness with wholeness. This creates the evolutionary magic. Being born during a paradigm of a consciousness of separation, where we disconnected from Source to come into physical form and then remember (for those that are choosing to) that we have been Divine all along, there is a sense of disconnect and connect. Yet in fact the connection was never severed; it has always been there. For me that is the purpose of *The Tablets of Light:* to reinvigorate our Divine connection, our Divine wholeness.

Since my first conscious connection with Thoth in 1997, my world has opened up to include the multiverse. Entering into a Divine partnership with Thoth and the Divine Council of Beings of Light has enriched my life beyond words. They are my family, friends, guides, and mentors . . . and they touch all levels of my life. These relationships are ones that I have devoted myself to deepening. At first the interaction was more kinesthetic, wherein I would feel energy in my hands. Then it became visual, wherein I would see pictures. Then it was auditory (I would hear words), and now it is fully embodied. I fully embody Thoth

100 percent at the times when it is optimal. Other times I connect with him through my aura.

Since our first connection, Thoth has asked me to bring in different bodies of work in direct connection with him. At first he taught me how to do body readings where he would scan a person and then provide a reading. This evolved to offering workshops on certain topics. Then he asked me if I would scribe *The Temples of Light, The Council of Light,* and now *The Tablets of Light,* to which I said yes each time. Our Divine partnership has also included bringing in bodies of work or activations such as Thoth's Magic Academy, a year and a day video course, SCRIBE retreats to support others in bringing in their unique bodies of work, and Divine Light Activation, a pathway to being a Being of Light incarnate and highly committed, in-depth 1:1 Divine partnership programs. Please see the resources section at the end of this book, or visit www.divinetransmissions.com. I am in awe of what comes through and the profound support it is to those that engage in these offerings. I have come to understand that the base of this is due to the fact that as Thoth and the Beings of Light are connecting with us, they are connecting with our wholeness. As such, this encourages the system to live in wholeness.

Part of the vision that I carry is that we reawaken our birthright to live as Beings of Light incarnate. One of the pathways for this remembering is to experience initiations and activations that reawaken the unique brilliance that we each carry. This is a time of leaders, visionaries, and pioneers, a time of evolving what leadership means. My connection with Thoth is leader-to-leader, Divine-to-Divine, visionary-to-visionary. My role with those whom I connect with through Divine Transmissions, Inc. is the same. Even though it appears that I am the one who is divinely transmitting this consciousness and you, the reader, is the one receiving it, it isn't that way. Instead, it is a simultaneous receiving and transmitting. There is no longer a leader and a follower or a student and a teacher: we are all individualized oneness in equality.

It is with great joy and delight that I give birth to this collaborative body of work with Thoth and the Council of Light, which I know you are a part of as well. I extend great blessings and love for your journey of evolution in consciousness and the brilliance that you carry. Thank you for the contribution you are and the role you have in our greater remembering and evolution.

WITH LOVE AND DELIGHT,
DANIELLE

THE BIRTH STORY OF THE TABLETS OF LIGHT

This is Thoth and the Tablets of Light Council of Light that are moving more into the forefront of this Divine Transmission. We are embarking on a sacred remembering journey. This sacred remembering journey is one in which you are rediscovering that which you have known to be true all along. This discovery is such that you are streaming into a wealth of infinite being-ness. This streaming is both the journey and the destination. They are one and the same thing.

SACRED REMEMBERING OF THE ANCIENT AND INNOVATIVE

As we begin our somewhat lengthy conversation about the infinite being-ness that you are, we are entering into sacred remembering territory. We are entering into the space in between the space. We are entering into the light in between the light. This space in between the space and this light in between the light is your Divine heartbeat. It is your Divine compass. It is your Divine knowing.

The Tablets of Light is a sacred text that is simultaneously old, ancient, forgotten, and new, innovative, and remembered. That is because as you are tuning into that which is old, ancient, and forgotten from the vantage point of where you are in this *now* moment, it can appear new, innovative, and remembered. The same is true in the inverse: As you tune into that which is new, innovative, and remembered it is old, ancient, and forgotten. That is to say that that which is scribed, that which is encoded, that which is sacred multidimensional wisdom is vibrating in many planes of light simultaneously. The simultaneity of these light codes is such that the codes are operating like many vortices within many vortices within many vortices within many vortices. These spirals of light, these multidimensional vortex energies, are unraveling—unmasking and revealing what has been there all along. Old is new, ancient is innovative, forgotten is remembered.

The Tablets of Light is a sacred text that has been waiting for its time to be reborn, and this time of being reborn is now. We are using this language of being reborn so that you may cognitively comprehend that *The Tablets of Light* is ensouled, it is alive, and it is a being with many incarnations with a purpose. Just as you, dear one, have waited in the streams of Divine light for the time to incarnate that you have chosen, so has *The Tablets of Light* been waiting in the interdimensional space, in the interlife portal.

The conception of this rebirth of *The Tablets of Light* actually was February 16, 1970, the same day that our beloved Divine scribe and transmitter of these words, Danielle Rama Hoffman, was born. This consciousness has been gestating as she has been evolving, growing, and becoming the one that she is at this time. This transmission is occurring on February 13, 2014, three days before her forty-fourth birthday on this Earth plane. This is the true birth date of *The Tablets of Light* and as such it is a celebration. She, Danielle, is a carrier and bringer forth of ancient and innovative wisdoms. There is a time to carry and there is a time to bring forth. She has carried *The Tablets of Light* within her during this incarnation and previous incarnations as well, and now it is time for her to midwife this Being of Light into form. The joy of this process will at times feel orgasmic.

THE REASON FOR YOUR INCARNATION
AT THIS TIME

The Tablets of Light is a scribed text that is alive, multidimensional, a Being of Light. Each person that chooses to read this sacred text is also a carrier and bringer forth of infinite knowledge of sacred codes of light. These sacred codes of light also have varying gestation periods. These gestation periods vary for each of you and each of the scribed consciousness, and yet the time to uncover that which you have held within your DNA records, your Akashic timeline is now. This is the reason for your incarnation at this time.

You have traveled across the multiverse to this place called Earth. You hold within you the sacred texts of other solar systems, of other times, of other ways of life. You are a light bearer, a way shower, a consciousness evolver, which means that you are on a journey of epic proportions, one in which you are self-creating, self-initiating, finding your own way. It is as if you are walking inside the bowels of Earth in the darkness, with your own light finding your way and bearing the light, showing the way to others and, in the process, evolving consciousness.

Sometimes the path that is laid before you, which you walk upon, is already opened. Other times you forge through the closed doorway, the forgotten pathway, the nonexistent path—because you know that is the way. When you know that is the way it is evident to you and to you alone. Thousands of other seekers will walk past the true path that is evident to you because it is yours to show the way, it is yours to illuminate, it is yours to shine the light upon. *The Tablets of Light* is a reactivation of Divine consciousness inhabiting the human soul. That is how it has always been. Again, it is simultaneously old, ancient, and forgotten—and new, innovative, and remembered. You are a diamond light seed of galactic divinity, multifaceted, exquisite, unique, and brilliant. *The Tablets of Light* is a text that you left for yourself to find in order to remind you of who you truly are, to remind you of why you're really here, to call back within your own heart an awareness of your Divine origin.

We will continue our journey in increments. We invite you to pause here and take a few breaths to absorb this increment thus far.

BEING MATCHED

A Divine Partnership
with Thoth

AN EVOLUTION OF RELATIONSHIPS

This is Thoth that is moving into the forefront of this Divine Transmission. The subject of this Divine Transmission is entering into a Divine partnership, a Divine partnership with me, Thoth, and the greater bandwidth of Divine consciousness and a Divine partnership with your multidimensional self, your fully realized self. This invitation to enter into this Divine partnership is in response to your asking, in response to your knowing, in response to your inner guidance. For you have the awareness that what you have been longing for is to truly be matched, eye-to-eye, peer-to-peer, Divine-to-Divine, from a place of equality, equanimity, and a knowing that all is well. This being matched and being in a Divine partnership with me, Thoth, as well as with yourself through the pages of this sacred text, will awaken the resurrected and evolved Divine Union.

It will awaken the evolution of relationship in unity consciousness, which will be based on mutual respect, love, and collaboration. In this, it transcends the old paradigm of relationships where there was power over or power under, or the idea or need that one needed an intercessor in order to access the Divine—whether that was a priest, parent, or teacher. There is no such thing as power over or power under; all beings are equal. The old paradigm of relationships is outdated.

This time of unity consciousness is one in which there is the return of Divine wholeness within the system, wherein you are directly connected to Source consciousness as a Divine Being of Light incarnate. You have a direct connection with Source consciousness. In this, you are able to connect, through multidimensional communication, with other Beings of Light (both incarnate such as yourself and in-light such as me, Thoth) on the planet as well as off the planet. This connection is from a place of wholeness to wholeness. There is awareness of you being fully who it is that you are and the other being (incarnate or in light) being fully who it is that *they* are on the same playing field, on the "fifty-yard line." This awareness includes the knowledge that no one is better or worse than another.

There is no one who knows more about what is best for you than you, and that includes me, Thoth, and the Beings of Light who are present in this Divine conversation—this wider bandwidth of the Council of Light. We have agreed and chosen to engage with those of you who have decided to engage with us in order to resurrect this Divine consciousness.

SPIRITUAL TECHNOLOGY
OF MULTIDIMENSIONALITY, ENERGY,
AND CONSCIOUSNESS

The methodology utilized in the pages of this sacred text is one of vibration and consciousness. As we are connecting with you, as we are collaborating with you and your system, as we are entering into this Divine partnership, there is the invitation for you to be engaged at the level of your full multidimensionality—the level of your Divine Union self. We are being with you, all of you, at that fully turned-on, awakened level. That creates an environment where your system naturally remembers what it is like to have all of your dimensions turned on and functioning optimally, to be in a state of Divine wholeness and Divine Union.

This is an evolutionary spiritual technology or methodology that

utilizes vibration and consciousness to awaken the divinity codes within
your system. The sequence of Divine light that is activating within your
system is a Divine light activation. Through this awakening process, the
full access to that which you already are is remembered. It's not that
you *weren't* Divine and now all of a sudden you *are* Divine. Rather, it's
that you were vibrating in different dimensions than the fully realized
multidimensionality of you.

Throughout this journey together, throughout this Divine partnership, you will have an awareness of reawakening, of that which has been
dormant coming back into life. You will also have an awareness of what
are naturally your origin Source codes returning to their fully calibrated
and turned-on space. This is an innovative spiritual light technology
and a different way of looking at who you really are. In the past paradigm of survival and separation there was much focus on what wasn't
working well. Or on trying to clear or release those aspects of yourself
that you didn't like or that you thought were holding you back. Yet
from our perspective, *all* of you matters and has purpose. When you
bring everything to the table—that which you prefer and that which
you don't prefer—you provide rocket fuel for your evolution in consciousness. This is viewed from the perspective of a vibration of inclusion; there's not any thought that you've ever had, any experience that
you've ever experienced, that isn't a part of the Divine wholeness, a part
of the Divine Union.

This isn't about releasing slower vibrations; it's about integrating
them back into the wholeness—the oneness of All That There Is. This
conversation is a conversation of inclusion. It is from being matched,
having an environment where the slower vibrations that you carry and
are connected to are welcome, and your higher vibrations are welcome
as well. This environment, where you can access the full brilliance of
you, the genius of you, vibrationally encourages you to embody and
express that fully alive and embodied Divine knowing. This totality is
your Divine Union, your brilliant self.

As this becomes your new set point, where it is that you come from, there is also the leaving behind of your old ways of being, which might include thoughtforms expressing, for instance, that it's not okay to be as brilliant as you are, or it's not safe to shine your light brightly. There is an awareness of being matched, really being matched—being matched at the level of your multidimensional, fully embodied Divine self. There is something within you that has been longing for this. It has been craving this, for it senses that there is so much more that resides within you than perhaps you are actualizing on a daily basis. Part of that gap between what you know is possible and what you created involved the old environment on the Earth plane. However, now that Earth's environment is evolving, those codes that reside within you, which can access the new vibration in consciousness, are awakening, for it is their time to do so. As such, you can be congruent between the infinite being that you truly be and what you actualize in your incarnation, in your life.

A COLLABORATION
OF GALACTIC PROPORTIONS

We speak about being matched. Being matched is how we are being with you on a multidimensional level throughout this sacred text and within the invitation to enter into a Divine partnership with me, Thoth, and Source consciousness. Being matched and Divine partnering is also the foundation to a wider collaboration that involves a revolution, an evolution, a remembering of an evolution that is not only about you as an individual and the Earth plane, it is also about the multiverse. You are co-creating with Beings of Light, ascended masters, teams of consciousness that are partners in this larger evolution in consciousness. This co-creation involves other Beings of Light who are incarnate on the Earth plane, who are visionaries in that they have visions that they carry within them. It is time to awaken these visions as well.

All of this is not just about those of you who are Beings of Light, who have incarnated as what are most commonly referred to as *human beings.* It's not just about the human race—although we wouldn't call you *human,* for we know that you are Divine and that the word *human* has so much charge to it that implies you are separate from Source. Being a human being also implies that you have a small self and you were born into original sin and that God is outside of you and above you and all those things. That's one of the reasons we don't say *human.* Also we don't say *human* because your origin is *not* Earth. Within you are other incarnations from other planets, as well as the consciousness of your particular role in deciding to come to Earth at this time, to be engaged at this level. However, it's not entirely up to the beings that are incarnated, the brilliant systems of the human race, to evolve consciousness and the future of the collaborative effort. There is much support from so many Beings of Light who aren't incarnate—who aren't necessarily in the physical dimensional space of the Earth plane—and who are here to support the process.

This invitation to enter into a Divine partnership with me, Thoth, and the Council of Light, the bandwidth of consciousness that is your access point to Source consciousness, is something to be chosen and engaged in from your level of free-will choice. Because you are within the tablets of Thoth you have a connection with me, Thoth, already. It may be very familiar and it may be brand new. Our Divine partnership is in tune with the awareness of the collaborative vibration and energy that is also returning the partnership between incarnate/physical and nonphysical/energetic. This partnership is very natural, not extraordinary or "out there." For us to have a direct connection with you, Being of Light–to–Being of Light, from a place of equality in your wholeness, and with your own inner guidance is indeed a Divine partnership. This partnership never steps over the "fifty-yard line"; we always honor your free will and your consciousness choice. That is why these tablets of light are placed on the altar of the heart, on the altar of inclusion. The tablets are yours to pick up or not.

We wanted to share this state of being matched and entering into a Divine partnership to really set the stage for your conscious awareness of how this particular book, this sacred text, is perhaps unlike any other that you have been engaged with. It's a vibrational environment, it's a conversation Divine-to-Divine, and it's encoded so that as you read the pages, as you interact with the tablets, you awaken your multidimensionality and your Divine wholeness. You may have a Divine partnership at this level with a Being of Light such as me, Thoth. Or you may have a stronger connection to another Being of Light and it may be directly with infinite oneness, Source consciousness, God, Goddess, and/or all that there is, and it may be your higher self. Yet having a place where you can be matched and being in a Divine partnership opens up worlds. It creates greater ease and grace. We look forward to engaging with you at this level and, through the process, supporting you in accessing the full breadth of who you are and the Divine light mission you came to Earth to contribute. We complete this segment at this time knowing that all is well and you are all.

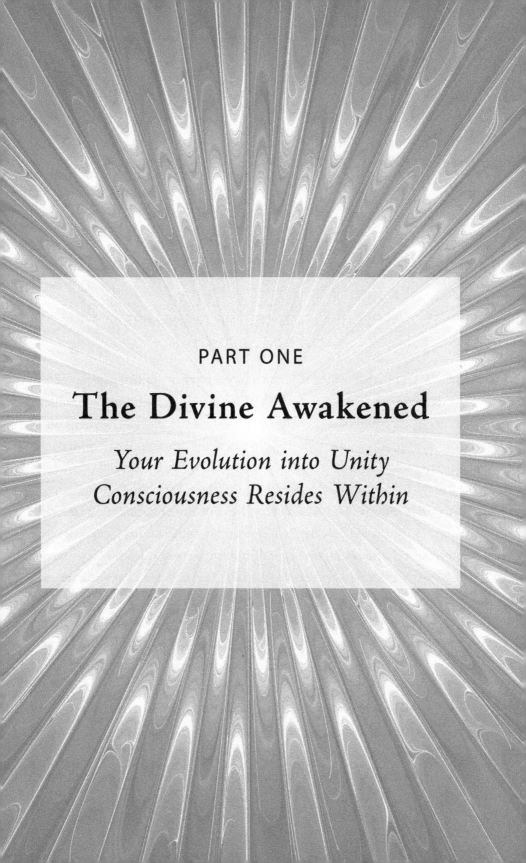

PART ONE

The Divine Awakened

*Your Evolution into Unity
Consciousness Resides Within*

1

Oracular Vision

Access the Vision You Carry

RECOGNITION OF THE SIGNATURE ENERGY OF THOTH

This is Thoth, that is moving more into the forefront of this *now* moment to continue our conversation of *The Tablets of Light*. Infinite knowledge, scribing, astronomy, architecture, Akashic Records, energy readings, conscious evolution council, healing, art, writing, communication, magic, pattern recognition, soul themes, energy movement, Divine embodiment, hieroglyphic speaking, palm reading, Tarot, the Emerald Tablets, Egypt, Atlantis, Lemuria, Mu, Milky Way, Keys of Enoch, Mercury, Hermes, Mercury the planet, blue heron, ibis, egret, ascended mastery, enlivener of dormant consciousness, unlocker of hidden treasures, Divine developer, maze pathfinder, teacher's teacher, healer's healer, aligner's aligner, are all energies, frequencies, and vibrations associated with me, Thoth.

They have been listed in this format to spark recognition within your system of our connection. This connection is one that's recognized within your connection to yourself. As you go within and tap into your inner awareness, your inner ibis, your inner sacred text, you recognize me, my signature energy. You recognize lifetimes that we have spent together. You recognize codes of energy that are vibrating within you. Recognition is re-cognition in fluid form.

This recognition stream of consciousness has been activated; it will be your guiding light through *The Tablets of Light*. This guiding light is such that you are illuminating inner awareness within your own Divine origin. The keys of recognition, the keys of a remembering of oracular visioning, are within your cerebral cortex. The cerebral cortex is within your Divine awareness.

These opening words have been heavily encoded on multidimensional levels, and as they have been heavily encoded on multidimensional levels their purpose has been to create an energy vortex for this conversation to occur within. In a sense we have been painting through words the setting for this conversation to take place, the energy location for this conversation to take place. For it is a vibrational conversation and as such there are times when it is necessary for your vibration to be guided into a spectrum of consciousness in which you can tap into the true meaning underneath, around, and within the words.

Then we can converse in a way that becomes fluid, self-evident, and with an awareness that it is the conversation that you have been waiting to have for eons. We are saying *conversation* because conversation is what this is. It is an interplay, it is a dialogue, it is a back-and-forth. A conversation also is an oracular experience. This conversation through words, the oral tradition, activates the oracular wisdom consciousness—the laser frequencies of truth—and catalyzes the active remembering of you as a vision holder.

THE VISION YOU CARRY

As we have now moved into vibrational proximity with one another through these opening words it is time for you to connect to your true vision for this infinite experience of evolution as a light being. What vision are you holding? What vision are you holding? What vision are you holding as a Being of Light incarnate? A vision in this expanded sense is a way in which you are seeing the world through the lens of infinite possibilities. As we bring in the invitation to uncover what vision you are holding within the energy location that we are having this conversation in, you are able to drop the lens of that which may be a finite view that you have taken on of how you see the world, and instead to really be the vision that you have been carrying since the inception of the molecules of this incarnation and beyond. You have been carrying a vision, carrying a perspective, carrying a way of seeing, a holding of a dream, of a life, of a civilization that actually is outside of your experience in your Earth walk.

This is where it gets fun. This is where you realize that you have left the tablets of light for yourself to find, to revitalize and to breathe life into the vision you hold. Up until this point you haven't even known it is the vision that you hold. As such it is a time of deep remembering. It is a time of moving out of your ordinary way of being into your extraordinary way of being. It is the evolution of that which has always been there, streamed forth in your awake and aware consciousness.

As a point of light, as a star seed on the Earth plane, you have this vision that we have been speaking of that is in some ways the mission of this developmental stage of your time on Earth and of the larger evolution of consciousness on the Earth plane. This vision and your developmental stage in your evolution of consciousness calls you forth to step into the unknown, to step beyond the borders of what you think you are, of what you have experienced, and what you have cataloged as reality. Your vision cannot be experienced from anywhere but the rainbow-rose, golden glasses of high perspective, of infinite knowledge, of heart wisdom. Vibrational consciousness, such as your vision, must be spiraled into. It must be delicately approached; it must be loved into being. As it is spiraled and approached delicately and loved into being it is an artistry of oracular weaving of threads of awareness that are unique to you as a point of light.

STREAMS OF ENERGY

There has been much awareness about an incarnation being an experience in which you travel through streams of energy, and that these streams of energy can have the impetus of remembering who it is that you are. They can also have the impetus of forgetting who it is that you are. It is truly optional which road you journey on in your incarnation. They are equal. It is a choice.

That you are within the temple of the tablets of light and having this conversation strikes the match that ignites the light of your choosing to have these streams of experiences of remembering. This is igniting your memory of who it is that you truly are: you are a vision holder. You are a Being of Light that has within you a hidden treasure. The way that this hidden treasure is found is by you recognizing you. You recognizing you. The ways that you recognize you are beyond just the color of your hair or the sound of your voice, and the activities that you do. It is the recognition of you as the wholeness of all that there is, of the divinity of you, of the infinite nature of you.

We have chosen this term, *a hidden treasure,* on purpose because it is a hunt that you are on, it is a stalking down, a tracking, a pattern recognition of molecules of consciousness, of drops of awareness, which resurrect the vision that you hold. The vision that you hold. The vision that you hold.

Now that we have transmitted more increments of consciousness, ask if it is your choice that the vision that you hold be remembered, be revealed to you, be re-accessed. This reconnection, this re-cognition of your awareness of the vision that you hold, can happen in an instant, can happen overnight, can happen over the span of a century. It can happen at a sacred site, it can happen within the pages of this text, it can happen anywhere and within any *now* moment contained within the multidimensional strings of *now* moments of time.

CONSCIOUS CHOICE EXERCISE
· · · · · · · · · ·
Choose to Recognize the Vision You Hold

This is not about, in this instant, going directly after the vision. It is quite the opposite. It is about choosing. It is about deciding to recognize the vision that you hold, the perspective that you carry, the wisdom of light that's within you, and to plant that seed. It's about lighting the match that sparks a remembering and to approach it delicately, to spiral into it, and to allow it to ripple out like water after a stone has been dropped into it.

Are you choosing to recognize the vision that you hold, that you carry? If you are, state out loud, "I choose to recognize the vision that I hold, that I carry." State this three times out loud with increasing levels of resonance and commitment. "I choose to recognize the vision that I hold, that I carry. I choose to recognize the vision that I hold, that I carry. I choose to recognize the vision that I hold, that I carry."

ORACULAR VISION AS A DOORWAY

Oracular vision involves the way you hold awareness, energy, perspective, light, and consciousness to funnel in new ways of being. The oracle was sought after for his or her wisdom and knowledge of energy trends, of possible realities or outcomes. The vision that the oracle receives holds a possible reality. This is like opening a door that holds a pathway into another chamber or room in a house. The oracular vision is such that there is the reading of a possible reality that then is expressed in a way that increases its probability.

We are not speaking of telling the future, of reading a book that's already been decided upon—the book of someone's life, their destiny, and events. We are actually speaking about opening a road to a possible reality through a vision, through a line of sight, through a perspective. As the light bearer, the way shower, the oracular vision holder, the carrier of infinite knowledge that you are, we are reminding you of a much-acquired skill that you have had from past incarnations, which is actually quite powerful and potent at this time.

Holding a line of sight, a vision, increases the probability of that certain reality coming into form, coming into fruition, coming into light. It is important at this stage to open up to receive the full dimension of what's being transmitted and to let go of any expectations of where you think this conversation is headed. It is important to likewise drop any recognition of where you think it is that we are going or what *A* plus *B* equals or leads to, because this book of Thoth's tablets is about creating, through ancient and innovative wisdom, that which has not existed before. It is about re-creation, the recreation of that which is new. It is a choice. It is a malleable weaving of strands of light in such a way that depending on who you are and the way that you are choosing or not choosing to interact with this material, the possibility of the reality you are here to remember and create is increased, it is formed.

It is approached delicately because if you approach it as the person that you *had* been, it is unapproachable. It is almost as if the person that you had been is a magnet that is facing a possible reality that is also a magnet. When this happens, these magnets then face each other in such a way as to repel one another. Approaching this magnet from the perspective of who you had been, including the visions that you took on that aren't actually the visions that you hold, pushes the visions that you hold away. It pushes the possibility of something to be created—that had never been created—away. It creates this invisible force field in which that which you are actually choosing to access jumps into another dimension.

We are saying this not because there is anything wrong with who it is that you had been. It is only to say that who it is that you had been had created the world that you had existed in and therefore it cannot create the world of this possibility that this vision holds open. We are wanting to stay on one stream of consciousness and yet we could place a placeholder energetically here to recognize that this conversation is happening within a larger conversation that we haven't provided a context for. We are doing that on purpose because if we were to provide the larger conversational context, that then creates a limitation because it's held within a context.

To provide a context of the context, the more you can be without a context the better, for this invites you to scramble old ways of thinking, old ways of being, and old neural pathways. It invites you to recognize that what has gotten you to where you are will not get you to where it is that you are choosing to go through the pages of this book, through the days of your life, through this incarnation. It is through the forget-ting that the remembering happens. It is through the awareness of the spiraling of who it is that you are that then allows you to be conducive, to walk down the line of sight of the vision that you're holding, to the reality that is yours to experience.

We did that outtake of sorts when we were beginning to speak about oracular vision, which is a light tool that you are remembering. For it's natural for you to want to categorize it to look like something else, to compare it to that which you think may be similar to what it is that we are describing. In that process, what we are actually describing gets overlooked. We have said that the oracular vision of the one that holds the vision creates an open doorway in which a probability of a new reality through a line of sight gets created. The interesting aspect of the one holding the vision is that it is being held from a position of absolute knowing of the vision. The absolute knowing of the vision.

This brings us into quicksand, for the more we begin to play with this concept, the more we invite you to wrap your mind around it, the more stuck and farther away from the concept we actually get. If we don't name what it's not and how *not* to be, then it's almost impossible to transmit that which it actually is.

This is not deciding that you want to create a certain future and visualizing this future into being, and then that future increases the probability of actualizing it. That process is not what we're describing in oracular vision. It is not the process in which you take an energetic picture of somebody's life and what it is that they're holding and then create a conclusion about what their future will be, and sharing that vision as what their future will be.

It is not reading the future, and, again, it is not actualizing some-thing that you would like by holding the vision of it. It is not receiving a vision from the spirit world in the form of a shamanic vision that is deciphered by your entering into an altered state and following a journey with your spirit guide and receiving certain images, sounds, or words, which then you hold and create.

We are not talking about these forms of visioning here. It is not the shamanic vision, it is not future telling, it is not visualizing what you decide you want and then affirming it into manifestation.

Rather, oracular vision is holding the vision of the reality that you know exists and the line of sight that you have on it that is unknown to anyone else. It is unknown to anyone else and it is unknown to you until it is known by you. The explorer, the leader, the way shower, the pioneer, the light bearer is out there in front finding a path that hasn't been traveled before and illuminating it into an open doorway that then creates a higher probability of a reality that didn't exist. As the oracular vision holder it is important to reactivate within you your capacity to see that which has always been there, which you hadn't seen before. You haven't seen it before and you can't see it in advance.

Let's circle back to an analogy about walking within chambers below the Earth and finding a pathway there. At times this can be like seeing through walls that seem to be solid but actually aren't. You are following a pathway that's already been laid out before. It is a process in which, if you are imagining it like a pathway that you are walking on within a cavern underground, you don't know what's coming. You know only the step that you took before and yet you don't even really know what has gone before. You know where it is that you are. Where it is that you are is where your oracular line of sight is seen from. Sometimes as you're walking forward you just know to walk forward. You just know to walk forward and then all of a sudden there's a crystal that sparkles out of the corner of your eye. It's above your line of sight and you're just drawn to it like a magnet and as you approach it and as you reach out to touch this crystal a secret passageway that wasn't obvious to anyone gets opened up.

PRESENCE

What we are speaking about above is literally about finding a pathway. We are speaking about opening a door and holding a vision of that pathway creating a reality so that it becomes more inevitable. And yet what we are also speaking about is a way of being in your life that has absolutely been forgotten by 99.999 percent of the beings on this Earth plane. Here we are talking about presence, presence, presence. It is through your presence in the moment that you clearly see what, to many, appears to be invisible.

If you have never been on a path before you cannot anticipate that three hundred steps along the path it drops down into a waterfall. You know only that it drops into a waterfall as you approach it and you begin to hear running water. If you didn't know what a waterfall was you wouldn't even know that it was a waterfall. As you approach it, you take in information about it that you couldn't take in if somebody was trying to describe to you what a waterfall is if you've never seen one before. By experiencing it, by putting your hand in the water or dropping a leaf if you're at the top of the waterfall and watching it fall, you can see what you couldn't have seen any other way. You can experience what you hadn't been able to experience from any other vantage point.

That's why we're saying that once you hold the vision, once you know the vision of that which you are holding in that line of sight, then it opens a pathway for that reality you're holding to then become a probability. The vision that you hold is actually outside of time, it is organic, it is always moving. It is always moving because you are outside of time and all that there is is organic. It is alive, it is always moving. That's why it is not telling the future, that's why it's not illuminating what you want to actualize and visualize until it comes into fruition. That's why it's not receiving a shamanic vision and deciphering it.

It is moment-to-moment holding the vision, one increment of awareness and consciousness at a time. The door opens, the pathway is traversed. It's traversed from the moment that you know it, that you follow it, that you become the oracle that has oracular vision once again.

We have transmitted much in this segment and we would actually invite you to rest at this time and, when you are ready, go through it again. Go through it again and go through it again from the awareness that you have now at the end of this increment. Find the hidden treasures that have been seeded within it. Choose to hold the vision that you carry and to recognize the vision that you carry. It is all that you have left for yourself to find at this time and it is a joyful experience to share with one another.

2
Evolution Hologram

The Sacred Architecture of Unity Consciousness

AWAKENING

Our purpose together is to unlock within you that which has been patiently awaiting. The awakening of that which has been dormant within you is what we are reactivating together. Because of the very nature of the dormancy, the reposed state that this has been incubating within, it exists in a dimensional space of that which is unknown to you.

As such, you are accessing something that is not familiar to you. It is not known to you. It is another realm of consciousness. As such, you could say that you are separate from the purpose that we hold together in reactivating now what you chose, before your current incarnation, to carry. That you are separate from that goal, from that charge, from that mission—and at the same time just as all separation is the idea that you are separate from that which lies dormant within you—is an illusion. What resides in the realm of consciousness of the unknown is in conjunction with you. It is in labor within you. It is developing within you. Because what we are speaking about awakening within you is consciousness, this consciousness is conscious and it has a growth pattern, an impetus to develop that has been placed within it by you.

Just as you know that babies who grow from embryos to birth have within them what they require to develop, so does this dormant consciousness have everything within it to become awakened. The same is true for separation consciousness—it has everything within it to evolve into unity consciousness. We have alluded to the fact that we are having this conversation within the context of a larger conversation and yet we have not spoken of this context up until this moment because it would have created a limitation rather than an expansion. Now it is creating an expansion where there would have been limitation or illusion.

To frame this conversation we will speak about the evolution of consciousness. The evolution of consciousness is such that it has evolved and it is evolving and it will continue to evolve. Just as we have spoken about this evolution in the previous phrase in the past, in the present and in the future this evolution of consciousness resides in all time and in all space. It is a spiral, it is an expansion capsule, it is evolution as evolution is spoken. It is evolution as evolution is experienced. It is evolution as evolution is because evolution exists in all time and space. There is the awareness that it is occurring simultaneously. It is occurring within the context of wholeness, within the context of unity, within the context of the hologram but every aspect of evolution has the wholeness of every other aspect of evolution within it.

We begin this way to speak about the evolution of consciousness at this time on Earth because we want to set the stage in such a way that it is apparent that this evolution exists within a larger evolution. The evolution of the Earth plane and those beings that inhabit the Earth plane exist within an evolution that is beyond Earth. This is beyond galaxies, beyond multiverses, beyond a timeline of various civilizations or a location line such as Earth, Venus, Saturn, your solar system, or the Milky Way, and those nameless stars as well. This evolution is happening within a larger evolution and yet the evolution that is occurring on the Earth plane has within it the hologram of all that there is, of the all, the evolution of the all.

It is this understanding of interconnectedness that models what has been spoken about regarding the Emerald Tablets, of as above so below, as within so without. It is the awareness of the microcosm and the macrocosm. It is the awareness of the library of consciousness within the DNA and the Akashic Records, the library of all consciousness. It is the drop in the ocean *and* the ocean. It is the nucleus of a cell within an environment of trillions of cells within a body that exists within a multidimensional infinite being that exists within a larger context of many multidimensional infinite beings that exist within the context of those billions of infinite beings that are embodied at this time that exist within a larger context of the infinite that exists within the infinite infinite. You can go in, you can out, you can go up, and you can go down yet anywhere you go you are within wholeness. You are within wholeness. That is unity consciousness awareness.

As we speak about trends of this evolution in consciousness that's occurring within the Earth plane we cannot do it outside of what you would call the larger picture, outside of the oracular vision. That is what we are doing at this time. We want to speak about this in more of a contextual manner. From this level of all there is to the level of your experience of living for that, is where you are within the hologram of all that is. You are within the energy location of the units of consciousness that are you. Those units of consciousness that are you are vibrating in a reality that you call your life, that you call your body, that you call your money, that you call your family, that you call your interests, that you call your career, that you call all of those experiences that you relate to as your reality.

EVERYTHING EXISTS IN WHOLENESS

From our perspective it doesn't matter if you are relating to your foot or you are relating to yourself as an enlightened being or if you are in the energy of the material or the physical or you are in the energy of consciousness and spirituality. It does not matter because it is all there is. It is within a larger context of evolution.

As we are getting into more of these unity consciousness universal principles, there is the awareness that every reality that each person on the Earth plane is experiencing is within a larger context of all realities. It is within a larger context of all consciousness, of the all that there is. Because that is the case, from an awareness of free will, there is nothing that is outside the wholeness. As such, someone can choose to play in whatever arena they choose to play in and they are still within the arena of wholeness. They are still within the context of a larger context. They are still vibrating with a hologram of the drops of water within the ocean. This is a beautiful awareness of unity consciousness to have.

To see it as such is to be free. To see it this way is to experience moments of your life as ones to choose or not, as the path that for you holds within it all that there is to become. This includes the developmental stage that you are becoming, the evolution that you are becoming, because everything within it has everything within it to evolve, including separation consciousness. In understanding this, you can be free. You can be at peace. You can live with presence because the whole idea of right and wrong, of good and bad, that you need to be fixed, that somebody else needs to be fixed, exists within a larger context that actually nullifies all of those ideas because within those ideas exists the awareness of the wholeness . . . exists the awareness of the wholeness.

We have done a beautiful job of setting the stage for the evolution of consciousness from the awareness that anything goes, that everything is connected to the wholeness, that it cannot exist outside of unity, and it has within it that which it requires to evolve. This involves moving from being active into dormancy, or from dormancy into being active, or to transmute or to change. This is the good news, the very good news, because it illuminates that every time you've experienced something unpreferred by you—whether that was sadness, abandonment, self-deprecation, an experience of powerlessness, survival, or lack—it has always had within it everything that there is to evolve into the wholeness of *all* that there is. In those moments of suffering, peace has also existed. The capacity for suffering to be peace exists because it exists within the wholeness.

THERE HAS NEVER BEEN A SEPARATION

We are weaving in this sacred text. Each word, each increment is a part of this larger tapestry and at times you may feel as if you are lost in seeing just a few threads at a time and yet, as we weave, the larger pattern is revealed, uncovered, and rediscovered.

The larger context of the evolution of consciousness that the Earth plane is in is that the separation has never truly been. It is an untruth; it is a lie. As you experience this lie it feels true, it feels awful, it feels as if your very life is in danger and yet that is a functionality of the dormancy of this consciousness that we are reawakening together. For it is almost as if you haven't had all of the facts, you haven't had enough information, and so based on the facts that you had been given and the information that you have had, you can draw one conclusion. Yet once there is more information and more facts then another conclusion may be drawn.

This is like when you're playing blackjack and someone is shuffling the cards and as the cards are shuffled you can see red and black, you can see kings, aces, twos, and threes. If you base your conclusion on what it is that you see when the deck is shuffling you may assume, with that limited information, that the cards you see as they are being shuffled will be the ones that will be laid out for this game of blackjack. Yet in this scenario you don't have enough facts to accurately know that the cards visible in the shuffling are the cards that are going to be turned over in the actual game.

This is the same as being in a state of what we're calling separation, a state of lack or survival. In other words, what you would refer to as your negative emotions and experiences, your suffering. And yet this slower vibrational experience of separation consciousness emanates from the perspective of you, from the vantage point of your incarnation as something separate from your infinite being-ness, your infinite awareness, your wholeness, your multidimensionality.

As that which has been dormant becomes awakened within

the context of the larger context, the way you view your experience changes. That which is dormant within you has been reactivated through this increment, through this conversation. This was the activation sequence that was required to jump-start the evolution of consciousness, of the awakening of what has been dormant within you. This evolution of consciousness, the awakening of that which has been dormant within you, is streaming in such a way that it illuminates pillars of light within your cellular matrix. This then illuminates other pillars of light within your cellular matrix, which then illuminates more facts and more information and a wider perspective and a remembering of the hologram that everything exists within wholeness.

At this time there is nothing further to do in this awakening process because the light codes have been given and have been received by your system. This is because this reactivation is your choice, because it is what you have left for yourself to find, because you are that powerful that we are showing up in this way, because you have spoken it into being, and because you have created it for yourself.

Continue to play with your oracular vision and your capacity to see the wholeness that exists within every unit of consciousness of your being and your life. When you are experiencing something unpreferred, see if you can see if something else preferred actually exists in that same moment.

THE BLUEPRINT OF UNITY CONSCIOUSNESS

We are delighting in this conversation and the continuation of it as we further explore the energy and consciousness of the hologram of evolution. The hologram of evolution illuminates a concept of unity consciousness in a unique way, for a hologram is known to be such that each part holds the sum of the all.

One could look at that from the perspective of a blueprint, from the perspective of a holographic inscription of energy. The blueprint holds the energy of the emanation of the blueprint or plan in its inception, in its conception, in its premanifested state in some ways. The building follows the blueprint. As we look at the evolution hologram, the hologram of evolution, and the idea that the part holds all the information of the one, of the wholeness, then it is likened to unity consciousness. It is a conceptual way of perceiving unity consciousness—for unity consciousness includes everything. Unity consciousness is wholeness. Unity consciousness is that which is vibrating from the awareness of everything being interconnected—of everything being in a state of wholeness. That is like hologram upon hologram, upon hologram, upon hologram.

As we have spoken about, there are trillions of cells in the body and the trillions of cells in the body are making up the body and so on and so forth. It is along this thought line that we would bring up the idea of you being a Being of Light, a being of holographic evolution, and that within you resides everything that you need to evolve into the next level of consciousness. Because this book in particular is coming into the hands of those who are leaders, pioneers, star seeds, it is evident that you have been birthed, conceived at a time in which what you require to be in a state of consciousness that is unified resides within you. It resides within you like a library holds books, like your DNA holds codons, like the blueprint holds the plan for the building.

The awareness of evolution denotes that there is an unfolding, there is an evolving, there is a developing, there is a growing. It is also the same with you and with the planet at this time. Every experience that you've had in this incarnation has held energy and purpose, including the experiences of challenge, lack, and separation. It is from separation consciousness that unity is remembered, is rebirthed. Via pollination, the life cycle of a flowering plant continues after the flower that's come to full bloom has separated from the plant.

As such, all that you have experienced has been important. Sometimes when you are engaged with consciousness of this caliber, of this distilled level of refinement by virtue of your proximity to it, your system may go into some kind of a deflection mechanism such as, "Who am I to be on this consciousness journey?" Or a sense of being afraid of the power that resides within these words and within you. Perhaps you experience separation patterns such as self-doubt, fear of being seen, unworthiness, and many, many, many other patterns that you are familiar with already.

We want to say that unity consciousness includes all that there is, including these patterns, including these limiting beliefs—including separation consciousness—that you may experience. Stating this at this time provides a context for you to continue forth on your journey and to understand that your patterns of separation consciousness and your patterns of beating yourself up or playing small or holding back or trying to fit in or trying to be perfect, or, or, or (fill in the blank of your preferred pattern) are not only welcome, but they are also instrumental in the hologram of evolution. Within that separation, within that challenge, within that darkness, within that unpreferred experience exists all that there is. That part also holds the sum of all there is and that part is in the energy of wholeness already.

THE ANATOMY OF EVOLUTION

Evolution also has the capacity to evolve in consciousness. Evolution is often thought of in terms of a species, how that species evolves. Evolution is thought of in terms of consciousness. Evolution is thought of in terms of a deepening or a developing. Your relationship evolves, your intelligence evolves, your level of mastery or consciousness evolves.

The interesting thing about evolution as it's frequently spoken about is that it often evolves in a way that is simultaneous, meaning that it shows up in the same way across multiple experiences. The evolution of the human brilliant system, the body, is thought of as showing up in a way that it is applicable to all humans. For example, the evolution of the appendix, from essential to nonessential, is universal to the entire species. The appendix doesn't remain essential for a few and not for others.

We know that your human brilliant system, and the juxtaposition of your human brilliant system in this larger shift in consciousness of evolution, is innovative, is unique, is calibrated to individualized oneness. The kind of evolution that we're speaking about in terms of you, and your becoming that which you are choosing by interacting with the tablets of light, is not an evolution that is going to crop up in every other person on the planet. In fact, it is quite customized to you.

It is a bit like vaults that are sealed by a series of locks keyed to your fingerprint or your eyes. When the retina scan is done, when the fingerprint is imprinted, then the door opens. That which exists within the hologram of you, your evolution, is such that it is only accessible by you, although you can be supported brilliantly in the process. That evolution will show up within you in a way that is unlike how it will catalyze evolution in others.

We don't want to give the impression that your individualized evolution is outside of the hologram of all there is because of course it exists within the hologram of all there is. It has an impact, a ripple effect out into the larger population. What we are describing is the awareness that our role with you here is to nurture and nourish that which resides within you, which is the evolution of your incarnation that is unique, innovative, and extraordinary.

It also makes sense when you look at the conglomeration of your life experience and your past life experiences and your future life experiences that nobody has had the exact combination of experiences that you've had. Your world, in the past, has liked to speak about some of what we're speaking about in terms of nurture versus nature. Your environment, your family, the conditions that you're born into, the experiences that you have, nurture you in a certain way.

We are singling this out: you as an individual are unique, you are extraordinary, and you have within you something that is essential to the larger shift in consciousness, because this is a time of individualized oneness. It is a time when the more that you are being you, the greater is the unlocking within you of the you-ness of you.

This supports the energy of this evolution in consciousness.

EVOLUTION OF LEADERSHIP

We are bringing this up for a variety of reasons. One of them is that sometimes there is this sensation that somebody else could do it, that you're not really important, a downplaying of the role that you have in life. From our perspective it doesn't serve you or anyone else to pass the buck, to come from the vantage point that somebody else could do what you could do, or be what you could be, or know what you could know.

We are bringing this up at this point to really shine the light on you, to put the spotlight on you, to stop giving yourself an out because somebody else could do it better, somebody else is doing it anyhow, somebody else could be the catalyst for the changing times. We are putting this on the altar of your offering plate, to reclaim—to reclaim and restate that much of tribal consciousness and the old paradigm of separation had to do with the coming together in groups in order to survive. There was a morphic field, like a school of fish that would swim together, and there would be a leader, a symmetry, an intercommunication between the fish so much so that the school of fish would move together. One turns and the others turn.

Or if you look at your society there are those who seem to be leading, who seem to be the ones in charge, in power. Whether you are discussing ancient civilizations, aboriginal tribes, or the current government, the proportion of those that seem to have the power to be the leader is small. One out of a hundred has a role of importance and the rest are worker bees. If you look at the queen bee there is one queen bee. The rest of the hive has important roles and yet there is this sense of what we were speaking of—putting it off onto the leader, onto the shaman, onto the president, onto someone who you perceive as having more to give than you. This is unconscious. It is programmed into you to look around and to see others in a light that posits that they are more suited to lead than you are, that they are more suited to express.

We are dismantling this untruth in this conversation because actually, equality is all there is. There is no better than or worse than. To put the charge of your life back into your hands and to gift you with the invitation, the purpose to unfold into the fullness of you, places the charge of your life in the domain of *you*. That is where what you are in the process of accessing, uncovering, discovering, and remembering resides.

It doesn't reside in what anybody else is doing. It resides within you.

✴

UNITY CONSCIOUSNESS EXERCISE

The Holographic Tablet of You

You may imagine—just as you may imagine an ancient tablet of wisdom or hieroglyphs or a beautiful goatskin scroll with emerald and lapis writing, or a crystalline chamber of ancient wisdom, or the Akashic Records, or a scribed text—that you are this as well. You are the book of you. You are the sacred tablet of you. You are the hologram of you. You are the beautifully inscribed library of consciousness of you. You are the Akashic Records of you.

As we are speaking, you may imagine a temple column in Egypt covered with hieroglyphs. These hieroglyphs not only tell a story or convey a message; they're also encoded with sparks of light, with remembering. You may begin to see your own body as this vertical column of light that has within it pictures, light language, sparks of light. Just as someone who cannot see can read Braille with his or her fingers, you who have not been able to see the sacred text of you, the infinite knowledge of you, the tablet of light of you, are now able to sense the sacred symbology of your evolution, of your hologram.

This is creating a bit of an unwiring, an unraveling, a reframing of the experiences that you've had in your life. Just as you could hold your hand over a part of the temple wall and receive almost by osmosis or energy transfer the story from the hieroglyph, you also can begin to receive, from experiences in your life, the full story of those experiences.

We are choosing to keep this broad. We are choosing to not funnel very much into any one experience yet in order to underscore that you are receiving an impression, a broad brushstroke impression of your signature energy, your uniqueness, your evolution, and your individualized oneness.

YOU ARE A KEY OF EVOLUTION

Now that you have this enhanced vision of you having shape, of you having texture, of you having consciousness and energy, you can also think about a key; you are a key of evolution. Just as a key has individualized grooves, a certain shape, pattern, texture, and color, so do you. The lock—that you as a key of evolution open—has taken on the form of your life at this time. Your life creates that which you can plug into to unlock this evolution of consciousness, to evolve from the states of being that you have experienced, into territory that is beyond your current level of experience.

If you're in a room that's locked, what is outside the room is outside of your current experience. Because the shift in consciousness is such that it is moving into territory that has been forgotten, that is unknown, it can only be moved into from a place of openness, from a place of forgetting all that you have known. This means that your patterns, thoughts, emotions, and ways of being don't apply in the dimension of consciousness that you are choosing to be aware of, that already exist within you. You're not really going anywhere, yet you're moving in energy and in location vibrationally.

As this forgetting to remember is required, there is the sloughing off of the old skin, just as a snake does, and yet it is bit more like those transformer machines in movies where there was a truck and then the truck dismembers and then it becomes a plane. There are some things in common between a truck and a plane. They are still objects of transportation and yet they operate in different realms— one on the Earth, one in the sky and on Earth. It is the same with you: as you refigure, transfigure, and evolve, some things will remain the same. You are still a vehicle of evolution. You are still a Divine being. However, the dominion, the dimension, the field you play in is different. It is different.

A TRANSMUTATION PROCESS

Imagine that this journey through *The Tablets of Light* is a bit of a weight-loss journey. Imagine that perhaps you weigh a thousand tons at the beginning of this journey. The journey will be like walking through a cavern under the Earth or in between two mountains in that as you continue on, the path narrows, squeezing you. As such, to continue on this path, you will be required to take off the thousand tons. You will be required to take off the backpack and the extra stuff that you're carrying, which is really outdated anyway. For you are going through a channel, going through a transmutation process, to come out on the other side transformed. You will emerge with a different shape, a different way of being, a different perspective.

We know at times that this process can feel intense, for as you are being squeezed and encouraged to lighten your load, there is a distillation process. One in which you take one step at a time. And although you may experience this time as intense, know that it has purpose, for you have everything within you, and all is well.

We will conclude this installment with the idea that you have packed for your journey before this incarnation and that everything you have packed has the capacity to transform into something that you need more of in each now moment. It may have appeared to be one way and yet actually it can become another way. In this process that which you have brought with you is transforming, up-leveling, upgrading, transmuting. In this, it is tapping into that which it actually already is.

Evolve Repetitive Patterns

Take a few deep breaths before moving into the exercise, the purpose of which is to identify your repetitive patterns. To help identify these patterns, bring into your awareness something that you want—a goal or a dream—and write it down on a piece of paper.

Once you have written down your dream, write down the ways that you hold yourself back from realizing this goal or this dream. It may be a belief like you're not worthy, you're powerless, you can't have what you want. Or it may be that if you have it you'll lose love. Continue to write the ways that you hold this dream out of your life. Maybe it's that you take two steps forward and one step back. Maybe it's that you pretend to be the most powerless powerful person. Maybe it's . . .

Write down your repetitive patterns, the ways of being that are very common to you, your go-to ways of being. Identify these repetitive patterns, the ones that you repeat over and over and over again, the thoughts that you have over and over again. We're speaking of ones that are unpreferred, that you may call negative.

Once you have identified them, set the intention before you go to bed that these repetitive patterns evolve and transmute while you're sleeping. Just let them rest overnight with the intention that these repetitive patterns evolve into their next level of consciousness with ease and grace for all levels of your system.

When you wake up in the morning you may see these repetitive patterns in a new light, in a new way of being. Perhaps you know that within these repetitive patterns resides the key of your evolution. Ask yourself upon awakening if these repetitive patterns are a key to your evolution, what are they unlocking, what are they telling you, what are they sharing with you.

We'll see you on the other side of this exercise.

3
Cosmic Choice

Resurrect the Energy of Infinite Choice

This transmission is about cosmic choice. Cosmic choice is such that you are in a space of awareness; you are in the energy of choice. This energy of choice is on the level of the cosmos, on the level of galactic proportions.

The energy of choice is something that flies under the radar. There can be a learned pattern of displacing your choice throughout each day, throughout each moment, and throughout your incarnation. What is meant by displacing your choice is that you can disconnect from choice and place it somewhere outside of you. Then, as you build a pattern of displacing choice, it can feel as if your life is over, that your life is predictable, that your life is in a groove or rut, and that you don't have any choice in the matter. Or if you have a choice it's one that's very limited. You may be able to choose between the right hand and the left hand and yet the awareness that you could choose both doesn't seem to be on the docket or in the cards.

As we speak about choice there is the awareness of the multidimensional energies of choice. As you are choosing, there is the placement of empowerment in the word *choice*. Someone who is empowered chooses. Someone who is a leader chooses. Someone who is a guide chooses. Someone who is a holder of an oracular vision chooses. Someone who is on a holographic evolutionary journey chooses. Someone who is

27

one of one chooses. By introducing the concept of choice at this juncture of our conversation we are resurrecting multiple layers of awareness that as one who chooses, which is you, you are empowered. You are a creator. You are on the leading wave of consciousness.

Without going into this very much (because it just doesn't serve our purpose together to go into it more deeply at this time), one who doesn't choose is one who is outside of their Divine birthright of empowerment. The Divine birthright of empowerment is such that at its base you're aware that you are an ensouled Divine being, you are an infinite being. One who has stopped choosing is one who has stepped out of Divine order with the capacity for and the birthright of empowerment.

How do you know if you're choosing or if you are outside of your empowered choice? You know because you have the sense of being aware of what you're doing, how you're being, and the culmination of what you're doing and how you're being over the time period of your life. To be conscious of what you're doing and how you're being from a place of choice allows access to infinite possibilities and allows access to what we're calling cosmic choice.

NOTHING EXISTS OUTSIDE OF CHOICE

When you're not choosing, or when you have the *sense* that you're not choosing, oftentimes what's happened is that you *are* choosing, because there really isn't any way to get outside of choice. Yet you're choosing to be powerless, you're choosing to let things happen to you, you're choosing to play the victim, you're choosing to allow a circumstance to be bigger than you, you're choosing to give up, you're choosing to play small, you're choosing to stay in a comfort zone, you're choosing to repeat a pattern.

That brings us to cosmic choice, because whether it feels as if you're choosing or not choosing, nothing can exist outside of choice. There is no assertion in the universe. Nothing can be added to you or taken away from you. You are perfect, whole, and complete, and you are a creator of worlds. This is true whether or not you choose to understand, align, or create from the awareness that you are creating your reality or whether you choose to feel as if you don't have any choice. Again, nothing exists outside of choice. There is a saying that people will do what they want to do. That is because it is their choice.

As we have entered into the domain of choice, and we have opened up the awareness that nothing exists outside of choice. The energy of choice is brought into your life once more. Reclaiming the energy of choice back in your life resurrects possibility because, as we are saying, nothing exists outside of choice and therefore you must exist *within* choice. Your life exists within choice, your relationships exist within choice, your finances exist within choice. On some level you have chosen everything that is in your life at this moment. You are in agreement with it.

Where the choice happens and when it happens isn't really pertinent to this discussion. The content of this conversation, the purpose of this conversation, is to resurrect the energy of choice into your awareness and into your life. Only you are powerful enough to choose less than empowerment.

That this choice energy is within all that there is, and all that there is is within choice, allows you the space to renegotiate your choices, to take a look again at what you're choosing and to choose something new, to choose something beyond. Part of the capacity to remember that you have a choice occurs from your awareness of being an infinite being. Would an infinite being have no choice? Would an infinite being be outside of choice? No, an infinite being has choice; it has within it the ability to choose.

As you are remembering your infinite being-ness through *The Tablets of Light,* through this conversation, you are entering back into the multidimensionality of you. This is where the spectrum of choice expands from the awareness of having one or two or three choices in a situation, to having an infinite possibility of choice. For when you are operating as the multidimensional infinite being that you are, your units of consciousness exist in a greater state of wholeness. Therefore, you're tapped into something broader, cosmic, infinite.

THE RESULTS OF CHOOSING
TO BE OUTSIDE OF YOUR INFINITE NATURE

When you are choosing to be outside of your infinite nature and your capacity to realize that you're choosing *not* to choose, what often happens is that you begin to operate in a smaller area of your dimensionality. You begin to operate very much in a predictable manner, very much in a repetitive pattern, very much in the domain of smallness. The domain of smallness is chosen by way of multifaceted ways of being to maintain that area of smallness. And yet even though it's chosen, it's not realized that it's chosen. Thus what this often looks like is that you begin to hang out in a comfort zone comprised of similar ways of thinking, being, and feeling.

It begins to be this hamster wheel where you're constantly in motion and yet you're just spinning; you're staying in place. To chunk that down into an example, what begins to happen when you are choosing to be powerless on a regular basis is that the domain in which you are operating from becomes one or two or three dimensions. It becomes fear, it becomes worry, it becomes holding back, it becomes blaming others, it becomes some type of resistance or some type of chronic way of being.

This is when you really stop living and you stop being engaged in your life. At this point, you are just in an echo. Just in an echo—an echo of decisions that have been made in past incarnations, an echo of repetitive patterns, an echo of emotional conclusions. When this happens, the magic of life isn't seen, the bliss of life isn't seen, the real choice that you're given each day when you wake up isn't seen. It just isn't seen.

WRITTEN EXERCISE
· · · · · · · · · ·
Own Your Choices

We would insert a written exercise at this point for you to become aware of what it is that you're choosing. To become aware of what you're choosing you can look at your life. You can look at your life and you can begin to describe that.

We understand that you have different areas of your life and that you may perceive that some areas are going better than others. We want to play a game here, as you're doing this exercise. We want you to say, "I have chosen, I am choosing, I choose," "I have been choosing to . . . "—whichever feels the most resonant for how you're going to finish that sentence. Then look at an area of your life. "I have been choosing to be exhausted. I have been choosing to be too busy. I have been choosing to be the victim. I have been choosing to be in this loving relationship. I have been choosing to have a career that I love."

There will be aspects that you will feel you've been choosing correctly, because you like those areas that are going well in your life. There will also be some that you will write about from the place of negativity or consider to not be going well in your life. Continue this exercise: "I have chosen, I am choosing, I choose," "I have been choosing to . . . " Go through the various areas of your life: your health, your emotions, your thoughts, your ways of being, your family, your home, your career, your hobbies—whatever they are. Spend ten to fifteen minutes on this exercise.

Ready to know the punch line before the joke? It's that the purpose of this exercise is to indicate to you that what's going on in your life is a reflection of your capacity to choose. When you tie together what's going on in your life with your capacity to choose, you're able to realize that you have a choice. You are able to access your capacity to choose in a way that allows you to choose something new.

We want to invite you to do this written exercise now: to spend the next ten to fifteen minutes doing this written exercise before continuing on with the information that follows.

TRIBAL CONSCIOUSNESS AND CONDITIONING

We want to speak about tribal consciousness and conditioning as it relates to this ability to choose. Part of what has occurred through tribal consciousness and through collective conditioning is that a choice that could be infinite in terms of its possibilities has already been narrowed down before you choose it. It already has become narrowed down to four or five different choices before you even choose it.

Our underlying purpose of this conversation is to create leaders, to create innovators, to create way showers, to reactivate leaders, to remember leaders, to provide a direct transmission that sparks something within you to remember that which you already have access to. Part of that process involves shining a light on where you've been conditioned to *not* lead, to *not* innovate, to *not* go for it, to *not* shine, to *not* play full-out, to *not* put your cards on the table, to *not* get out of your comfort zone. You may understand that this is what you've been conditioned to but that, as you become anchored in unity consciousness, no longer applies to you. At this point you are able to regain what we're calling cosmic choice—you regain infinite choice, you regain multidimensional choice.

Let's explore this in a slightly different way to spiral more into the awareness of conscious choice. Let's look at an animal experiment wherein animals who are conditioned to press a red button receive food as a result. But maybe there's also a green button, a purple button, a white button, and a yellow button. This is assuming the animal can see colors and yet the animal doesn't even see those other buttons anymore. Actually, the white button would open the enclosure and the animal could leave it and then have access to an infinite supply of food. However, the animal has been conditioned to just press the red button, get the food, eat the food, and stay in the enclosure. It no longer even considers pressing the white button, getting out of the enclosure, and having infinite access to all there is.

This is a rough analogy that we're building. We know that it's not exactly a seamless analogy or example and yet it gets the point across. Perhaps it gets the point across a little too harshly when we say that you're a conditioned animal inside of an enclosure just pressing the red button every day. When you wake up you get the food that you need in order to survive. If we say it this clearly it'll irritate you, it'll ruffle your feathers, and that energy creates momentum—it creates consciousness.

YOU ARE A HOLOGRAM OF EVOLUTION
AND AN INFINITE BEING

We began this conversation speaking about how the ancient and forgotten and the new and remembered are one and the same. The ancient, old, forgotten wisdom and new, innovative, remembered wisdom are one and the same. You are in a hologram of evolution. We can go into any one point of your evolution and access all that there is in the evolution. You can go into one point in the hologram to find that everything to create the entire wholeness resides within that hologram.

What, from our perspective, you have forgotten is that you are an infinite being, that you are the Divine, that you are Source. As such, when that is remembered, really, really, really remembered—and is not just something you tell yourself to get through the night or a spiritual belief that you have—and you have embodied this knowledge, you're playing in an entirely different arena than the one that you're playing in now. The one that you've been playing in says that you are a finite being and that each day is a finite game, it's a finite experience, it's about survival, getting by, it's about pushing the red button.

But what if you say, "Okay, I've chosen to participate and to be incarnated during separation consciousness, during survival consciousness, and I've chosen to be conditioned to the responses that are going to help me survive, that are going to get me through, that are going to get me by, that are going to get me to be part of the tribe." Then you can say that all of those skills that you've had in survival consciousness have the capacity within them to evolve. Ask them to evolve, ask them to move into their next level of evolution. *Choose* to evolve them into their next level of evolution.

As you are choosing to reactivate your cosmic choice you can begin to remember the white button, operating outside of the enclosure, and having access to that which you can't access from doing the same thing in the same way, which you've done up until this point. A leader of a shift in consciousness doesn't do the same thing that's been done up until this point. The innovator, the new thought leader, the exponential consciousness evolver, accesses something in a way that is beyond what has been accessed before. It is cosmic; it is exponential.

Let's say that in the past when you've pressed the white button you've gotten a shock, and so pressing the white button isn't a choice anymore. It gets taken off the table—the choice isn't even there. You're not going to put yourself through that again, you're not going to get shocked. What about in the meantime? The button doesn't have any electricity in it anymore and the battery has died. You can press it and not get shocked and yet you don't know that unless you press it and you don't know that unless you also dismantle the electricity that was giving the charge to give the shock. The electricity that gives the charge that gives the shock resides in your DNA, it resides in your Akashic Records, it resides within the collective consciousness, and it resides in some very general ways among people. It also resides for you in a very specific way.

Some of the general ways are that if you really express an idea that is a reflection of you then somehow you will be shocked, you will be killed, you will be rejected, you will lose love, you will disappear, you won't survive. You could look at that from an evolutionary standpoint: the one who left the cave, who was the pioneer, who was the innovator, went into the tiger's territory and got eaten. Or the one that said, Let's do it this way, got silenced. The one that was the prophet got persecuted. You could look at this from a past life experience, from the times before when you innovated and accessed that which you have access to. Things didn't end well for you, or for someone else.

You can look at this from an illusion of control, which you've displaced to exist outside of you. That illusion of control says that the choice to press that white button isn't really yours to make, and that if you press that white button then you're going to get shocked. The only choice you have is to *not* press the white button and to *not* have what's outside the enclosure and unlimited access to everything. That doesn't feel like a choice and it puts the choice on others.

YOU ARE A CREATOR BEING

When you come from the awareness that you are a creator being and that you've created everything that exists in your life—including the shock—you can trust your creation and put the empowerment back in your hands. Put the empowerment and the awareness back in your hands. Put the choice back in your own hands. Nothing happens outside of the arena of choice. What is it that you're choosing or not choosing?

We have spoken about choice and the capacity to choose and we have encoded this with an energy and scribed consciousness to go beyond just the words. For words create their own mazes, they create their own sticking points, they create their own conclusions. The purpose of this conversation about choice is to unlock choice, to free choice, to take it out of shackles, to take it out of conclusion, to take it out of limitation, and to resurrect it into the infinite choice that it actually is.

As was mentioned in the example of the animal that's in the enclosure, in your life it may appear as if the actual choices that you have are quite limited or quite small. This is especially true just as you step onto the precipice of tapping into something beyond what you've tapped into before. When this happens, that part of you—that is so powerful that you're pretending to be powerless or that's stopping you—can get even louder.

We know that because you are in this conversation with the tablets of light that you are on this tipping point; you are on this precipice. With this tipping point comes your capacity to identify untruths and illusions as they arise for what they are. For example, as the old belief arises that the control and the choice of your life exists outside of you, you can see clearly that this is untrue. You can see the dimensions in which you're operating in repetitive patterns also aren't true. Those are just echoes, those are just echoes, those are just echoes, those are just echoes. Through this conversation we're providing the opportunity to dismantle everything, and to resurrect your capacity to have free choice, to have conscious choice, and to have cosmic choice.

We will talk more about choice and no choice, and yet let's introduce the energy of cosmic choice at this time to tap into your evolution as an infinite being in the arena of the cosmos. The part of the no-choice choice that becomes so familiarized, so routinized, is that you operate within the concept of one incarnation of one day of one you. You wake up, you have your body, you have your life. It's all going to be pretty much the same as yesterday and that will evolve plus or minus 10 percent in somewhat of a default future for a decade, two decades, three decades, four decades, five decades, six decades, seven decades, eight decades, maybe nine decades, maybe ten decades.

There is a simultaneity of the absolute denial that this incarnation is sitting within the concept of time, of a lifespan and a lifetime. It always feels like there is a tomorrow, that even though there is the awareness that your body does stop at one point, and there is a transition that is called death, it's not something that is lived with often (although for some it's *too* lived with).

Simultaneously there's the sense that it doesn't really matter who you are on any given day or what you do on any given day because there's always tomorrow and what you do really doesn't make that much difference. So why do something outside the norm? Why do something extraordinary if you're only connected to this lifetime? The idea of cosmic choice takes the supposition that you're being in your life outside of the arena of a lifetime or a lifespan to a cosmic level, to a multidimensional level. It takes it to a certain level of awareness, an understanding that there is much more happening beyond what you can see, feel, taste, and experience in your daily life.

You have a cosmic choice and what you're choosing right now actually is creating a direction of energy that will be experienced in a hundred years, two hundred years, three hundred years, four hundred years, five hundred years and counting, from now. From our perspective if you can really plump out to be beyond the context of your lifespan while at the same time maximizing the momentum of your lifespan, you are in a sweet spot. You are in a place of freedom, you are in a place of connection, because there's the sense of what you would call building a legacy. There's a sense that the choices you're making now are creating consciousness on a cosmic level beyond Earth, this incarnation, other planets, other civilizations. This is a cosmic perspective, a cosmic choice. You are up-leveling your awareness while simultaneously having it absolutely be about this moment, this incarnation. Your choices on this day create this powerful combination, this powerful combination.

We know it's easy for us to say that what you like to call your purpose is not probable, it is inevitable. Who it is that you are and what it is that you're meant to express and experience is a given. It's going to occur and yet we're stringing together an awareness of multidimensional living. Some speak of that multidimensional living as follows: You're not only living this lifetime right now; you're living in all lifetimes right now. You're not living only in this incarnation or this planet at this time; there are parallel realities or parallel lives. We don't find that way of thinking very pertinent to evolving the units of consciousness that reside in this incarnation. This is because this way of thinking also begins to split your energy to some idea that maybe there's another you in a parallel universe that's just got it all figured out or that's doing worse than you are. That's the problem in this.

You have multidimensional choice, multidimensional *cosmic* choice. The awareness that what you choose or don't choose to be and to do and to have in this incarnation is in the context of a cosmic choice. A choice that you've made and continue to make on a

Divine level, on a soul level, is plugged into and is interacting with this lifetime.

If you woke up tomorrow with the idea that you had absolute infinite choice on that day as a cosmic being, as an infinite being, then what could you choose that isn't available when you wake up with finite awareness and a range of possibilities that *is* limited?

We know that you could be misinterpreting this conversation to say that we're blaming you or we're saying that you're not doing it right or that you're just stuck in a small hamster wheel or pressing the same button. That we're saying this to simply point out that you're doing all these types of separation-consciousness things without a deeper purpose. However, we're sharing this to say that you have set it up for yourself exactly the way that it is. As such, in pushing the red button again and again and again and again, exists multidimensional cosmic choice.

Where in your life right now, where in a pattern that you've had over and over again, is more choice? What's right about what's not right in your life? What's right about being in survival consciousness? What's right about being within the multidimensional temple of the pages of *The Tablets of Light* having this conversation?

CONSCIOUS CHOICE EXERCISE
· · · · · · · · · · ·
Remember Your Cosmic Choice
to Incarnate with an Innovative Mission

As you go to sleep on this night, if you choose, we recommend that you begin to remember your cosmic choice, your cosmic choice. We recommend that you tie this incarnation to that cosmic choice to incarnate, to come with a mission, to understand that a part of your mission is to pioneer something, to innovate something, to lead something, to access something—and that you are the one that actually has within you that which unlocks everything for you.

YOU ARE THE KEY
THAT UNLOCKS THE LOCKS

We're saying that you are the key that unlocks the locks because it is an interesting thing to create this book of Thoth's tablets with you with the understanding that we are discussing certain concepts and certain arenas. And yet those concepts and those arenas are simply just locks that are being unlocked, that are sparking within you that which you know. There comes a time in your life, in the life of a leader, in the life of a pioneer, that you know what actually will light you up, what actually is within your awareness, and the way to access it uniquely for you. You have that within you.

We are creating a platform that many of you, who have called it forth, will plug into. It contains the blueprint that is designed to activate your uniqueness within you. That is a different proposition than providing a training manual that you follow wherein A plus B plus C plus D . . . and then you arrive at Z. What we're doing here together is igniting dormant codes of consciousness within your system that then activates within you what you already know—what it is that you know.

It's not about what *we* know; it's about what it is that *you* know. To create an environment, to create a temple of these pages that creates an environment for you to know what it is that you know, represents an extraordinary threshold of consciousness and of awareness. That's where your multidimensionality, your cosmic choice, interfaces with these words, energies, and multidimensional concepts in such a way that what is in, around, and through each of the words gets accessed by you and to you.

It's a little bit like different coded messages on a piece of paper. They are not to be read by just anybody who finds the piece of paper. There's a key that goes with it wherein every O equals a letter or a certain thing. Then, as you read it that way, you pull out the words that are actually embedded within the context of a seemingly innocuous page of words. Breaking the code of what the deeper message is, without the key, is impossible. Accessing what's embedded in these pages, without you—for you are the key—is impossible.

Each person that engages with these pages will access something unique, something different, because their key will pull out different information. It's like with DNA—what gets created in DNA gets created from the same letters: *A, T, C, G.* Depending on where you start reading those letters, either a protein is created or a toenail is created. There is an inner librarian, so to speak, who is a creator. That is the same with *The Tablets of Light,* that is the same with the Akashic Records, that is the same with your life. You are the librarian. You are the key that decides to start reading the fabric of creation in a certain way, which then creates the perfect people, places, and opportunities in your life.

If you've been on autopilot, if you've been sleepwalking, if you've been in a domain of concluding that that *O* equals an *A,* when actually the *O* could equal an *O,* cosmic choice allows you to be aware that there's something beneath the key. It's like those dolls that are placed within dolls that are placed within dolls. If you didn't know that the doll opened up, the head and the body opened up into two parts, you'd never know there was something inside.

If you thought that, after the first time it was over, you'd never know that there was another doll inside and another doll inside and another doll inside and another doll inside and another doll inside. It's the same with these pages. If you are interacting with them without your key of conscious cosmic choice engaged, then what you tap into is a certain dimension. And yet throughout each page you access more dimensions, more dimensions, more dimensions, more dimensions. You being you full-out is what is the key, is what opens up possibility, is what opens up your cosmic choice, your creative choice.

As you sleep on this night, if you choose, choose to access your cosmic choice and, as such, begin to operate in the awareness that nothing exists outside of your choice. If it's in your life you've chosen it and therefore you can choose something else. You can have access to more choice than you ever thought possible.

It is with great joy and appreciation that we complete this segment of cosmic choice, knowing that you are in agreement with what you are in agreement with—nothing more and nothing less. That agreement can be augmented, enhanced, renegotiated, or expanded at any moment.

4

Ring of Inclusion

A Path to You in Wholeness

CREATE AN ENVIRONMENT OF STILLNESS
THROUGH THE RHYTHMIC PULSE OF INCLUSION

We are gathering strands of consciousness like a bird gathers branches to create a nest. We are traveling into various dimensions to find these strands of consciousness to weave into the awareness of your evolution, your contribution, and your awakening from the illusion.

We are, in a sense, slowing down the rhythmic pulse of this installment of consciousness for the purpose of creating an environment of stillness, an environment of complete acceptance and oneness. This energy spiral or rhythmic pulse is one of inclusion. You can think of this environment that's being created for this transmission as a ring of inclusion, a spiral of inclusion. This ring of inclusion has an elevator of dynamic energy assimilation that is moving vertically like an elevator, ascending and descending, and yet also spherically like a spiral, like a ring. This spiral of inclusion is assimilating energies, and the outcome of assimilated or included energies is a sense of stillness, unity, and peacefulness.

This environment is reopening a tablet of consciousness, Divine Union, which resides within *The Tablets of Light*. This remembered Divine Union transcends so much of what can transpire for you in a day when you're in a state of separation consciousness and excluding

42

or not accepting or assimilating experiences, impulses, and energies. As you choose to come with us into this ring of inclusion, the sensation that you may be aware of is one of feeling as if things are simplified, bottom-lined, and cohesive.

It's like someone who is drilling for oil, for example. As they're drilling there is a lot of vibration, there is a lot of hard substance that has to be broken up. There is resistance. It takes a lot of energy. Then once things are pushed through into the oil there is a softening, there is a change in the density and the texture, and in the rhythmic pulsation.

As you are drilling in your own way for Divine Union, you may experience a sense of being fractured from yourself, splitting off from yourself, or separating from yourself. The way that this can show up is as a friction within your own being. This friction may show up to you as a lot of activity within pockets of activity. Here's an example: You may just be sitting in a chair, and yet while you're sitting in that chair—where your body isn't active in terms of running or walking or jumping—your mind may be very active. It may be like a jackhammer, creating a sense of tension. Or your emotions may be spiraling out of control with worry, force, fear, having to be and do more, and to go all of the time.

Your awareness of continuity within your own system begins to become fractured. It is as if there are particles of consciousness that are frozen in certain repetitive patterns and certain ways of being. This can result in a sensation of survival, when there is nothing to survive. There is no imminent danger, there is nothing that needs to be fixed or changed, and yet the inner drive is pushing to find that oil. The inner drive is on high alert. This can result in a sensation of being fractured, of being what often is referred to as anxious, and a pulsation of consciousness that is uninformed.

We're using this language very intentionally when we say that what can occur is that there are aspects that get frozen in a repetitive pattern because that exists in a dimension that's outside of this environment of inclusion that we're speaking of. This ring of inclusion defrosts the frozen vibration back into oneness, back into wholeness.

For the ease of conceptualizing, imagine that you have been a magnet and that as you have been traveling through this journey called life you have picked up all kinds of screws, junk metal, nails, iron filings, and discarded rusted barrels. You have picked up all kinds of fractions and fractured energy that, as you are walking in the *now* moment, create a sensation that you are stuck, powerless, separate from that which you would choose to have or be.

This ring of inclusion, this environment that we're creating, this Divine Union, is creating the sense of everything being simplified because it's stripping away all that scrap metal that you've picked up along the way that isn't really uniquely you or yours. Once all that noise and weight is stripped away then things become clear, then things become still, then your vibration is optimally functioning.

We want to specify that we are not speaking about action and non-action in terms of being active or being still. You can be very active with a lot of projects going at once or very physically active, moving your body quickly. At the same time, you may still be connected to this ring of inclusion and be connected to this rhythmic pulse of Divine Union, which then creates a distilled awareness within each *now* moment that is awake, aware, and conscious. You can energetically vibrate into what it is we're speaking of, this ring of inclusion, this Divine Union, and reintegrate what has been displaced and include what has been frozen. This occurs all from within the inner planes.

This brings us to an interesting conversation about the inner planes and about the outer planes. The outer planes are your external life. *The Tablets of Light* has much anchored in the awareness of the potency of you that can be accessed through awakening on the inner planes.

With that there is a tendency for less is more when it comes to activity that is accompanied by consciousness, meaning that as you move into inspired action from a state of Divine Union it is more potent and therefore less activity may be required. And yet you may have gone too far into inaction or what may have gotten turned upside down within your pursuit of remembering, awakening, or your awareness of the potency of your inner planes, is that which signifies, in this distorted way, an unplugging from being engaged in your life, from having activities. Meaning that you may have created for yourself a pulling back in some way—whether that is an introversion, a reclusiveness, or a pattern of disengaging induced by mind-numbing chemicals, foods, activities, books, or TV—whatever it is.

The outcome of adding a lot of disengaged experiences, which has less to do with what the experience is than how it is that you're being with the activities, is a sense of not being engaged, and a frenetic energy. Because actually to be in this ring of inclusion and alignment with Divine Union you are hyperaware, you are highly engaged, and yet what you're aware of and what you're engaged with is simplified, it is wholeness and union. It is the ease of the universe.

Much of what we provide in *The Tablets of Light* is a process by which you can dismantle from those ways of being that have been creating a restlessness, a frenetic energy, a sense of survival, and an illusion of separation. You may have been operating from a very complicated formula of awareness and of awakening. What we are proposing or inviting you to remember is that it is all much easier than that.

INCLUSION, DIVINE UNION, AND A STATE OF ZEN

There is much more to be expressed on the subject of inclusion, of Divine Union, and yet what we are truly transmitting is the experience of it. The experience of it is like going from not seeing to being able to see with crystal clarity. It is like going from striving, struggle, survival, to realizing that all is well all the time. A slight shift in consciousness creates another dimensional perspective of what's occurring.

The word *Zen* comes forward at this time to describe how one can be on one's journey of life. One can be in a state of Zen, in a state of stillness, in a state of being plugged in, and that rapidly changes the journey of the life experience. Many times you have tried to change the outcome, the destination, so that it is better, more fixed. That process is such that, at times, what has ended up happening is a greater alignment with the idea, the concept, the illusion that something isn't right.

That mimics the impulse and the system that has been broadcasted through separation consciousness that something's not right, that you're in danger, that you have to act a certain way in order to survive. Even as the things are changed in the external environment your inner sensation that there is something wrong remains. You may have an experience of this from your own life. Maybe you always wanted a partner and you didn't have a partner and then you *did* have a partner. What you thought would come with having a partner actually didn't come. This is because you had a sense that the partner would complete what was missing within you, yet in reality, he or she did not.

Or perhaps you wanted to have more money and then you had the experience of having more money. Yet that experience of having more money didn't create the sensation that you thought it would. It didn't change anything much on the internal plane because there was a memory pulsation that (and we know this is very subtle) the having of what you wanted—more money or a partner—proved the lie that there was something wrong with you before.

One of the deeply embedded, old paradigms of consciousness is that if you actually allow yourself to have what you want in terms of the outcome of your life, the destination of your life, this proves that you're not whole already. If you think you need something external to complete you, you are buying into the idea that you are incomplete without that thing. Another separation-consciousness illusion is the idea that knowing you are already whole will prevent the destination from occurring, that somehow you need separation, fear, and lack in order to create. Yet if you create from separation you must always be separate from that which you are wanting. That is why, from our perspective, it is the inner evolution that we are leaning toward, illuminating more and more frequently. Because it is through the inner illumination that the journey is experienced in a way that signals to your entire being that all is well, that you are in Divine Union. Then what is created from that energy and vibration is ascended into an awakening process.

STAYING IN THE GAME

You're the only one who can take yourself out of this evolution in the consciousness game. Not that it's really a game, yet if you use the analogy that you're on the playing field, that you're in the game, you're engaged. A lot of times in a game there's a coach and there's a team and there are two ways you can get taken out of the game as a team member. The coach can say, "You're out. You're on the bench. You're not playing anymore." You can also say, "I'm injured. I'm tired. I need a break." Whatever it is, you can take yourself out of the game. In this evolution in consciousness playing field there is no coach that says you're out: *you're* the only one that can take yourself out.

You may have learned that an acceptable way to get out of the game is by having slower vibrational or unpreferred experiences be the reason you sit out on the bench. We know this is a very tricky segment, yet that may be the acceptable way that you would use to take yourself out of the game, to take yourself off the playing field, to take your foot off the infinite energy that's propelling you forward. That is something in separation consciousness, in collective consciousness, that is accepted. It's accepted that if you have a headache you don't go to work. If you're sick you stop. If you're in pain you don't move forward.

We're saying it's a tricky segment because we know that you could interpret this as us saying, "Well, just ignore any pain that you're having. Just keep going. Just push through," which is a way of being that is associated with the paradigm of separation consciousness. You may even have moments of this yourself, where you show absolute stoicism and a disconnection from the body, an inattention to it, if you will. There's just a sense that you must keep going, going, going, even if the arm is broken. That no matter what you would just keep playing and not be in tune enough to recognize that it's time to stop—it's time to take care of this broken arm.

However, we're speaking more on the level of what's unpreferred, or nuances of those patterns that might say, "Take yourself out of the game, take yourself out of the game." In some ways these are more mild manifestations of concern, things that would easily pass through—a headache, let's say, or being tired, or having a body pain, or feeling sad, or feeling depressed, or feeling afraid. When you evolve your consciousness, anything that's hidden or in a slower vibration becomes visible. There's a transparency that you have with it. You can see it.

It is natural, as you are in this process of evolving your consciousness, that you may experience adaptation sensations. These may take the form of slower vibrations coming to the surface to be included in the ring of inclusion. As you know ahead of time that slower vibrations coming to the surface as you are moving into a higher vibration is par for the course, when these sensations come up, you can reframe them as a sign that you are moving into a higher vibration and include the slower vibrations back into the wholeness. Whereas without this awareness, you may have stopped or taken yourself out of the game at the first sign of a slower vibration coming to the surface.

UNITY CONSCIOUSNESS EXERCISE
. . . .
Awareness of Ways You Take Yourself
Out of the Game

What are the ways you would take yourself out of the evolving consciousness game, should you choose to do so? What's your flavor? How would you do it? You know. You know how you would do it because you've done it before. Would you hide out, hold back, or play small out of the fear of being seen? Would you play nice, go into patterns of people pleasing or approval seeking out of the fear of losing love, or being ostracized or killed? Would you tell yourself that it isn't safe, that you're not ready, you don't know enough, that if you play full-out you or someone else will be in danger, be harmed, or disappear? How do you take yourself out of the game? You know. There is zero judgment in what we're sharing. Again, we know you could interpret this to mean that we think you're doing something wrong or you have yourself to blame or you took yourself out of the game before or you took yourself out of the game yesterday.

That's not what we're vibrating. We're vibrating awareness. We're vibrating consciousness. We're vibrating truth. We're allowing that which may happen unconsciously to be conscious. Here it is. We're talking about it. It's a part of the fabric of The Tablets of Light. It's a part of the tablets. It's a part of your evolution in consciousness.

Take a few moments and bring awareness to the ways that you take yourself out of evolving your consciousness. What are your stopping points? If you are able to identify the ways in advance, when a slower vibrational experience or adaptation sensation comes to the surface, just recognize it as a part of the process and keep going. After a few minutes of contemplating the ways you may stop yourself, take a few deep breaths and set your intention to include these ways of being back into the ring of inclusion, back into the wholeness, back into Divine Union.

Then continue reading.

TAPPING INTO POSSIBILITIES
OF HOW THINGS ARE ACTUALIZED

A children's book called *A Wrinkle in Time* speaks about a tesseract. From the perspective of this book, time is a line, and in order to time travel, one can create a wrinkle in this timeline and put the ends together, so to speak. This is a jumping of dimensions. When you have the capacity to shorten the distance by folding the line, what you are choosing to experience within and without is much easier than if you are putting in the miles to arrive at your destination.

As you are tuned into your awake and aware consciousness, the possibility of adapting the experience of your day and the outcome of your day to Divine Union, to this place of stillness, to this place of crystal clarity, is exponentiated.

Let's say you're in a room that contains snakes slithering on the floor. There are children who are playing and yelling and enjoying their time. They're not in danger from the snakes. There are lots of televisions on, all on full volume to different subjects. You are on a treadmill that can go fast, slow, uphill, downhill—and yet no matter how much you go you're staying in the same place. At times you are more exhausted than at other times.

Also, the room is in total darkness and there's an overpowering scent of eucalyptus in it. Your sense of getting off the treadmill and walking out of this room becomes overwhelmed by your awareness that there's something slithering on the ground. Even though you may sense that the snakes wouldn't hurt you, you don't want to step on them.

There are all these noises around you. You don't know that the TV is actually just broadcasting something that's not even in the room. There's this smell, there's no light. In this environment it would be natural to pull in, or to just stay on your treadmill. Getting off the treadmill or even utilizing your voice command to turn off all the TV's, to turn on the light, to ask the children's parents to pick them all up, to get the snake-zookeeper to come and collect all the snakes, to stop the eucalyptus from pouring into the air vents—all of that could be actualized by tapping into the possibility of how it could be actualized. As we're saying, you could, in this scenario, use your voice commands or you could just walk off the treadmill and use your third eye like the ancient initiates to see through the dark and to walk out of this illusionary environment, which in some ways is a rather arbitrary environment.

You could also pull out your ring of inclusion and your ring of inclusion would just absorb everything in the environment back into the oneness, back into the wholeness. It would do this until you're in that state of being plugged into Divine Union. Yet what often begins to happen before it occurs to you to do this is that your environment seems to be larger than you. It seems to have more power than you. It seems that you may have chosen to disengage more and more from life and disengage more and more from empowerment and from choice and from your awake and aware union—and from enjoying the experience.

TRANSCENDING LINEAR TIME

As we are continuing to pulsate this ring of inclusion it's like turning off all those TVs. The kids get picked up and those snakes get picked up and the scent of eucalyptus evaporates and your treadmill disappears. Now all you can really see around you is a blank canvas. Now that you know you have within you the capacity to create this anew, you can create it from a sense of stillness, and in a way that transcends linear time or transcends lots of activity that are based in being in the energy of something needing to be fixed.

We are collecting branches from various dimensions to create your nest of unity consciousness and to return your awareness to that crystal clarity. You can bend reality, fabricate a moment to be whole, to be peaceful, to be still because it already is.

CONSCIOUS CHOICE EXERCISE
• • • • • • • • • •
Invitation to Include Separation
Beliefs into Wholeness

For the remainder of this section we would invite you to choose, if you choose, to turn off the overwhelming environment in your energetic system that is based on the illusion that something is wrong with you, that something needs to be fixed, that life is a struggle, that you are separate from your union with self. You can do this by saying, "I choose to include back into the wholeness this artificial environment. I collapse any untruths, illusion, and false identities back into oneness, back into wholeness."

We are broadcasting a neutralizing energy that is a big one. This neutralizing energy, if you choose to receive it, is including into the ring of oneness, of wholeness, the echoes of original sin, of survival, of not enough-ness, of self-created chaos. As that's being transmitted we want to be clear that we're not suggesting that you won't continue to create more in your life, for the desire to have more doesn't need to go away. That's natural.

What we're saying is, "Where does the desire to have more come from?" Does it come from a sense that once you attain more, you will then be complete? Does it come from a sense that something is wrong with you and you need to prove that you're okay, that you need to fix what is fundamentally wrong with you? Does it come from believing that life is a struggle? Does it come from all of these illusionary beliefs?

Allow this neutralizing energy to take these illusionary beliefs out of the equation so that you're coming from crystal clarity, from Divine Union, from an environment of simplicity, of wholeness. When you do this, the internal environment is positioned to receive even more in each and every moment. This "more" is actually present, but otherwise gets overlooked.

INTERNAL AND EXTERNAL EXPERIENCES

There is the internal experience and there is the external experience. The internal experience, for example—how much you enjoy your life, your moments, your relationships, your career, your finances, how much you're enjoying, how much you're Zen-like, is how you're being on the journey. Your external environment is your destination; it's what's happening on the journey. It is your relationship, it is your career, it is all of that and more.

Let's say that you were to change your external environment for the better, in your estimation by 10 percent, by 15 percent, by 20 percent, by 30 percent, by 50 percent, by 100 percent, and yet your capacity to enjoy that stays the same or gets worse. The external environment in this scenario has not changed your journey, the way that you are in your life.

Now let's flip that equation. Let's say you enhance your internal environment, your capacity to enjoy, the way that you're being on the journey, from the place of oneness, from the place of wholeness, from the place of inclusion, from this rhythmic pulse of stillness and simplicity 10 percent, 20 percent, 30 percent. Then it appears that, within the same external environment, a dramatic improvement has been experienced, because there's always more in your life right now without anything more having been added. It is on the internal side of the equation, it is in the *way* that you experience what you have in your life.

Part of the reason why the environment had seemed so powerful in the past and why the pleasure capacity to enjoy or to be at peace didn't seem accessible was that there was an association that if you were at peace right now, if you were in a state of unconditional joy right now, if you were in a state of unconditional freedom right now, that would be dangerous. The danger was that you would stop paying attention to your external environment. That's not what we're talking about at all. We're talking about bending reality, bending awareness to the inclusion of what exists already, which is harmonic resonance, which is Divine Union, which is wholeness.

How you're being, where you're coming from, has everything to do with the journey and the destination that is experienced and arrived upon. We would share that a lot of the effort that you're expending each day gets eliminated or freed up when you take the time to vibrate in this ring of inclusion before you start your day. Take the time to come into that place of stillness, that place of simplicity, that place of awakening, of crystal clarity. From that space and that place, the enjoyable experience of the journey and the destination are amplified magnificently.

We understand that we are unraveling quite a bit of the fabric of your reality, as it was based in separation consciousness, and we are doing that on purpose not to disorient you. Instead, we are doing it, if you choose, to liberate you.

We will end this chapter with this: One unit of consciousness vibrating in Divine Union is more creative than seven trillion units of consciousness vibrating in distortion, illusion, separation, and lack. Receive this one unit of Divine Union ring of inclusion, right here, right now. Remember it resides within you already.

The simple truth is that the truth is simple.

5

Vibrational Proximity

Divinity Codes to Access the Fullness of You

We are continuing to spiral into the consciousness of *The Tablets of Light* and the awareness that it is encoded with a multitude of energy pockets that are opened by each person who is calibrated to open them. This consciousness is coming forward to be a guide on the journey of the evolution of consciousness by reactivating the dormant divinity codes within. These codes have been waiting to come back alive, into awakening, into an awakened state. As you read these words, your system is interacting with them to access keys of consciousness. These keys of consciousness are related to your personal remembering, evolution, and awakening.

You may be wondering how it is that a book can be interactive and customized in this way, for that is what we are saying. *The Tablets of Light* that you read is unlike any one else's experience of reading the same book, because it is an encoded text just for you. It is designed just for you—to recognize what you have left for yourself to find, what is residing within you already, and what the activation codes of empowerment and of your empowered consciousness are.

You are a leader; you are someone who houses vibration and consciousness. That is your contribution to this evolution in consciousness. And yet it is as if you didn't know that you housed this consciousness until coming into connection with this book. You can imagine that it's like someone who had a tattoo underneath their hair and they never knew it until they shaved their head and then this tattoo was visible. Or someone that might have left a very special key for themselves to find and yet when they find it, they're surprised.

We're describing it in this way because it is such that your Divine awareness has been with you all along and yet it hasn't been the time to access this awareness until now. Nor has it been necessary. Through you accessing your Divine awareness there is a particular ripple effect on the planet that also has a ripple effect intergalactically and throughout all there is. This is the level of presence that your presence has, which is now being remembered through your interactions with this consciousness. You may wonder how it is possible for you to be interacting with words on a page as if you have been in the desert for a long time and they are water, as if they are the missing piece of a puzzle that you've been working on for eons. This coded text is designed to support your full remembering and awakening process and, through that, you're born anew and your contribution is expansive and extensive.

THE FULLNESS OF YOU

It is understood that the way the Earth has been presented to you and the way that you've experienced living on Earth is not *all* of the experience, meaning that Earth has been home to a time of absolute vibrational proximity with the authentic expression of all that there is. Earth has been home to each being experiencing their being-ness fully without doubt, fear, or hesitation—just as a given. That is what these pockets of energy in this chapter are especially about: the remembering of your authentic Divine expression. It is also about remembering that your authentic Divine expression, as it's fully awakened, is gorgeous and exquisite—it is Divine.

Be the Undiluted Version of You

Have a sense of this alchemical awakening occurring with these words. Imagine that if you were a pineapple, as you're reading these words the sun is ripening your fruit to perfection; the sweet juicy fullness, the ultimate pineapple. It's not that before you started reading these pages you weren't already the pineapple in this example; however, through the reading of these pages your full pineapple-ness gets catalyzed.

Anywhere that you've been a diluted version of yourself, a watered-down version of yourself, a safe version of yourself, the interaction with these pages shifts that so that you embody the very fullness of you. For it's not that anything ever needed to be changed about you, or that something was wrong with you or needed fixing. It was simply that you were utilizing some of your energy to try to be less of you, and that isn't who you are, and it isn't who you are in an enlightened state. Engage your conscious choice to become the full concentrated version of you.

RECONNECTION TO SOURCE CONSCIOUSNESS— RIPENING INTO SUCCULENCE

We know that you've had a desire to be reconnected to Source consciousness, to be at one with the beauty of the Divine, to evolve personally and spiritually. At the same time, as you've held that choice, that decision, that desire, you also wanted to hold on to being a diluted, smaller version of yourself. It doesn't work like that. Being re-Sourced and a diluted version of yourself doesn't go together. For as you know yourself as Source, as you know yourself as enlightened, as you know yourself as fully realized, you reclaim being the juiciest, most exquisite pineapple that's ever existed.

We use this example of the pineapple because a pineapple, as you think about it, has a place in your awareness on a sensory level. You can imagine a pineapple that you've eaten that's been tough, dry, bitter, or unripe. Or perhaps you've had a pineapple that's been overripe, soggy, or sour. Maybe you've had a pineapple that has been the true nectar of the Divine, that's been sticky, sweet, nourishing—a vibrational explosion of flavor in your mouth. You interacting with these pockets of consciousness that catalyze your ripening is the process of becoming reconnected to Source in such a way that your Divine design is shining through brilliantly.

You could say, "Well, a pineapple is just a pineapple and what's so important about a pineapple?" We chose this example on purpose because it is about the pineapple being the pineapple-iest it can be. It's not about the pineapple trying to be a plum, kumquat, or raisin, for those are all equally beautiful in their own right. It's about the pineapple being the pineapple, the kumquat being the kumquat, the plum being the plum, the raisin being the raisin. They're all fruits and yet they're all different. *The Tablets of Light* allows you to remember the difference that you are and to be vibrating in the succulent brilliance of that difference—authentically, unapologetically, and deliciously being in vibrational proximity to you. You as Divine, you as you, you as Divine you.

We want to really bring to light this paradox you may be holding yourself in when you say you want to experience oneness, you want to experience God/Goddess, you want to experience all there is. You want to experience spiritual evolution, you want to experience whatever word you would use: *feeling good, ascension, unity consciousness, your Divine birthright, your Divine lineage, your Divine design, your purpose.* Whatever it is that you have been asking for, desiring, choosing, and then simultaneously living the paradox of trying to be a dry pineapple.

Again, it doesn't work like that. We're shining the light on this because it's so subtle and obvious and simple and complex at the same time. Some part of you holds your awareness so clearly of what you know to be true about Source consciousness, about your own being-ness as Source consciousness, and then at the same time you are trying to be a diluted version of yourself, or you feel like you'd rather be an orange than a pineapple or that the oranges that you know seem to have a better life.

BEING IN VIBRATIONAL PROXIMITY TO YOUR WHOLENESS

We like to talk in these ways in order to highlight some ways of being that you may not have realized you've been holding. This chapter, with its pockets of energy that are designed to unlock your fully ripened Divine design, is highlighting the Earth grid of being separate.

We've said that Earth has had a time or two when vibrational proximity existed. What we mean by "vibrational proximity" is that the pineapple is a pineapple, you're you, the lawn mower is the lawn mower. There's a simplicity and an alignment with the Divine design of each thing and each being and how it expresses. Some of you are reclaiming this for yourself. You are choosing to be one who is in vibrational proximity to your own wholeness even in the midst of others choosing being next to themselves or a diluted version of themselves or separate from themselves. In this they are comparing, they are manifesting self-deprecation, self-judgment, holding back, playing small. There is an Earth grid for that overlay, that distortion.

With *The Tablets of Light*, however, for those who are choosing to engage in it in this way, that Earth grid of separation is being purged from your pineapple, from your core essence, so all that there is is the most beautiful, exquisite, yummy pineapple that you can be.

Imagine what it would be like if one out of every thousand people, one out of every ten thousand people, were the full expression of who it is that they are. Imagine what that would be like. Imagine, when you see it already right now, that it's extraordinary. It's why we use the example of the pineapple because you might think of people who are really being the fullest version of themselves are the elite, the Olympic athletes, the Mozarts and the Picassos.

Those are examples of the pineapple being the pineapple. Yet you can also see the pineapple being the pineapple in someone who has never been famous, but when you are with them there is a radiance about their being-ness that just shines through. Maybe they have a simple life yet when you eat a meal that they've prepared or take in their smile it's like you're in the face of magic.

We aren't talking about bigger, better, faster when we're saying "be the pineapple that you are." We're saying, "Be the fullness of you and the fullness of you is authentically you." Maybe you're a mom and you being you is the radiance of the Divine mother energy. Maybe you being you is a quiet authority. There's a disintegration of the judgment of anyone being better than anyone else, to allow everyone to be the brilliance that they are, which is equal to everyone else's brilliance. It was that discordant vibration, which was a part of the Earth grid, which created the disharmonious paradox to begin with. It was thought that apples were better than pineapples or apples had a better life than pineapples and so then the trying to *not* be who it is that you are started to happen. Really, what more would you want from your life or from your loved ones than for them to be, to really be, authentically who they are? As these pockets of consciousness are coming through, you may notice in the background a freedom energy bubbling up. The freedom from trying to be something that you are not opens up a beautiful presence, which is who you authentically are.

THE ILLUSION OF HIERARCHY

There's a difference between comparison and creating a hierarchy of something being better than another thing, and the awareness of the uniqueness of everything there is. This disintegration process that's available through this segment is the disintegration of that comparing up and down, better or worse, to the allowing of the brilliance of what is.

Maybe for you your optimal state of radiant health is manifested in a way that's absolutely right for you. Let's use body weight as an analogy. Let's say you're five feet tall. As such, let's say your optimal body weight is one hundred and five pounds. Let's say you're six foot four and that two hundred and five pounds would be optimal for you. You wouldn't say that a body weight of two hundred and five pounds is best for everyone, or that a body weight of a hundred and five is best for everyone, because for one person it's one thing and for another person it's another thing. To have a hierarchy, to say that "This is the best weight ever," doesn't make sense.

It's the same thing with finances. Maybe for one person a billion or two billion dollars is their ideal wealth. For another person it's ten thousand dollars, or twenty thousand dollars or Euros or whatever. What's important is not just to lock into the notion by saying, "Well, this is the number, this is the right number for the year, this is the right number for life," based on the randomness of it, because maybe for you one hundred and five pounds is optimal, or maybe for you two hundred and five pounds is optimal.

It's not an arbitrary selection that reflects, "Well, this is what's got to be." It's realizing what the you-ness of you *is*, what the radiant health of you *is*, what the radiant wealth for you *is*—what's the best expression of your gifts and talents, the expression that's right for you. That's what's being disintegrated is the one-size-fits-all kind of idea. Meaning that if you are really having an amazing life, it looks like *X, Y,* and *Z,* and that this has somehow been randomly decided that that's what you look like.

That's why we use the example of the pineapple because the pineapple has some certain qualities about it. It's not going to be a coconut and it doesn't try to be a coconut. These are the subtle ways that you may have been wobbling your vibration to be, in some diluted version or some distorted overlay version, rather than just being the most wonderful pineapple you could be.

We are, as you know, really deeply connected through the words on these pages; they are like an interactive session that you're experiencing.

We would just have you, if you would, pick one way that you're comparing yourself and coming up short to a coconut when really you're a pineapple. In other words, pick one way that you judge yourself or that you see yourself as a diluted version of yourself. Maybe it is around your health or your weight or your wealth or your money or whether you have a family or don't have a family.

Where are those ways that you tell yourself you're not good enough, that you long to change something in a way that creates a ripple or a wobble in who it is that you actually can be? The pineapple doesn't want to be the bitter coffee bean. It doesn't apply for the job of being a pineapple; it is the pineapple. Where are some areas or some ways that you think about yourself and think that you've fallen short? Just let these come into your awareness.

TRANSMITTING SUPPORTIVE
POCKETS OF ENERGY

Now we're transmitting more pockets of energy that are supporting you and unlocking more of who it is that you are as your fully realized self. This allows you to be in the vibrational proximity, the vibrational location of who it is that you are. Trying to be a coconut when you're a pineapple is a distraction. It takes away from you concentrating on realizing your own uniqueness, your own path, your own soul agreements, and your own Divine awareness.

We like where we've gotten to energetically so we'll complete this segment at this time knowing that you being you and you being in the seat of your fullness are one and the same.

6

Vibrational Autonomy

A Return to the Uniqueness of You

As we continue our conversation within the energetic vortex environment of *The Tablets of Light* we are brought to the subject of vibrational autonomy. Vibrational autonomy is something that is fostered through the pages of this book, through being within the walls of this temple. It is an environment that allows you to be you without any other vibrational confusion. It allows you to be you in a way that you are streaming forth more of your vibrational essence because the energetic space and invitation to do so exists.

Just as water will fill a vessel that it's poured into, so does your essence fill your incarnation. *The Tablets of Light* is the widening of the vessel of your incarnation. It's creating infinite space for you to occupy your unique essence, your vibrational complexity, the full bandwidth of your being, which is that of a Being of Light who happens to be incarnate at this time.

As we speak about vibrational autonomy there is the awareness of this widened vibrational landscape of you. As you have the space to occupy more of who it is that you are, you can reclaim your vibrational autonomy. An analogy is this: If there are several trees in a small area they'll begin to grow together, to become intertwined. Yet if a tree has ample space to grow as large as it can, it will. It doesn't require intertwining with the other trees around for it to grow. Yet it does require an environment that's conducive for that expanded growth, for that fullness of who it is, to optimize its height, width, and type.

AN OUTDATED PARADIGM
OF SEPARATION CONSCIOUSNESS

As we speak of vibrational autonomy it's as if you have been vibrationally intertwined with consciousness, people, events, and expectations that are not uniquely you or yours, or that you've outgrown. Separation consciousness has, as its foundation, the construct of surviving through the tribe. This, by its very nature, is not an environment that amplifies vibrational autonomy.

It cultivated various forms of survival patterns that created a sense of consistent separation in order for you to be part of the tribe. That there was a greater awareness perhaps of what was going on outside of you—whether that came from the perspective of trying to keep yourself safe or trying to survive, looking for what might be dangerous, being invisible, hiding out, playing small to stay safe, anticipating what somebody else's mood might be, wanting their approval, not wanting their disapproval, a fear of being isolated, of being kicked out of the tribe, of being left behind. And all of that equaled death, all of that equaled danger, all that threatened the very core of survival. Yet that entire paradigm is not only over and outdated, it's based on the faulty premise that you're not eternal, that you're not Divine, that you're not already whole.

We're extending vibrational units of consciousness to the origin of this illusion. If the premise of your incarnation is built on the fact that X equals 3, when X equals X or 3 equals 3, then anything that comes after that, in that equation or in the solution of that equation, will always be off because it's built upon a faulty premise. Any place that you have separated from your vibrational autonomy and have not made it a top priority to remain connected to it, we invite you to dismantle that, to bring it into the wholeness, the oneness of all there is. By *vibrational autonomy* we mean you being you and you staying connected to you, your essence, your fullness, your Source consciousness, no matter what. That you utilize your cosmic choice, if you choose, to no longer being willing to separate yourself from Source consciousness.

Wherever you have built this incarnation on the faulty premise that you need to separate from you, we invite you to deconstruct that, to include it back in the wholeness, to include it back in the oneness, to include it into the ring of inclusion, to let it fall away. Allow yourself to be, do, and have, what's yours to be, do, and have. Allow yourself to be in a state of vibrational autonomy where you're so connected to yourself as a Divine Light Being that you're re-Sourced. From that place of being re-Sourced, you interact with others. You contribute. You have relationships.

FREEDOM AND INCLUSION IN VIBRATIONAL AUTONOMY

We're not saying that vibrational autonomy is equal to being a recluse or living on an island. We're saying that your vibration, unique essence, signature energy, signature Source field, your being-ness, that which makes you uniquely you, is whole and complete and it's so solid, it's so known to you, that you don't leave it. You don't leave it when you drop your body when you transition at the end of this life span. You don't leave it when somebody else around you wants you to be something else or when somebody else around you is disconnected from his or her source. You don't leave it. Period.

It's the capacity to stay in your own rhythm, to stay on track with your inner compass. Vibrational autonomy is a part of your oracular vision, your capacity to see a pathway and hold that vision open. It's like being able to keep your own rhythm in the midst of many other rhythms. If you're a drummer and you have a certain part of a song that's yours to play, you don't leave your beat to play the part of the song that's the guitarist's part. You don't leave your beat even if you're one of a hundred other drummers playing the same song. You stay in communion with your song, with your vibrational autonomy, and you don't leave it for any reason. This is giving yourself full permission to be who you are.

As you're being who you are, there's a flow, a luminosity, a knowing, a connectedness—there's an impenetrable wholeness. As you're in that vibrational autonomy you're aware even more of what your givens are, what the principles of your vibrational autonomy are, of your unique essence. There's freedom in that. There's inclusion in that. The tree that grows to its full expression, that has the space to do so, is still part of a larger landscape of a larger forest. It still produces its fruit and offers it up.

UNITY CONSCIOUSNESS EXERCISE
....
Unwind Any Reason You Use to Separate from You

We're providing energetic consciousness to unwind and unravel the entanglements, the distractions, the repetitive patterns of leaving your unique essence of separating from you for any reason. Some of those reasons appear to be noble. For instance, leaving yourself to help somebody else seems to be a noble cause. Yet leaving you is never supportive of you or of anyone else.

We know that what we're inviting you into is simultaneously exactly what you already know. It's familiar. It's what you've been aware of in your consciousness. At the same time it calls forth within you the awareness that there's a threshold to cross and that threshold will have a particular flavor and voice for you.

It may be that as you're in your vibrational autonomy there's the voice that says others will think you're being selfish or that you don't care about anybody but yourself or that you're not pulling your weight or that you're a freak or that you're crazy or that you're weird or that you're unlovable or that you have to face the disappointment or the lack of approval from those that you have been intertwined with. Yet only the tree, only the tree, can grow its fruit. The tree next to it cannot grow its fruit for it. It doesn't work like that. These distorted ways you tell yourself there is something wrong with you or you hold back from being you are faulty premises that the incarnation gets built upon as you're born into one paradigm of separation and survival consciousness and you live into another of unity consciousness and wholeness.

Take a few breaths and engage your conscious choice to include back into the ring of inclusion anywhere that you have been holding yourself separate from you. Include any infrastructures within which these patterns resided, back into the wholeness. Step into your full vibrational autonomy.

RECOGNIZING WHAT *ISN'T* YOURS

It's not as if your vibrational autonomy didn't exist in the height of survival consciousness. It does. It did. You're upping the ante of it, the awareness of it. For some of you this vibrational autonomy can appear so foreign. It's like the more vibrationally autonomous you are the less you recognize the you that you knew yourself to be. Especially for those of you who are highly sensitive, highly empathic. You may have thought that your personality was a certain way. Maybe it's that you have a propensity for sadness or a propensity for fear or a propensity for depression or a propensity for the highest highs and the lowest lows or a propensity for suffering or feeling so deeply that there isn't vibrational autonomy. Yet the more *you* you actually are, the more you get to know your true self without the overlays of sensations that weren't uniquely you or yours to begin with.

As we're speaking about the emotional body, you may experience a certain range of emotions that you thought were yours that weren't really yours. They belonged to your neighbor tree or they originated on the other side of the Earth where there was something happening: an earthquake, a tsunami, a plane crash, a child who didn't have enough to eat.

The more into your vibrational autonomy you move, the more you may feel as if you're not the you that you knew yourself to be. You may also experience the opposite, wherein you breathe a sigh of relief or have a recognition of who you were, perhaps as a child, when you were in an empowered state, when you were in a vibrationally autonomous state.

We've spoken about this in the emotional body yet it may also be physical; your body physically begins to change as you're more and more in your vibrational autonomy. You may have more energy, there may be different foods that you're drawn to, there may be a lightness of being or a physical vitality, a shifting of the way your body looks.

This process of standing in the potency of being the galactic pioneer that you are, the leader in consciousness, the visionary, is a process of letting go of who you thought yourself to be or how you thought the world worked. As you do this, you tap into what you carry, what you know—that unique expression that you're here to actualize. You can't get here (unity consciousness) from there (separation consciousness) and yet separation consciousness, vibrational enmeshment, is rocket fuel for being here as you include it into the oneness, into the wholeness.

We know that at times it seems as if we're encouraging you toward a certain direction. We also know that your system may interpret that encouragement to go in a certain direction as something to strive for, or that we have an expectation of you. Or that in order to gain our approval you need to become the best unity consciousness vibrational autonomous being on the planet. It is not like that. We always meet you at the fifty-yard line, eye-to-eye, peer-to-peer, heart-to-heart, Divine-to-Divine, wholeness-to-wholeness.

Yes, this book of Thoth's tablets has a direction, an invitation, and an oracular vision that it's holding the door open for and yet it is not that that is being brought to you or done to you or done *for* you. It's always in response to your asking. It's always what you've left for yourself to find. You're the origin of this material. Anywhere in the pages of *The Tablets of Light* that you might have been trying to please me, Thoth, allow that to fall away. There isn't a right or a wrong path. All there is is you. Be the you that you're divinely designed to be.

As we provide divinity codes at this stage of this vibrational autonomy conversation, you're invited to step into your vibrational autonomy, vibrational autonomy, vibrational autonomy. It's as if you've been an octopus that's had all its tentacles out, using them to stick onto other vibrations. Now it's time to unstick them from this vibrational enmeshment. It's time to bring all the tentacles back to you so that you can use them to propel yourself forward.

It's as if you've been this power strip with five different electrical cords plugged into you with an extension cord going to one part of the wall. Rather than having your power source on an extension cord, plug back into Source, to your vibrational autonomy.

Here's another analogy: It's as if you'd had your roots intertwined in the root system of all those trees around you and you take that root ball and you transplant your tree to be in its optimal environment. Or it's as if you've been impersonating Elvis and you take off the hairpiece, rhinestones, guitar and boots, and you play the character of you flawlessly, full-out, committed.

EVOLVING SEPARATION CONSCIOUSNESS; FEAR OF BEING ALONE

As we're transmitting this consciousness to all those that will be within the pages of *The Tablets of Light* we're noticing an absolute terror of being alone. It's brought up when we speak about vibrational autonomy because to be alone in tribal consciousness meant that you no longer lived. Again that's built on the premise that you're separate, that you die, that you're not eternal.

This deep-seated fear of being alone is within the DNA, within the body memory of the collective consciousness. Vibrational autonomy does not mean that you're alone. We're not speaking about isolating, being reclusive, being lonely. When you're rock solid in your vibrational autonomy you'll be even more connected to others because there's more to connect from and to. There's more to commune from and with. The connection, the communion, the collaboration happens in a whole other plane. It happens from the absolute respect of everyone else's vibrational autonomy. It's pristine. It's Divine love.

Sometimes when there is this, let's call it this echo, from the tribal consciousness, from the collective consciousness, that says it's not okay to be alone because being alone is scary, then that can be an overlay on your vibrational autonomy. It can be like a hook that pulls you back from your vibrational autonomy that says you have to leave you so that you're not alone.

Usually whatever you're trying to avoid, you're already creating. If you don't want to be alone, for example, you've probably created a sense of being alone in your life already. Since you've already experienced "the worst thing that could happen," allowing yourself to consciously move into and be the energy of being alone often dissipates the stuck energy.

Maybe in the fear of being alone you've separated from yourself and then you're not with yourself. It's already happened and yet to just be willing to go into the energy and include it into the ring of inclusion already shifts it. It's not even true. It's impossible to be alone. Even the tree that's in its section of the forest is not alone. It's part of the forest.

Vibrational autonomy. We've described it as your capacity to stay with you, your unique vibration, your unique essence—no matter what's going on around you. This capacity to have your vibration be autonomous is self-regenerative. This is because as you're in vibrational autonomy you're in your wholeness and fueled from the infinite Source of all that is. Vibrational autonomy is true freedom.

AWARENESS, PEACE, AND ABUNDANCE

Then there's also the awareness and the peace of being who it is that you are, having what is yours to have. When this happens, there's not a vibrational dependency on an outside circumstance to complete you. You're already perfect, whole, and complete. When there's vibrational autonomy you're also tapped into your birthrights. You're tapped into the birthright of abundance. You don't have to wait to experience vibrational autonomy when you create a certain level of abundance.

This vibrational autonomy is a game changer on a lot of levels because tribal consciousness, survival consciousness, says you'll be happy when *X, Y,* or *Z* occurs: when you retire, when you're married, when you have the job that you want, when you have a certain amount of money, and/or when your body has a certain level of health and vitality. There's always something that you come from in separation consciousness that says you're not vibrationally autonomous.

As we've discussed in the evolution hologram segment, everything exists within every moment. All that there is exists within every moment so there's nothing that's out there. When you have true vibrational autonomy then you're in a state of being where there's not resistance or striving. There's a flow. There's a receiving and a transmitting of what's yours—what your Divine design is like.

You may have heard stories of people falling in love and meeting their life partner when they'd given up on dating, when they'd accepted being alone. They no longer were looking. That creates the capacity to care less because you care so much. There's a positioning to it. When you have vibrational autonomy you're vibrating with your abundance, your soul, your health, your peace, your happiness, and you can self-generate that vibration within you.

As a conscious creator you absolutely have the capacity to be in oneness with all there is. You can move into joy because you choose to. You can move into a state of feeling abundant on command. It's your capacity to be able to access the vibration that already exists within the vibration of all that there is. Vibrational autonomy is a paradigm shifter because it transcends the duality perception that this is preferred and this is unpreferred; this is good and this is bad.

Perceiving through duality is built on the judgment of what it is that you think that your life should be like based on what the collective consciousness, morphic field, or tribal consciousness says that it should be like. You've also experienced having what you thought you should have, but it hasn't made you happy. It's because the vibration doesn't exist in the object attained. The vibration exists within you.

Sometimes when you come into vibrational proximity to what you're choosing to actualize it touches the vibration that already exists within you. That's why sometimes you do feel happy when an experience shifts. It's not because you weren't whole already or that vibration was outside of you. It's because as you came into vibrational proximity with that experience it unlocked the vibration that already existed within you.

As you utilize vibrational proximity and vibrational autonomy together you're able to be in vibrational proximity to your vibrational autonomy. Through your vibrational autonomy you're able to access through your vibrational proximity that which already exists within you. Then it's like you're able to roll, flow, and move forward.

MOVE INTO THE UNKNOWN

The Divine light code, the sacred geometry, the language of light in between, through, and all around the words of this book, give the same message: "Move into what you may have previously perceived as the unknown." Being within the walls of the temple of *The Tablets of Light* continually, word by word, vibration by vibration, says this same thing.

But survival consciousness says the unknown is dangerous. If you go into a cave that's unknown and a tiger is there and you get eaten by it, the unknown becomes dangerous. Yet the unknown is also what the pioneer follows, and then comes upon the ocean or a waterfall. These pages are saying, "You can't get here, unity consciousness from there, separation consciousness." You have to step out of the known, out of the sameness into that which you previously would have called unknown. And yet as you're in your vibrational proximity, you're in a state of knowing. It begins to feel more like you.

As we spoke about earlier, as you move more into your vibrational autonomy, there may be a phase where you just feel weird, as if you don't recognize yourself, you don't know yourself. The habits that you had, the thoughts that you had, and the emotions that you had really weren't uniquely you or yours to begin with. They fall away and then you get to know yourself all over again. As you're getting to know yourself all over again there comes a point where you may realize, "Ah yes, this is really who I am. This really feels right." Then what was previously perceived as unknown is known because you're connected to your full-on awareness.

When you leave you, you shut down your awareness. When you're vibrationally autonomous you're connected to that wider landscape of oneness, of wholeness, of your Divine knowing.

BREATHING EXERCISE
· · · · · · · · · ·
Be in Vibrational Proximity
with Your Vibrational Autonomy

Take a few moments as we're completing this segment to come into vibrational proximity with your vibrational autonomy.

To complete, take ten long, slow, deep breaths, knowing that you are the one who is breathing these breaths. We can encourage you to take these ten long, slow, deep breaths but it's not us who is breathing the breaths. It's you. It's you. Enjoy these breaths.

7

Source Light

Illuminate the Light of Your Presence

THE RETURN OF THE DIVINE AWAKENING

We are beginning by transmitting units of consciousness, blocks of consciousness, energy downloads, sacred geometry, and light codes to prepare the energetic template of this next segment. Open to receive even more of what's here for you to receive.

This is an extraordinary conversation that we are having. Let it be extraordinary. Let it take you into new arenas of consciousness. Let your cosmic choice guide your involvement in this energetic template. One way to look at this evolution in consciousness is that it is the return of the Divine awakening. It is the return of Divine unity. It is the return of the embodied Divine Being of Light incarnate. Receive the expansiveness of that. Receive the reuniting with your Source light.

We know who you are. We see you clearly. As we converse within the pages of this sacred text we are providing a direct transmission of your Source light. Your Source light is that which animates you, that which embodies you, that which is you on the essence level. You are Source light and that light is luminous. That light is brilliant. That light encapsulates all that there is. You as Source light are embodying downloads of consciousness of the possibilities available to you in this incarnation as you live as the Source light that you are.

More sacred geometry is being transmitted.

SENDING LIGHT TO YOURSELF

How is it that you would send light to yourself? Perhaps you would send it through a scribed text such as this. As you hold these pages, as you gaze upon the words of this energetically encoded text, you receive the package of Source light that you sent to yourself.

It's like those that go on a trek, perhaps the Appalachian Trial or the Camino de Santiago. They are going to be hiking, walking, and trekking for days, weeks, some even months. It's not possible, it's not practical, to carry a month's supply of food, of water, of clothing on one's back. So hikers plan ahead. They mail packages to the next destination, or five destinations from the last destination, when they know they'll need another pair of shoes. Then, when they arrive and their pockets are empty of food, and they open that package, it's like Christmas in July.

We're sharing this concept of resources and mailing resources in advance so that as you're on your journey of a hike you have the supplies you need. These are supplies that you need when you're hiking day after day, mile after mile, or kilometer after kilometer after kilometer. They're kind of the same supplies that you'd need if you were in your daily life. You'd need food, you'd need water, you'd need clothing. And yet they're specific; they're a specific type of supply.

You wouldn't mail high heels to yourself on your hike. You wouldn't mail a winter coat in the middle of the heat. There's a specific blend of fabric that is capable of supporting your body as you're moving, sweating, and in the elements. You might have some supercharged foods or some minerals to augment what's naturally in your system or to replace what you're dispensing.

How is it that you would send Source light to yourself? We've used this concept of the hike to be just that—a way you can conceptualize what it is we're speaking about. Your incarnation is like this trek. It's like this journey. When you incarnated, it was as if you were starting a hike in December. But now it's summer, and because it's summer you don't need your warmest sleeping bag, heaviest coats, hats, gloves, and scarves. You don't need all that.

This process of being incarnated during separation consciousness and then evolving into unity consciousness is one that you can dismantle; you can let go of the outdated supplies. You can leave behind those winter coats, gloves, goggles, and scarves because they don't apply in the infinite summer. Instead you pick up some things that *do* apply.

THE PACKAGE THAT YOU'VE LEFT FOR YOURSELF

This segment, this pure transmission of Source light, the Source light that you are, the package that you've left for yourself, is in some ways the heart and soul of *The Tablets of Light*: for you to be reunited with the Source light and the energy vibrations that your system in unity consciousness requires. Those supplies that pertain to the environment that you're now in energetically and vibrationally, on a frequency level.

That your journey, your hike, would bring you into these pages, would bring you to the destination of this book, is an ingenious way to employ your cosmic choice! All the things that led up to it, all the steps, all the magical ways that this consciousness has found its way into your life designed by you and for you, is nothing short of ingenious.

Activate, receive, and absorb this Source light. You may have a sensation of how it would be if you were to open a package that you mailed to yourself a year earlier. What's in there, what you packed for yourself, might be a surprise, for you may not have remembered exactly what you packed in there. As you open it and as you go through it there is the excitement of what you're unpacking. This is analogous to your unpacking your Source light to reconnect with, for you to access from within, to unlock from within. In addition to finding those things that may be quite surprising, there may also be those things that you've been really looking forward to.

Again, let's use the example of the hike. If you were on a hike and knew you were going to get a package that you had sent to yourself six months prior, and in it you find your favorite pair of socks, your favorite thing to eat, something really special, your . . . whatever it might be. During that six months you'd be thinking about it. You'd be thinking about how much you're looking forward to having that favorite pair of socks or having that special thing to eat.

You may also have that same sensation as you're unpacking this segment of your Source light. It's what you've been thinking about, what you've been thinking about, what you've been thinking about, what you've been thinking about. Now it's not thinking about it—it's more than that. It's really experiencing it.

Some examples of that may be some of those beliefs that you've had for a long time, or those knowings. You know that you're a Divine being, for example, and yet there's been this disconnect of experiencing yourself as a Divine being. Or you know that you have a heightened awareness, an intuition, a Divine knowing—yet you haven't been living it. Or you know that really following your bliss is the actualization of your Divine light mission. Or you know that things have changed, that the Earth has shifted, that the consciousness has shifted, and you've had some ideas of what this might mean.

HOW DOES LIVING IN UNITY CONSCIOUSNESS CHANGE DAILY LIFE?

This is something that your Divine transmitter, Danielle, has asked us over and over again for years now. How does living in unity consciousness change daily life? How does it show up here, not out there in some meditation? *Here.* How does it change your life? This is something that she's asked us over and over again. We love that because we're also interested in having this be in your incarnation. We're interested in having your Source light be embedded, and embodied in your incarnation. We're interested in what gets illuminated as a result.

What do *you* notice that's different?

When we say that some things that you've been looking forward to receiving in the package of Source light are familiar, that's what we mean. It's like ease and grace. You've had the idea of ease and grace, but not really the experience of ease and grace. Then you have the experience of ease and grace. And yet not everybody wants ease and grace. We know that sounds funny but it's true. Or if you experience living from equanimity and know that all is well and you are all. That knowing is what is experienced; it's different from believing it or thinking it.

There are items in this Source light that are like that, that you've been looking forward to. Some of the looking forward to is a moving away from wearing the winter coat when you're hot. There is a moving-away-from energy and that's okay. You've been looking forward to moving away from feeling separate from yourself and separate from Source. You've been looking forward to moving away from feeling the illusion of lack, of scarcity, of struggle.

It's like thinking about swimming versus actually swimming. You can think about swimming and if you've swum before then you have a better idea of what the experience of swimming is like. But it's not until you swim that you feel the absence of gravity.

That's a beautiful example because you're used to feeling the pull of gravity in everyday life on Earth. Then, you get into a pool or an ocean where the gravity is different. Instead of being weighed down, you're floating. You feel the coolness of the water. You feel a connection to all parts of your body because of your interaction with the water.

It's different from air. You may not feel the air around your body right now but that doesn't mean it's not there. Your sensation of the air, your sensation of the atmosphere, is less palpable on your skin than if you're in a body of water, if you're in a cool lake. Then you feel your skin, calves, feet, and hands. You feel your whole body as it's interacting with the water.

SURPRISES THAT YOU LEFT FOR YOURSELF

This conscious experience of Source light is multidimensional. It's simultaneously what you've been looking forward to and what you've remembered. Now you get to be in it, play with it, and experience it. An aspect of the purpose of *The Tablets of Light* is to awaken the evolutionists, the carriers of Divine awakening. That may be a surprise to you. You may have thought that it was somebody else who would be an awakener of consciousness, not you. Or that it would look or feel like something else.

This may also bring forth within you a desire to pivot your external experience of life in a way that's surprising to you. Perhaps you've been living in the same place for twenty-five years and then one day you just know it's time to move and you move. Or you hadn't really been actively engaged in a particular creation methodology. Then all of a sudden you are, you do. You write a book or you pick up photography. There's some pivot for some of you. That may be the surprise part.

We know that may also be why you haven't wanted to reawaken what you carry within you. It's due to a fear that everything that you've built thus far will be destroyed or that you'll outgrow the people around you, that you'll have to leave your relationship or your job. We want to say that although sometimes that happens, for the most part everything in your life has positioned you to be exactly where you are right now.

You can trust. You can trust the people in your life are there for a reason. You can trust your life is the way that it is for a purpose. The surprise may be that something within your life that has been there for a long time evolves. Maybe you've been in a relationship for a long time and then something awakens within the relationship that hadn't been there before ever, or in decades. The evolution is surprising to you. You think you know that person or family member but you are surprised and this is in an exciting way.

As this Source light is streaming in and through and around you we're noticing that for some of you we're coming to a place of lockdown or shutdown. There's this opening of the package and then an interpretation of what it means and then an, "Oh, crap!" Then the package is closed back up and given back to the post office. That's okay. It's really okay.

We're pausing to deepen the energies. . . . Take a few deep and integrating breaths.

We know that as we bump up against these lockdowns, these shutdowns, these thresholds, that they have a certain vibrational context like fear of the unknown or fear of change. That is a part of the old consciousness, of the old paradigm that when you get to a precipice of something being different there's self-preservation of survival consciousness that shuts everything down. It freezes it.

That really is an illusion because you can't stop. You can't stop energy. You can't stop evolution. You can't stop movement. There's no such thing as staying the same. It's not even possible. You're not the same as you were a few paragraphs ago. Everything is always in motion. Everything's always moving. You're organic. You're dynamic. There may be the appearance that something is still; you don't feel necessarily the Earth moving. But the Earth is moving.

Sometimes there's that clamping down to keep the familiar. Your system says, "This is known, so let's keep it this way." "I know this. I know my discomfort or I know this unpreferred experience or I know this and because it's known I'm going to try to keep it this way." But that's not even possible. The givens in your life are change and new beginnings. Each moment is a new beginning. Each moment is a new beginning. Each moment is a new beginning. Each moment is a new beginning. Each moment is a new beginning.

LET GO AND LET YOURSELF
BE SURPRISED

Sure, you can buy into the illusion that things are staying the same. You can buy into the illusion that things are staying the same. You can use a lot of your energy against yourself trying to keep things from moving. It's like you're on a bike and you're going downhill. Sure, you can squeeze your brakes as hard as possible. Then you go down the hill perhaps more slowly yet you're still going down the hill.

Or if you're in a raft on a river-rafting trip, you can try to hold on to the bank but the water keeps moving. It keeps moving, it keeps moving and it takes a lot, a lot, a lot of energy to hold on to the side. Let go. Even while you're holding on to the side and you have the appearance that the boat's not moving, the water underneath you is not the same. It's not the same. It's moving.

You're not the same. Your cellular tissue is not the same. Your connection to the quantum field is not the same. We know that you can put a lot of energy into trying to keep things the same. You're powerful so you can use your potency and power to try to keep things the same and that can be very exhausting. You're the only one who's powerful enough to stop you yet even while you're stopping you, you're changing. You're in the unknown.

Let go. Let yourself be surprised. If you don't like it go back. Go back.

We know that sometimes as we're speaking you may feel like you relate less or more to the words that we're speaking. As we're sharing this or as we've shared different concepts at other times, you might say, "Well, that's not really where I am. I'm leaping into the unknown. I'm embracing change."

We're speaking to you multidimensionally and so most of your energy may be embracing change. The majority of you may be leaping into the unknown. There may be some echo within you that's still anchored in the old paradigm that we're speaking to. Trust that whatever words come through, whatever subject is a part of this book, it's because there's a facet of you that is being spoken to, that's being included, welcomed, loved, and encouraged to evolve.

Now more Source light is coming through. It's like you've opened the first package and you're on to the second one.

UNITY CONSCIOUSNESS EXERCISE
. . . .
Discover What You Left for Yourself to Find

We invite you to pause here and to be present with the Source light that you've left for yourself. Receive and ask your inner knowing what you have left for yourself to find? What is the Source light package including for you? It may be an energy download, a message, an action step; it may be a key. It could be anything. What did you pack for yourself? What's in this Source light package? Spend some minutes in the silence tapping into that, being present with this Source light download.

You may notice that as you're connecting to this Source light that it's like a string of pearls. As you're within this pearl of Source light you're noticing other pearls on the strand. You're aware of other points in your incarnation that were also packages of Source light that you left for yourself to find. Maybe it's a sacred site. Maybe you've met somebody that you have a really profound exchange with. Or you've seen something or gone somewhere, you've read a book, or taken a workshop, or you've studied with someone. That's Source light. You've picked up a hobby. That's Source light; that's been the Source light you've left for yourself in these experiences. As you're vibrating into this Source light it's activating the Source light you've left for yourself at other points.

SOURCE LIGHT CLUES

Some of this Source light that you've left for yourself may be conscious, it may be unconscious, it may be hidden in the depths of experiences that you've found challenging or unpreferred at the time. As you're continuing to absorb this Source light think about that.

You as a Creator Being of Light before this incarnation had the choice, the agreement, to have an incarnation be one in which you could experience the Divine forgetting and the Divine remembering. Yet you could leave clues for yourself along the way. These clues are

Source light–based. How would you divinely design that? How would you fold that into the incarnation?

We're asking this because it's an alchemist's question. As you, the alchemist, the creator of your life, of your incarnation, a master with light, how is it you would mold and play with this light in an incarnation? Some of the fun ways would be through the people you meet, through the experiences you have, through the scribed text you're reading.

We're speaking about a level of adeptness because this took creativity. Even in your infinite nature it took creativity to embed this Source consciousness throughout your incarnation so that you would find it. It's like having a course in which there are clues along the way. The course is designed in such a way that every person in the course doesn't find the clues. It's not because you kept it secret it's because it's vibrationally encoded in certain landscapes and not others.

It takes you being the vibrational key that you are and being in your life in each moment to then access the multidimensionality of what's there. Let's say you're on a course like a cross-country course in which you have to travel from one place to another. In the process of traveling over this course there are certain changes in the environment. You have to go from walking to flying or walking to swimming. There's some change that has to happen throughout the course or something you have to find in order to get to the next level.

We're using the word *course* because it's fun. It's as if you are on a course that you're going to go through, like a horse would have a cross-country course that it would travel through. The horse would have to jump various jumps: some comprised of water, some of rails. Some of it would be certain terrain that would have to be traversed. As you're on the course of your life, the journey of your life, there are these certain keys that then you find along the way. You only find them from the vibration and with the support of your oracular vision.

On this course you might have different vehicles of transportation. You might walk it on foot, you might drive it in a car, you might bike it on your bike, or you might ride it on a horse. When you're walking you're aware of different things than when you're biking or than when you're in the car. There's a different vantage point that you have. We're not saying that one is better than the other but each presents a different vantage point.

Here's an example. You may have seen *Highlights* magazine in a doctor's office when you were a child. A fun exercise in the magazine is to find hidden images. Maybe there's a picture of a forest and you have a key and you have to find the things in the key. You have to find the brush or the comb or there are certain objects that are hidden in the forest. If you look at it from one vantage point it seems like a forest but there's something else there too.

Or like a picture that, if you look at it with a soft gaze, becomes three-dimensional. If you just look at it regularly you don't see it. That's what we mean by your oracular vision. That's what we mean by this course. This Source light that you've left for yourself to find takes a certain vibrational frequency for you to access. Not because it's hidden, but because there's a level of adeptness to it. Only *you* can find it.

Let's say there are a hundred sources of water that only you could find, and that water is something that is essential to the human brilliant system. If you don't find the water then the water is not found, it's not utilized. That's a dramatic example, we know, yet we want you to feel some fire, some urgency—not because of lack, not because there's anything wrong, not because there's not going to be enough water. We're not saying that at all. What we're saying is that it's only you. You're the only one. There's not anybody else that's going to do it. If you don't do it, it doesn't happen.

SYNCHRONICITIES AND SIGNPOSTS

In this adept course of your life, you've left sacred symbology, synchronicities, signposts, packages of Source light for yourself. Where, as you're tapping into this Source light package right now, did you walk by one? Now that you have access to this one, you're realizing, "Ah, there it was.

There it was. I just walked by that." When you realize this, you can go back and get it.

We love to use analogies because it helps anchor the vibrations. Another analogy to express the oracular vision of your Source light is that of a video game. There are video games that as you enter into various levels of them you gain points or tools that you couldn't access on the previous levels. You have to go through one level to get to the next level.

Or think of this like a temple. There are secret compartments in the temple and you have to be in a certain part of it to access them. The temple happens to be multidimensional, so vibrationally you have to be in a certain vibrational proximity to access the secret passageways. Another way to describe the purpose of *The Tablets of Light* is that it is a vibrational passageway that then supports you in accessing your Divine light. Continue to absorb this Source light and let it create some ah-ha moments, some connections, some pings and some pongs of "Ahhhhh! *That's* what that was."

PROJECTING YOUR SOURCE LIGHT ONTO OTHERS

Sometimes you may interpret something in a way that wasn't intended. Sometimes the Source light package that you've left for yourself may take the form of another person, someone you might call a soul mate. You meet somebody and it's so intense; there's so much recognition, so much light, so much love, and then you glom on to that person as if that relationship is supposed to be your relationship for life and yet it wasn't about that. They just had a package of your Source light.

With that example we're also seeing anywhere that you may have projected your Source light on somebody else—whether that's a teacher, spouse, parent, priest, or a Light Being. For the truth is, you're the only one who can drink water for your body. Your connection to the Divine is direct. No intercessor. We're not intercessing here. We're with you as you're accessing your direct connection. *You* have to access it.

Focus on Your Capacity to Absorb

As this segment is coming to a vibrational momentum, a launching pad of sorts, focus on absorption, focus on your capacity to absorb. It's not about more, it's about your capacity to absorb.

Let's say your system needs vitamin C and you have an infinite supply of vitamin C. You keep putting vitamin C into your system. You keep drinking orange juice, eating oranges, taking vitamin C tablets, more and more and more. The input of more can't be utilized by your system after a certain point because whatever you're not able to absorb you just eliminate. It just flows right through you. The example of vitamin C is a good one because you don't need all the vitamin C in the world. You only need the vitamin C that your system needs.

Let's say you're not absorbing all the vitamin C that your system needs and you keep putting more and more vitamin C in, more and more vitamin C in, more and more vitamin C in, and yet you don't absorb anymore. There is a disconnect. Things aren't lining up. It's not intersecting. It's not meshing up. When we say that we've reached this place of vibrational momentum, this Source light, it's pumping, you can feel it.

We say, focus on your capacity to absorb. That's so much. Your capacity to absorb could be its own segment because everything exists in this moment. So whether you're accessing or not has to do with your capacity to absorb. How is it that you can enhance your capacity to absorb? Every time we say "absorb, absorb, absorb, absorb," we get your attention. Are you absorbing, are you absorbing? How can you absorb to the optimal potency of you? It's not more. It's not always about more. It's actually absorbing what's already there.

It's the same with food. You can be putting the most nutrient-rich foods into your body but if your digestive tract is not able to absorb it because it's filled up with something else or it's shut down in certain ways it doesn't matter how many nutrient-rich energies you've brought in. This

Source light that you've left for yourself is pulsating. It's on fire. It's there.

How do you access it? How do you absorb it even more? For example, if you're hiking and have a pack of water on your back, a sack full of water, you have to have a straw that you can then suck on to get the water out. Or it's like those juice boxes: the juice is in the box but you need that straw to be able to get the juice out.

Have your capacity to absorb be in your awareness. Focus on your capacity to access the Source light that you've left for yourself to find. Maybe something comes to you right now as you're reading these words. "Ahhh, that's how I can absorb more of this Source light," you may think to yourself. It may be something practical that comes to mind, like exercising or doing something you enjoy. Or it may be a meditation or a body movement, perhaps a state of mind. It may be circling back to that Source light package that's still waiting there for you. You can go back. You can go back and get it.

Absorb Source light. Take all the time you like to bask in this Source light before moving on to the next segment.

8
Source Light Embodied

Actualize Being the Divine Incarnate

Being an incarnated being during one of the most extraordinary evolutions of consciousness is quite a profound experience. You are Source light. You are the essence and luminosity of Divine proportions. *The Tablets of Light* recalibrates and guides your system into the unified field of ease as a Being of Light in form. It creates more moments of feeling at home within the Divine light codes that are pulsing through the molecular structure of your brilliant system and light body.

Part of the spiritual technology of evolution through Source light is the full integration of duality. As light becomes unified in your system, you are in congruence with your Source light and your soul's evolution. You're in accordance, agreement, congruence, resonance with the full spectrum of your luminous, Divine nature and your cosmic choice to express it through the lens of your life.

As such you may notice outdated ways of being coming to an end or coming up to the surface to be assimilated in the ring of inclusion. For as this absolute ease with the Divine light that you are occurs, the overlays or patterns of discordance, dis-ease, fighting, striving, or struggling are no longer active in the fully integrated system of the Divine incarnate being that you are.

There may be some subtle ways those echoes are playing out. Maybe you're coming from a sense of "have to." You have to go to work, you have to do your to-do list, you have to take care of your body, you have to pay taxes, you have to . . . whatever it is. Your life isn't a "have to." It's not something to get through. It's not something to survive. It's not something that's being done to you or that you have to overcome or a test that you're undergoing or an obligation.

You get to be this Divine Light Being who plays in the realm of what appears to be matter on the Earth plane. You do and are and have certain things because they're yours to do, to be, and to have. And there's a cleanness to that vibration. There's a seamlessness to that vibration. There's an overflowing awareness of that vibration. Your life is an emanation of you. Your life is an extension of you.

Yes, there are some things that are falling away and others that are moving more into the forefront now that you're more you. You are moving into congruence with your life, truly being an extension of your Source light and not an extension of your distorted, disconnected resistance. You are becoming an extension of the full breadth and magnificence of you.

EMBRACE YOURSELF AND STAY THE COURSE

What if you stopped resisting the full potency of you? What if you stopped resisting the profound gifts that you carry? What if, rather than hesitating, holding back, pushing, forcing, or striving you were in absolute right relationship with your soul's evolution, with the oracular vision that you carry within you? That there isn't any begrudging or dragging your feet around the full expression of who it is that you are.

The cat is a cat. She or he purrs, plays, climbs trees, stalks, eats, naps, and enjoys being petted. The cat is congruent with who the cat is. The acorn tree is the acorn tree. It doesn't feel obligated to produce acorns. It doesn't do it to please anyone. It doesn't try to get out of it. It is the acorn tree.

That is one of the fundamental ways of being of this evolution in consciousness: you stop fighting against who it is that you are and you embrace yourself. You embrace yourself. You're congruent with yourself. If you look at energy, it takes an enormous amount of energy to stop yourself from being you. It takes an enormous amount of energy for you to be in the dance of illusion where you're not really free or where you have to do things you don't want to do. It takes an enormous amount of energy for you to feel that you're powerless or that your life is happening to you.

This is analogous to a train that's going three hundred miles an hour. It's easier at that point for the train to continue to go three hundred miles an hour than to keep moving forward with the same propulsion and the brake on. That three hundred miles an hour of combustible energy on your trajectory with the brake on slows it down to a hundred and fifty miles an hour. That takes a lot of energy to have full throttle speed while the brakes are forcing it to go half speed. Don't go and stop at the same time. Go three hundred miles an hour and stop when it's time to stop. If you can do this, then your life becomes the true pleasure that it's designed to be as a reflection of your unique vibration.

We understand that the full expression of who it is that you are as Source light can be such that there's a sensation that you would be judged, or that you would be too visible, or you would be persecuted. Yet living a life that's half unlived is being in a state of disconnection from your true Divine purpose and expression.

LIVING A HALF LIFE

Let's say you're riding through the desert on camels and you have a mission to carry sacred tablets of consciousness through the desert on these camels. One camel is carrying a sacred tablet and the next camel has water and supplies and the next camel has sacred tablets and the next camel has water and supplies.

You're going through the desert and you have the life-supporting energy of the water with you on the next camel. It's with you, it's a part of your experience, and yet you don't drink the water. The water isn't helping you when it stays on the next camel. It doesn't do you any good after you've become dehydrated, after you and your camel can't go any further.

The sacred tablets remain in the desert, unutilized. The water isn't able to fulfill its purpose, again, not because it isn't there but because you didn't access it. Saving it in this analogy doesn't help because there's nothing to save it *for*. The camel isn't able to access the water for you to drink, even though it's carrying it. All the camels, all the people, all the water, all the sacred tablets are not able to make it across the desert to carry this consciousness because the water isn't utilized. The water was overrationed or you didn't take the time to stop and drink it.

This is like going through life half lived. This water is symbolic of Source consciousness. It's right there with you, partnering with you. If you don't access it, it doesn't matter. Trying to keep the lid on how much power, potency, and empowerment you have is like living life by half. Again, it takes a lot of energy to stop yourself from being who it is that you are.

If you decide to put down this book at any point in reading it, to stop being in the Divine Transmission of it, being in the sacred tablet of it, one of the reasons you may do so is because you want to continue to live half of a life. We don't mean that you want to continue it or that you're even conscious of what you're doing. It's more that your half life has gotten familiar, comfortable, that that's the norm. There's this sense of trying to get out of life; you get out of life by retiring, or you get out of life on the weekends, or you get out of life by going on vacation, or you get out of life by numbing out in some way. There is a sense of wanting to play hooky from life; this idea that work or responsibilities are something that you have to get through.

What if all of your life was embedded with Source light and you lived it fully? You lived it fully. We know that in the paradigm of separation consciousness or survival consciousness, this kind of living at half-mast, living at half speed, comes from the sense that there's not enough. There are not enough resources, not enough energy, not enough time, not enough food, not enough water, not enough money, not enough love, not enough clarity. There's this sensation of not enough. When that is habitually felt, each day is entered into from this place of holding back, this place of having to save the water for a future time. But then you're not able to drink the water because the future time never comes because you didn't utilize the water to begin with.

BEING RE-SOURCED

When you are connected to this Source light in a way that you are illuminating your Divine Union, then you're connected, you're living your life to the fullest. Therefore, you're re-Sourced in each moment. As you're re-Sourced vibrationally by light codes, by your light body, by your soul and by your Source light, there's a flow, there's an ease, there's an awareness. Then each moment gets fully lived and is fully expressed. Everything exists in each and every moment and so as this full expression is experienced from a place of being re-Sourced, you're able to access that which is there. You're able to drink the water from the camel next to you.

We're not speaking about action or inaction, doing or being in this moment. Or that living your life fully means that you're going three hundred miles an hour all the time. It's not what we mean. Sometimes you'll go a hundred miles an hour. Sometimes you'll stop. Sometimes you'll go faster. It's not about the being or the doing or the fast or the slow or the yin and the yang.

As you're re-Sourced, you'll naturally be flowing in a rhythm that supports your Source light. That rhythm is informed from within, from your conscious illumination. You're hooked up to your multidimensionality, to your Divine being-ness. As such you're able to access the water and also the consciousness of the sacred tablets you're carrying. The water and the tablets are no longer separate from you or the vehicle of transportation. It's your life, it's your vessel, it's your body, it's your being, it's your incarnation. That's your vehicle. That's your camel. That's your vehicle of transportation, your vehicle of evolution, your vehicle of transformation. There's so much more within you than you realize.

By embodying this Source light, you're re-Sourced—you're hooking up with the full breadth and vibration of your universal consciousness and awareness. We know that one of the sensations that you carry is an awareness that there's more within you. There's more potential, clarity, gifts, talents, there's a sensation of a super version of you that you remember.

You remember this and you feel separate from that fully lived version of you. There's this fierce longing to know the Divine within and without. You know. You know that sensation of having the tablets and the water within you and not being able to or not choosing to or not knowing how to or for whatever reason not accessing it.

The Tablets of Light is the access point, the field of consciousness that naturally guides you into remembering there's nothing that's keeping you separate. Those false doorways just fall away.

ALLOWING YOU TO BE WHO YOU ARE

In this segment we're talking about many things: your Source light, the ease of being you, and living each day re-Sourced. As you're living each day re-Sourced, then you're being the cat, you're the acorn tree, you're allowing yourself to be that which you are. There's an organic flow. There's an internal rhythm. The cat has different segments in her day. She plays, she eats, she sleeps, she hunts, she purrs. The train covers ground. It stops, it picks up passengers, and it lets other passengers off. Life is not the same. It's not the same. The acorn tree has developmental stages. That's the built-in rhythm of you being you.

If you've been coming from some kind of lack or fear, that may create the illusion that you have to always monitor your energy or monitor your creativity to ensure that you don't lay it all out there and have nothing left. The opposite effect actually happens because as you express your energy, which is connected to your Source light, you're tapped into an infinite vibration. That infinite vibration feeds you.

As you expend the energy you receive the energy. As you're really being who it is that you are it regenerates you, it recharges you. There's this illusionary fear that if you're being who you are full-out, if you're really expressing what you came here to be, that means that you will burn out somehow. It implies that every day is like running a marathon. But you have the capacity to run a marathon. It's within your cellular structure. It's within the Divine mind.

Let's say you're a runner and at some point in the future, you plan on running a marathon. Every day is not a day that you run a marathon. Some days you don't run at all. Some days you run a 5K. Some days you run a 10K. Some days you do yoga or you climb a mountain or you do something else. Even though there's the capacity to run a marathon, living your life full-out doesn't necessarily mean that you're running a marathon every single day.

We know that you've had the feeling of coming from a perceived lack or place of not enough—there's not enough energy, not enough food, not enough money, not enough time. Thus when it is time to bear those acorns, to grow them, to run the marathon, there may be that holding back. Or there may be a fear that if you let go you'll be out of control and then you'll not be careful and then you'll be in danger.

What if you didn't monitor your energy? What if you came back into right relationship with you, and within that you there was an inner compass to let you know? Just like your marathon training manual would let you know that today is the day you run and bike, today is the day you do nothing. It varies. There's a rhythm to you being you. That's why we love the example of nature so much, the example of trees.

Roses aren't blooming all year round, yet the Divine design of the rosebush is to have those blooming roses. Even when it seems like the roses aren't there, they're there. Everything is positioning to be a part of the wholeness. It's not that the time the flowers are blooming is better than the time when there are no roses. All of it counts. All of it's important.

LET YOURSELF FLOW WITH
YOUR SOURCE LIGHT

Whether you've been underachieving or overachieving or trying to have roses every day, the same amount every day of your life or pruning yourself back, let yourself go through a full cycle. Let go. Take a break. Let yourself flow with your Source light; then embrace who it is that you are. Embrace what it is that you're here for. Being, doing, and embracing who you are and what it is that you're here for regenerates you. It rejuvenates you. It doesn't drain you. It doesn't leave you empty. It doesn't overextend you.

When you breathe, you're able to absorb more of that life-giving energy that the breath is providing. That's why we focus so much on your internal experience. As your internal experience and your capacity to absorb and to access what is already here in your life—in your body, in your experience of this incarnation—deepens and expands, then you naturally are accessing more of what's available.

This capacity to access, absorb, to be in union, to be in congruency with your Source light, with your oracular vision, with what it is that you carry in this incarnation, allows you to bring it forth. For this conversation is happening with you because you are on this evolutionary wave of consciousness. You are on the forefront of this evolutionary wave of consciousness. What you carry that's been this hidden treasure within you is what then creates the landing pad of this newly evolved state of being.

It's as if you're building a bridge and you're the one that's building the bridge. You're the one that's on the edge, where the bridge doesn't have any more road on it. As you're there, the knowledge that you have within you, everything you've been prepared for, the positioning, is what then puts that next hundred meters of the bridge there.

Or it's like if you're building a train track. You're the one who has that next piece of track so the train can keep going. You're the one opening the way, clearing the way, and providing the platform for this evolution in consciousness to continue. That next piece of train track or that next piece of bridge comes from deep within the well of you. It resides deep within your Source light.

These examples of the bridge and the train are very functional, they're very industrial. We chose them because they're pathways of getting from one place to another.

DEEPENING AND EXPANDING YOUR INTERNAL VIBRATION

That's what the shift in this moment is about. That's why we're not saying to go and change your external life so that you're happy on the inside. We're saying you already have within you on the inside the capacity to access more joy and happiness with how your life is right now. That's a paradigm shift, saying you can be unconditionally free right now.

That's why we're not focusing on eighteen steps to evolve your consciousness. We're focusing on your internal vibration and deepening and expanding your capacity. It's already there. All you need to do is to allow it to be in its fully realized optimal functioning. This will enhance your capacity to access, to absorb, to go within the unknown and pull forth something.

It's like in the Indiana Jones movie where he's on the edge of a cliff and there's a precipice before him, which is only open space. It's not until he takes that next step that there's a place for his foot to go onto. Then he takes the next step and there's a place for his foot to go onto. He cannot see it. It looks as if it's just the abyss and he's just going to fall off into it.

It's why being in the now and accessing what's available to you in the now is what creates this quantum evolution. If you just skip over the now, if you're not used to accessing the water and the sacred tablets in the now, then you just walk by that oracular vision, that place in between the mountains, the path that seems invisible.

But it's not invisible to you because it's what you came here for, to realize and to recognize. It doesn't so much matter what the path is or where it takes you. It's that you can see it, that you're accessing the capacity to realize what seems to be unseen, and what seems to be unknown, and what seems to be not present. You can see the unseen. You can experience the unexperienced. That's how you know yourself to be the Divine.

Technically it seems as if it's impossible to be having this conversation, Source light to Source light, yet we are. We are because you called it forth into being. We called it forth into being. Your scribe, your Divine transmitter, Danielle, has remembered and developed her full adeptness to translate what appears to be unseen, to collaborate with us, to transmit Divine light in a way that it goes from being unknown to being known. It goes from the wordless to the word. It goes from the ephemeral vibration to the absolute laser transmission of energy.

MIDWIFING ORACULAR VISION

Let's say you're a coach or a personal trainer and you have a person that you're working with and they have a certain goal. Let's say that their goal is to activate their Source light, or to know the Divine within and without, or to communicate with Beings of Light, or to find a treasure within and then translate it and express it without.

How is it that you would support them in midwifing the oracular vision that they have, that which isn't even known to them, that which they carry that they haven't accessed before? It's not about giving them cardio workouts and weight-lifting workouts and preparing them for a triathlon—although those things may help with the vibrational capacity to access or embody more light. It's coaching them. It's guiding them to be able to have certain states of being on demand as they choose them.

If the goal, the journey, and the destination are to be the incarnated Source light, then the way that you might coach them is to be able to absorb and be aware of the light that already exists right here and right now. It's not about going out there for it. It's not about leaving the body to go into the light body to travel somewhere. It's in the life, right here, right now—it's in that person's life.

Where is the light? Where is the Divine consciousness? How do you access the brilliance that resides within you? How do you access the genius that resides within you? It's a way of being. It comes from being in Divine Union. It comes from knowing and expressing that Source light within you, that Divine genius within you. It comes from being in proximity to others that are truly embodying their Source light.

UNITY CONSCIOUSNESS EXERCISE
· · · · · · · · · · ·
Live Life Fully as Embodied Source Light

As we've continued this conversation of Source light, you're able to access even more of your Source light. And added to that is the ability to come into dynamic flow and rhythmic union with Source light. In this, you have the water on your camel. Drink from the water. Live this day as if it is the joyous ride of a lifetime, as if each moment has everything within it that you need and beyond. You're re-Sourced; you don't have to wait for some "out there" reality to be who it is that you are.

How would this day be different if you lived it fully? You have a Divine design. You can resist it within these pages, yet this is not easy to do. Or you can live it, be it, vibrate it, access it, and express it. When you do and as you are, there's a sense of being buoyed. There's a sense of being buoyed in this life.

What does your life fully lived on this day feel like? What does your day fully lived feel like? It's not about the doing or the being. You could fully live this day and never get off your chair, couch, or out of bed. You could fully live this day by running that marathon, or anything in between. No matter what activity level or stillness level you're being or doing, live it fully. Access the jewels that it has within it.

You may sense that there is an urgency in our vibration, there's an encouragement in how it is that we're speaking with you right now. We're saying to do it, be it, live it. Keep going. Don't wait any longer. It's not because there's anything missing or because if you don't there's anything bad that's going to happen. The urgency isn't from any lack or any separation. The urgency is from you because you don't want to live another minute half lived. You remember now, and that remembering sometimes creates a sensation of pain or a sensation of separation. You remember what it's like to live fully as Source light, vibrating, re-Sourced.

Allow yourself to live this moment fully and to absorb and access everything that resides within this segment, vibrationally, and on all levels.

9
Light Sequence Decoded
Evolutionary Sequence of Divine Awakening

A JOURNEY OF VIBRATION
AND FREQUENCY

You are decoding the light codes that are within your crystalline cellular structure as you move from word to word, page to page, and segment to segment within this book. Decoding denotes that there is something that needs to be ascertained, that needs to go from unknown to known. This is the joyous unfolding of your soul's evolution in this incarnation.

You are decoding the Divine Source light codes within your crystalline structure. As you do, what had been under the surface or hidden or unknown becomes seen; it becomes known. This may be tangibly realized or experienced for you in that something, some knowing that seemed to be beyond your reach, is now within your reach.

Maybe you've been asking what your purpose is and now you know. You know that you always knew. It may be very tangible. It may also be very energetic; you may move into an energetic vortex of these decoded Source light codes. This is a journey of vibration, a journey of frequency that you take, all within your being.

We began this sacred text with the recounting of the birth story of these sacred scribed tablets. They were born, conceived alongside of your Divine transmitter, Danielle, on her birth day. She carried them

100

within her, unseen and unknown to her conscious awareness until the first tablet, which began this book, was decoded. It was transmitted, transcribed. She crossed the threshold from carrying something in the space of the unknown to then bringing it forth into that which is known. That process doesn't and didn't happen in a vacuum. There was nothing outside of the ring of inclusion in her life that was outside of this project or this process. Every moment, every thought, every experience, led to the crossing of those thresholds.

We're using this example to illuminate that there's some version of that for you as well. It may or may not be a sacred text that you carry, one that you're deciphering, writing, scribing, and bringing into visibility. Yet there's something, there's something, and everything in your life has been a part of the illumination of this something that you carry. It's time to bring it forth out into the world.

There's nothing outside or excluded from this process of you illuminating, decoding, and deciphering what's inside of you. As you have accessed more of your Source light you're able to tap into the embedded consciousness that resides within this Source light, this hidden treasure that you carry within you.

As the waves of energy pulse through these pages, the words—the energy environment of this sacred text—have a sensation of your system matching the key or the decoding information with what has been hidden and heavily encoded within you. The waves of energy are washing away the cobwebs from this once dormant consciousness, clearing the pathways to access it and reactivating the infrastructures to realize it.

All of entirety exists within you; all that there is exists within you. Your inner universe is also very specific to you. This means that even though all that there is exists within you, not all that exists within you is being tapped into at this moment. There's a special sequence of divinity codes that reside within your system that are going from unknown to known, crossing the threshold from undecipherable to deciphered.

LEARNING A NEW LANGUAGE

It's like when you're learning a foreign language and you're exposed to that language. When you initially hear it, it doesn't make sense. You don't know what you're hearing. You can see people speaking and as they're speaking this language you can sense that they're not different from you. They're using their lips, their voices, and their tongues to string together letters, sounds, words, sentences, and paragraphs. They're expressing something.

Sometimes you even know through a hand gesture or what they're holding what they're speaking about. You have a word for *orange;* they have a word for *orange.* You have a word for *sun;* they have a word for *sun.* In the beginning, as you're exposed to it, as you're in the same vibrational proximity of the language, it sounds like gobbledegook. It's nonsensical. Then slowly you may pick out a word, theme, or body movement that keys you into the subject of what's being shared. You may still use your code at that point, your key, so that when you hear the word in another language you translate it in your mind to *your* language.

As you continue to immerse yourself in this foreign language you get to a point where what was unknown becomes known. You know it. You know what the person is talking about. Maybe at first you know 20 percent of the words, 50 percent of the words, or 80 percent of the words. It's not unknown anymore and you're not decoding it word for word, because when you decode word for word or you translate it into your original language word for word and the person keeps talking, you're left way behind. You're still at the beginning of their sentence and they've moved on to a totally different subject. Your comprehension becomes automatic.

Then not only are you able to understand what was unknown, you're actually able to express it for yourself. Perhaps you go through the same process. You translate your word for *orange,* for the word for *orange* in this language. Or perhaps that one word or one small percentage of communication leaves your mouth. Maybe at first what you're saying to the person who's listening to you doesn't make any sense to them. They don't understand your accent, your pronunciation, or your attempt to express in this other language.

As you continue you also go through these developmental stages with the language where you're able to get your point across. Maybe it's not pretty, maybe it's not grammatically correct, but you're able to be understood. Then it goes deeper and you're able to talk about what really matters to you. In this, you move beyond just the functionality of "Can I buy some bread?" to expressing your innermost feelings, sharing yourself in a way that is deep and profound. Then you start dreaming in this other language, you embody it, you live it, and it becomes automatic.

That is one way to wrap your mind and your being around what we're speaking of right now. It's like that which has been put there by you in silent repose, which has been residing or resting in a deactivated state, in a dormant state, has been talking to you. Maybe the last few years, months, days, or decades you've been hearing something. As you've been hearing it, it hasn't quite landed. You're hearing something and your attention is drawn there, but it just doesn't make sense. You don't know what it is. You don't know what it is because you don't have a context for it. You don't have the vocabulary for it.

Soon, however, you will have gone through the developmental stages of your soul and you will be able to access more. For as you've been carrying it and as you've been hearing it and as it's been awakening as you've been awakening, you begin to have certain codes within your system, certain signature symbols where you recognize that, "Ah, this equals that." Or you just throw out the whole key of what you've known before and you create a new one.

THE LARGER EVOLUTIONARY SEQUENCE
OF DIVINE AWAKENING

A useful analogy is it's as if you're an explorer and you go into an environment that you've never been in before. In the beginning you may try to relate it to what you already know. Let's say you've always lived in the woods and then all of a sudden you're on the beach and then you're in the ocean and you try to relate to it. "Well, that coral reminds me of a tree. Or that fish reminds me of a squirrel." You can to try to create correlations yet the same givens or principles of being in the ocean don't apply to being in the woods. You can't breathe underwater. You can't see with the same level of clarity when you open your eyes under water as you can when you're in the woods.

You have this very unique sequence, consciousness, and information within you that's been left for you, by you, and through you, which you're decoding right now. As you access it and decode it, not only does it imbue and touch your life, it's part of the larger evolutionary sequence of Divine awakening. Let's say there was a grand mission to resurrect light, love, and Divine consciousness on Earth and before you incarnated you took a part of this sequence. You took a part of these light codes within you. You carried it.

For example, if you're going on a trip, you have a week's supply of food, water, and clothing, and a week's supply of stuff for twenty, fifty, or a hundred people. Perhaps it's a hiking trip or a road trip. You don't put all the supplies on your back or in your car. You divide them up. Then you meet at a certain time and a certain place and you empty your pockets. You say, "Oh, I have this part. Oh, I have that part. I have the tent. I have the water. I have the stove."

Each person brings with them what they're carrying. They put it on the table and in and of itself it already has value and importance and offers positive support to the person who's carrying it. It's not random. What you carry is not random; it's particular to you. Just as in ancient tribes or in the realms of healers or medicine men and women the one who tends the fire does so for a reason. The one that has the altar for water has the altar for water for a reason. It's the same with you. What you carry for this trip, this incarnation of life, is unique to you. It's particular to you.

As you pull your items out you may say, "Ah, I've got water. I've got the matches"—whatever it is. "I've got the love. I've got the Divine sequence of harmonic resonance. I've got the galactic keys to the evolution in consciousness. I've got the bliss vibe." Whatever it is that you've got, as you pull it out and you partake of it, it already touches you, for it's already been within you. It's already been within you.

As it touches you, it ripples out. If it stays in your backpack, if it stays in your car, you're not partaking in it. Thus it's not available to be a part of the Divine sequence of this full remembering, of this Divine mission of this time. That's why you feel an urgency to empty your pockets to get what you know is within you outside of you in a way that you can express, tap into, and understand. You've been carrying this fire, water, or these Divine sequences that aren't random, they're particular to you, and you have an innate knowing of them. There's a proximity to them already; they're not out of left field. You understand the nature of water. You understand the nature of fire.

Or you're divinely designed in such a way that you've already been on this path of consciousness. Or you've been on a path that maybe seems different—you've been an engineer, you've been an architect—and all of a sudden you find yourself in the pages of *The Tablets of Light*. That's positioned you. What's come before has positioned you so that what you carry, the divinity codes that you carry, may be brought forward.

As we mentioned, this may be very tangible to you. Now you clearly know something that was unknown to you. Maybe this is your mission or your purpose or your next step. It may be in that stage of being a bit fuzzy, where you can only pick out a few handfuls of words, or maybe one word that lets you know the subject of the thing. You may be at various levels of the developmental stage of accessing what you carry within you. We know you've been hearing it. We know you've been feeling it. We know you've been longing to reunite with it. It's not random or an accident that you're within this decoder of *The Tablets of Light*. You're within this key of this Source light.

THIS BOOK AS
A CALIBRATION SEQUENCE

At times, as we're together in this conversation, you may think, "What's the subject of this book? Where are we headed? What's going on?" It seems so different from other books that you may have read. That's because it's not a book per se. It's an environment, it's a key, and it's a calibration sequence. This calibration sequence as you go through it— oracular vision, evolution hologram, ring of inclusion, cosmic choice, vibrational proximity, vibrational autonomy, Source light—as you go through each of the segments they're a part of the unlocking, like a long combination lock that you put in different numbers: 1, 8, 5, 7, 43. You put in one number and then you put in the next number and then the next number and then the next number. Once you have not only the numbers, but also the numbers lined up together in this sequence, you can pop open the briefcase that you've been carrying this whole lifetime and you can empty it, share the contents, and get them out there.

Have a sense of this decoding process happening and that you're not only tuning into these words as you're reading, at times you may enjoy reading them out loud, too. You're not only tuning into the words but you're also aware of what you're carrying. You're carrying the Divine sequence, that which is specific to you. You're decipher- ing it, you're pulling it out of your pockets, you're finding it, you're locating it, you're accessing it, you're beginning to understand more of it.

This is an acceleration, an accelerator segment accelerating your knowing about what you carry. As this acceleration, this decoding, this deciphering is happening, you may be aware of it. You may be having thoughts, images, sensations, ah-has, callings, or awarenesses. What you've been drawn to may even make more sense. Out of all of the infi- nite possibilities why is it that you've been drawn to the possibilities that you've experienced in your life?

WHAT YOU CARRY CONNECTS
TO THE WHOLENESS

What is it that you carry? Decipher it now. As you're deciphering it, as you're being with it, you may have a feeling tone that you begin to identify, or signature symbols that let you know you're in the vicinity of this consciousness. Maybe you feel peaceful, or excited, or tears come to your eyes. You may feel a body movement, a tingling, or a twitching. You may feel heat or a clicking into place in a certain part of your body. Maybe you hear the words or you know. You just know. You know what it is you carry.

We've spoken about this Divine mission, and spreading out what each being carries so that you have a sequence, somebody else has a sequence, somebody else has a sequence, somebody else has a sequence, and somebody else has a sequence. As they are vibrating into that sequence they carry, they put it out in their incarnation, they express it in some way in their incarnation. (This will get interesting in a minute here.) As they express it in their incarnation, it's available vibrationally to be reconnected to the wholeness of all that there is—to the other parts of the tent or the other parts of the building or the other parts of the meal, to the other parts of what everyone else is carrying.

What's interesting about where this is going is that it may not always be a direct translation and that's not even necessary. This means that you can empty your pockets of whatever you carry by vibrationally tapping into what you carry and living your life. It doesn't always have to be an exact translation, like in the example of *The Tablets of Light*. That's a pretty exact translation. These are sacred tablets carried by your Divine transmitter, Danielle. She translates them, they are scribed into these words, and they become this book. It's a direct translation.

You may not have that kind of a direct translation. It may be something that you carry in your eyes, which as you look at someone, maybe someone you don't even know, the sequence gets expressed. You are encouraged to be in the proximity to what is uniquely yours and your Source light and then to express it through your incarnation.

There's not anything that is outside of that expression, meaning, this is who you are, and you're transmitting that sequence in all areas of your life. It's not only when this book is being scribed that Danielle transmits this Divine sequence. It's in all parts of her life, whether she's with people or not with people. That's the recalibration for you as well.

Again, you may experience yourself as someone who is an unlikely candidate for carrying these Divine sequence codes. When we say this, we mean unlikely by your own perception. That unlikeliness may be because you perceive that someone who would be carrying these Divine light codes would be a certain way. Maybe they'd be visible, have a career in personal transformation, have written a book on the subject, are conducting a class on it, or are expressing it in an art form or have some other external expression of it.

You may be a lawyer, cherry picker, retired grandmother, or a librarian. It doesn't matter. It doesn't matter because the sequence of light is carried in your field and it crosses the threshold of the unknown to the known as you access it. As you decipher it and then as you come from it, it imbues and informs your incarnation.

The Divine sequence will have a certain characteristic. That's why we're such big fans of you being you, of you amplifying your signature energy and your vibrational autonomy and that which makes you uniquely you—because it's not random. There's a match there. The more you are you on an essence level and a vibration level, the more you're accessing what you carry. There's a synergy, synchronicity, congruence, and simpatico to you and what it is that you carry. You being you is a part of taking your language skills to the next level, and you understanding what is within you in such a way that it becomes tangible and realized.

As you've tapped into it, been basking in it, and as you've been deciphering and decoding it, allow it to inform you. Allow it to become more known, allow it to bubble up into the field of your vision, into palpable signature symbols or signals that are unique to you. Be the expression of this Divine light.

TRUSTING THAT YOU CAN SHARE YOUR PART OF THE LIGHT SEQUENCE

As we're tuning into the field of each being who is a co-creator of these pages (meaning you the reader), there are a variety of experiences that we're noticing as we've gotten to this point. For some of you there's a sensation that you can't let it out, that it's not okay to empty your pockets or to put it out there because you've been carrying it, this precious cargo, for so long.

To put it out there, to empty your pockets, to have it be available, to reunite with all the other sequences, brings up echoes of the times that that didn't go well in past lives. Or the times you felt like you put it out there and then it was in the hands of those that didn't fully understand it or didn't utilize it very well. Or you may feel that if you share it you'll be separate from it. Right now it's a part of you and if you share it, if you get it out there, then you think that maybe you won't have it anymore.

In the example of water, let's say you've been carrying some water and you've always known you have the water there. You could always take a sip of the water. Then, as you place your bottle of water on the altar of life for all of those who are also divinely designed to be accessing that water or to be connected to that water or for that water to then flow into a larger body of water, there could be a sensation of panic that you won't have the water for yourself. That's the illusion. That's the illusion.

It's what we were getting at in the previous segment on accessing your Source light. As you're accessing your Source light, you're tapped into an infinite supply. There's always more. You're re-Sourced. You know that when the need for more water arrives, you'll have it. There's no lack. There's no scarcity. As you add your water to the infinite supply of this Divine sequence your water is exponentiated.

We want to be very clear that we're not suggesting or that you don't infer from what we're saying here that we're recommending that you give away all that you have and that you don't leave anything for yourself. That's the old paradigm: You'd give the shirt off your back to someone who also was cold and then you'd freeze to death. No, that's not what we're suggesting. We're suggesting that as you share the template for the shirt then others can access their own shirt. They have everything within them. You accessing what's yours models to others this possibility so they might likewise access what's theirs.

We're not sharing this for you to turn it around and think that's what we're saying because that's not what we're saying. We're not saying to not take care of yourself out of the righteous idea that you're helping somebody else. What we're saying is that you're connected to Source light and you're sharing the Divine sequence decoded of what it is that you carry. In this, there's a quantum effect; there's an exponential expansion.

TRUST AND NEUTRALITY

Another thing that we're picking up on in the fields of those reading these pages is a sense that your Divine light sequence, if you put it out there, could go to waste or that it wouldn't be utilized or that it wouldn't be understood or that it's so advanced. There's that kind of sensation as well. That it's been your responsibility so long to carry this, that when you put it out there you will also have to monitor it. It's like you put it on the altar, the fifty-yard line of life, through the expression of your incarnation, by you being connected to you and you living your life by being connected to you. What happens from there, what gets created from there, what other sequences it joins, is not yours to continue to monitor, measure, or try to control. That's because there's a Divine design.

We're also transmitting the consciousness of trust and the consciousness of right relationship, the reallocation of your awareness of what's uniquely you and yours and what's not. As you look into somebody's eyes, for example, and you transmit what you've been carrying through your gaze, it's up to the other person to receive it or to choose it or to take it or to have their sequence also be lit up or not. We invite you to include into the ring of inclusion anywhere that you're wrapped up in the belief that what you're doing has to have a certain outcome or that somebody has to do the right thing with it or that it might get wasted. This is like working for the post office and you deliver packages and you pick up a package at the post office and you drive it to the address. You take the package to the front door and you ring the doorbell, and the person whose package it is comes to the door. They sign for it and they take it.

Once it's in their hands it's no longer a part of your role or your job description. Maybe they'll take that package. Maybe that package is absolutely everything that they've been asking for, choosing, praying for; it's the key. It's the key to unlocking their heaven on Earth. Maybe they just shove it in a closet or throw it in the trash. Or maybe they consciously open it and take every single thing out of it and combine every single thing with their Divine sequence and they get the full benefit of it. Yet if you, as the delivery person for the post office, stood in the open doorway or you were looking in their window to see what they did with the package, you'd get fired. You'd be outside of the bounds of what your part in the process is.

In much the same way as being this postal delivery employee, as you've incarnated by reincarnating on Earth, you're carrying Divine light sequences. Here, now, on Earth, it's time to empty your pockets of this consciousness and these sequences. This is all about you being the vessel: the conduit, the carrier, and the bringer forth—the empowered creator being.

Trust yourself that you chose this role. You chose what it is that you're carrying; you chose the timing of the delivery of it. There's nothing outside of this process in your life. It's all within the scope of your life. It's all within the sequence of your life experience. There's nothing to lose; there's nothing to gain. It's an expression of you being you. It's the acorn tree having acorns.

As we speak about these signature symbols you may experience a feeling tone as you connect to this consciousness you carry. That may be one of the sensations you have: an expanded neutrality. You just know. You just know that it's right. You just know that it's your next step. You just know that it's yours to be and do and have. There's a peace with it. There's an ease with it.

As we said, you also may experience yourself as an unlikely candidate so there may have also been resistance as a part of your ring of inclusion up to this point. Or you may have tried to get out of it, thinking it's up to somebody else. When we say that only you can be you and only you can be and do and have what's yours to be and do and have in this incarnation, we mean that. If these Divine light codes stay within your system, they don't get added into this larger Divine sequence.

We're not saying that to shame, push, or trick you, or to say that there's a right or a wrong. It just is. That's a viable choice. That's a viable choice to not share, to not express, to not have it be outside of you. From our perspective that's not the choice that you're making. It may be a part of the process to get to your yes. It may be a part of the process that you wobble, that you're unsure, that you say, "Ugh, forget it. I'm not going to learn this foreign language."

And yet there's something bigger within you, something that draws you continuously to keep moving forward, to keep pursuing it, to keep with your conscious unfolding, to continue with the evolution of your own consciousness, to position yourself so that you're unpacking, decoding, unlocking this Divine sequence.

We're looking for any other themes or patterns that you may be experiencing as we're decoding this Divine sequence, until it is clear of all overlays and you've calibrated to what you're carrying. We know that sometimes when we speak of signature energy, signature essence, Source light, or you being you, there can be an immediate response within your system to put pressure on yourself, to move into some kind of forcing, stretching, striving, or struggle—or that you have to be somebody that you're not.

It's not like that. It actually feels more like you and your life looks more like you in it. There's a vibratory resonance with it and your incarnation. It's also unique to you, what it is that you carry. You being more of you helps decode, decipher, access, transmit, and share this consciousness that you carry, this sequence of light codes that you carry. It doesn't mean that then you change your personality or try to be bigger or different than you are.

THE FREEDOM TO BE YOU

If you're someone who has a quiet power, it's not all of a sudden that you become this in-your-face, loud person. It's that the quiet power thrums, hums, purrs. There's an amplification of it. There's an embodying of it. You're standing in it. There's no longer any bouncing around of trying to be somebody that you're not. There's a freedom to just really be you. Really be you. Then as you're being you, the deciphering, decoding, accessing, expressing, understanding, and moving from that which is unknown to known happens.

UNITY CONSCIOUSNESS EXERCISE
• • • • • • • • • •
Decode the Divine Sequence Within

Spend a few minutes at this point being in the silence. We're transmitting in the silence the pulse of this environment of decoding. Be in the silence and decode more fully. Tap more fully into the divinity codes that you carry, the sequence that you carry, the consciousness that you carry, and move it into more of the known. You may choose to meditate; you may choose to write. Spend five, ten minutes in the silence, decoding what is within you, crossing the threshold of the unknown to the known.

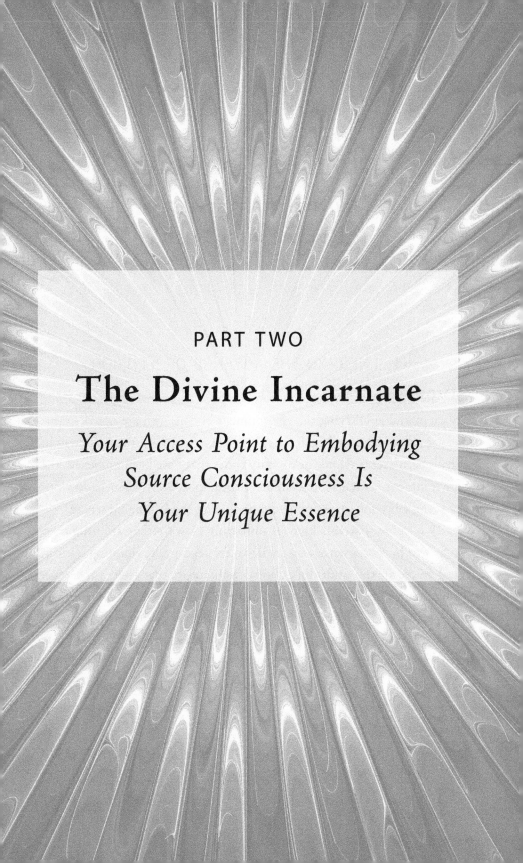

PART TWO

The Divine Incarnate

*Your Access Point to Embodying
Source Consciousness Is
Your Unique Essence*

10

Source Cohesion

You Are the Access Point of Source Consciousness

STILLNESS IN THE ABSENCE OF ILLUSION

We are circling back to the environment that this conversation is taking place in and amplifying the environment because you are not the same as you were when we began speaking. Therefore, with the Source light that's been accessed and the divinity codes that have been unlocked, the environment is even more conducive to support your wider bandwidth of being vibrationally autonomous and being the Divine incarnate.

We know that this book is unfolding in ways that are unique to you. You have the sense that while you're reading it, vibrating with it, and you're in the multidimensional walls of it, that there's a certain vibration and frequency that you can recognize. It's like you had been moving at a hundred miles an hour in your mind, in your thoughts, in your day, and then you sit down to read, to really be with me, Thoth, and the wider bandwidth of consciousness that's streaming through. Then all the noise and frenetic energy quiets and stills and there's this noticeable absence of illusion. That's your cohesive vibration connected with Source light.

It's the consolidation of your energy and at the same time an amplification of your energy. As you recognize the sensations that you have while in this conversation with me, Thoth, and the wider bandwidth of Source consciousness—the *we* that we refer to throughout this sacred text—you have an awareness of your presence without all of the interference, noise, distractions, and fragmented energies. You recognize that sensation of cohesion here and you also recognize that at other points in your life where there's been that sense of a breath of fresh air, a sense of relief from being reunited with the full breath of yourself as Source consciousness.

The focus of this segment is augmenting—now that the light codes have been decoded—the highlighting what was unknown to now being known. One of the universal unknowns that becomes known if you're choosing it through *The Tablets of Light,* through these sacred tablets, is that cohesion, that Divine Union, that stillness that's been described as neutrality, the zero point, clear field of the mind, the pulse of the universe, God, Goddess, all that there is. We describe it as an absence of chaotic or collective illusionary consciousness.

It's like the absence of something that you've been living with without even realizing that you've been living with it until it's gone. As you lean into that absence, as the first sensation of the absence of outside noise, of noncohesive vibrations, you can notice the presence of what's augmented.

There's an absolute knowing, thrumming, pulsating light from that state of being, a cohesive power place of Source consciousness, a Being of Light. There is a right relationship, a given-ness to your existence, your being-ness, your life. There's a clarity and of course-ness, a peace, an ease, a breadth, a power. Yet as you're first communing with your cohesive Source embodiment, the first thing you may notice is the absence of the noncohesive, the absence of the white noise, the absence of all the other frequencies that aren't uniquely you or yours to tune into.

When Danielle lived in downtown Seattle there were planes that flew over her house every few minutes. In the night, train horns would blow and ambulance sirens would wail. (She was close to several hospitals.) For her sensitive, empathic, intuitive nature there was the awareness, albeit unconscious at times, of the people in the city: their thoughts, their frustrations, their noncohesive vibrations. There was noise that could be heard with the ear and there was noise that could be sensed by the tuning fork of her being. We are talking about hundreds of thousands of people and they were not limited to just Seattle. For her nervous system, for her sensitivity, it was like constantly being bombarded with vibrations that emanated from outside.

We're sharing this story because you may relate to being the empath, to being sensitive. In the midst of that, it was perhaps more challenging for her to hear this inner thrum that we're talking about, this cohesive vibration, this inner clarity, the inner compass of Source consciousness. When she spent three months in the countryside of southern France without any neighbors, without being under a flight path, without any trains or ambulances or input from a highly populated area, the first thing she noticed was an absence of all of that noise she'd heard with her ears, yet also had felt with her whole system. It was so refreshing to her system.

As you're in this cohesive vibration, relief or an absence of illusion may be what you notice rather than being acutely aware of all the frequencies and vibrations around the world—of the seven billion–plus people, and all of the free-floating fear, suffering, negativity, righteousness, anger, and illusion. All that ceases to exist because you're in a vibrational communion, you're in a unified field of oneness, and in this, it's a relief. It's a relief to feel and hear your inner voice, your inner rhythm, your signature Source field.

THE STREAMING FORTH OF THE EMERALD TABLETS

Given that these are tablets of consciousness there is an awareness of the Emerald Tablets being accessed in an evolved way. Be within. And as you are within in this cohesive vibration, you're aware of the cohesive vibration without. Your system is thrumming to Source consciousness and as such you're aware of that communion with Source as well as other points of the universe. These other points are in nature, in the other Beings of Light who are incarnated, who are part of this larger mission to bring forth these Divine light codes. You're aware of their Source cohesion. The animals on the planet also are part of this absence of noncoherent vibration.

As the Emerald Tablets are streaming forth in this segment, in this sacred text, have an awareness that other tablets of consciousness like this have had a role in other pivotal times, civilizations, planets, and locations. Know that these sacred tablets hold the memory of this cohesive vibration. You are also a sacred tablet. You hold the memory of this cohesive vibration.

As you're in this cohesive vibration of your decoded light codes and in communion with the Emerald Tablets that have opened again at this time, there's a connection process, a discerning process, a matching process that's happening. Your cohesion within taps into some cohesion vibrations in the Emerald Tablets. Or to put that another way, because you're in a cohesive vibration you're able to be within the walls of the Emerald Tablets, which are also a cohesive vibration. It's almost as if you can't enter without that cohesive vibration.

It's like trying to go across a bridge in between buildings. Maybe this bridge is on the fifth floor and you're trying to cross this bridge but you're on the third floor. So you can't. You have to go to the fifth floor to cross the bridge to get to the other building. It's not that the bridge didn't exist, it's not that the bridge isn't open, it's not that there's not a pathway into this other building. It's just you have to be on the fifth floor. As you're on the fifth floor, metaphorically, you're welcome to be in cohesion with the Emerald Tablets that are coming forward at this time.

A DEEPER REMEMBERING AND THE EVOLUTION OF THE EMERALD TABLETS

Being in communion and connecting with these Emerald Tablets is augmenting and enhancing your cohesive vibration. Yes, you're here to receive from the Emerald Tablets but you're also here to gift the

Emerald Tablets with your decoded Source light consciousness, with what you've been carrying. As you, and all those who are within *The Tablets of Light,* put forth their light code, their divinity code, a deeper level of remembering is possible.

It's as if you are holding the letter *A* and the other people that are also within *The Tablets of Light* have other letters, and everybody puts their letters out on the table. Then as they're together, they reorganize into the pattern that is their origin, and a sacred text is created. An Emerald Tablet is resurrected, because consciousness, or anything in the universe, is never still. It's always evolving and never the same. This is the next evolution of the Emerald Tablets. Every segment of *The Tablets of Light* has been a reading of an Emerald Tablet.

Here is a message that's being transmitted from the Emerald Tablets directly. You, a cohesive Being of Light, are remembering the constant presence of the unified field of oneness. This unified field of oneness is ever present. It always has been and it always will be. Yet the memory of it is what illuminates it, what activates it.

You've had many choices that have led you up to this moment. You've remembered you are Source light. This activates the codes within these tablets and resurrects the memory of the unified field of oneness and the state of cohesion in the vibratory field of anyone who has the cosmic choice to remember it. Earth and those who have this cosmic choice are remembering the unified Source field, the true origin and Divine nature of all that there is. If your hands are full with illusion, with separation consciousness, they're not ready or available to catch the ball of the unified Source field. That is why you've had to, and chosen to, let go, drop the old stories, the old ways of being.

This is a sequence of Divine awakening. Empty your hands of anything else that you've been holding onto so that they're fully open to receive the Emerald Tablet of cohesion. If you're invested in noncohesive vibrations, that's okay. That's okay. There's not a right or a wrong here. In order to fully receive the Emerald Tablet of cohesion you have to untether yourself from these old investments of noncohesion.

We know what's being asked in this moment is a shift in consciousness, because there's been such a familiarity with the illusion of things not going well, or the illusion of lack, or the illusion of something that needs to be fixed, or that there's something wrong. When there's cohesion, when there's peace at first, it can feel odd, and so it's not for everyone. It must be chosen. Are you choosing to receive this Emerald Tablet of cohesion with Source consciousness? Yes or no? If it's yes, say "yes." If it's no, say "no."

As you've said "yes" there's a collapsing of these illusionary ways of being. As you've said "no" there's an anchoring of these illusionary ways of being. As you've said "yes" and "no" there are two conflicting vibrations that create noncohesion. It's natural to say "yes" and "no" at the same time because there are aspects of yourself that are invested in the old paradigm. It's not to try to convince or cajole or kick out the "no." It's to be in absolute cohesion with the "no" and with the "yes" that then shifts it from being noncohesive to being cohesive.

It's like a bee charmer. Bees can still sting them yet they're in communion with the bees. They're in cohesion with the bees. They're not afraid. They're not freaking out. They're calm. They're centered. They're connected. They're going to get the honey. Then they're in cohesion with the bees. They're in cohesion with the bees. Don't be afraid of saying "no" or "yes." Either way, bring it into the ring of inclusion, into a state of cohesion.

THE SACRED TABLETS ARE STATES OF BEING

At this point in our journey together you're becoming aware that each of these tablets that comes forward in each segment of our conversation is a state of being. It's a way of being. It's consciousness, energy, and vibration that then, from the inside out, resurrects the full Divine awakening of your soul's memory.

Your soul and your Source light travel through dimensions all the time. They travel through various incarnations throughout time and space. There are interlife periods, those periods in between lifetimes where the soul is in the full memory of Source connection, of Source cohesion. This memory exists within your Source light. It exists within your soul. It exists within your signature energy.

As you amplify your signature energy, your Source light, your cohesion with Source, you remember and you claim your seat at the table of life unapologetically. You sit at that seat of life—claiming it, claiming it, claiming with it your birthrights. You claim it with your adeptness with spiritual technologies. You claim it with your awareness of how the universe is actually working in the full-on memory of the connection with Source. This is not for the purpose of shaping what then happens in your life because what then happens in your life is beautiful, given that you're connected in cohesion with Source.

Because that's what you're here for. That at its base is your raison d'être, your reason for being. You can bottom-line it. You're here to be the access point of Source consciousness because that's who you are. That's who you are. That's what this incarnation is about and as you reclaim that, evolution happens.

Our focus within *The Tablets of Light* is not so much about what becomes of your connection to Source because that can never be taken away, yet rather strengthening your internal awareness of this connection. For even as you have it, then you pop out of it, and then you have it, and then you pop out of it. You are always it, you pop out of it, you are it, you pop out of it, you are it, and you pop out of it. Your experience of being it is in the Akashic Records, always present.

When we speak about that you may feel as if you're an unlikely candidate to be a revolutionist, an evolutionist in the Divine awakening because of what you've experienced in your life, or how you perceive your life, or what you think a leader or a pioneer or an evolutionist would look like. It's not about how you're presenting it. It's about you *being* it, you *accessing* it. That makes all the difference.

It's like in the old paradigm, the mode of operation was to be spending most moments in disconnection or separation from this Divine truth that you are Source consciousness. That was the way of being in which many experienced the tribal consciousness, the mass consciousness grid, and the illusion. Then you say, "Wait. I can be in connection with Source right now. It doesn't matter how much money I do or don't have. It doesn't matter what my life is like or not like, what my health is like or not like, what my relationships are like or not like, or what my work is like or not like." Because your Source cohesion is inside of you. Nobody can take that away from you. No situation can take that away from you.

As you reclaim it as your way of being, as your vibrational vortex where you hang out in a state of cohesion, in a state of Source being your top priority, that catalyzes quantum evolution because it happens in your incarnation. It happens in this Earth grid. It's the absolute freedom that you have.

YOU ARE INCARNATED SOURCE AWARENESS

You have your unique flavor of Divine embodiment, Divine awakening, Source cohesion, and that's also what creates a different access point, the unique thread in the field of oneness. As you're in this unique thread of individualized oneness, it's expanded even more fully. It's illuminated even more fully. You're able to be in this state of consciousness awareness of cohesive vibration, of universal light, of universal flow. That is your infinite nature.

Be, if you choose, this cohesive, unified Source field. Be the incarnated Source awareness. Be this fluid trajectory of consciousness and light. As you are, recognize it. That's the brilliance of being conscious; that you can recognize your consciousness. As you recognize your consciousness, as you're a witness to your consciousness, as you're noticing your consciousness, there's a consciousness to the consciousness. You're utilizing your capacity to be ever present in a way that magnifies ever presence, that magnifies your cohesion even more fully.

If you choose, direct your consciousness—your capacity to be conscious of yourself as a Being of Light incarnate—to be looking for, witnessing your communion with Source, your cohesiveness with Source, and to be looking for Source cohesion around you as well. This pivots your consciousness from looking for noncohesion to looking for Source cohesion.

It's as if you're on a treasure hunt and you have a list of items to find on your treasure hunt. You're going to look for a rose quartz crystal or a maple leaf or a birthday cake. As you're going through your day and your journey you're looking for a rose quartz crystal, you're looking for a maple leaf, you're looking for a birthday cake.

Perhaps, though, in the old paradigm, you had a different list for the treasure hunt. On this other list you're going to look for noncohesive vibrations, for distortions, for lack, for separation, for the illusion. You're going to look for what's not going well, to look for the gap. Then, as you go through your days, that's what your consciousness is directed toward. It's what it's looking for. It's what it finds. In order to be finding it, and this is quite interesting, in order for the consciousness to be finding it, it has to also separate, it has to also be in vibrational proximity to those experiences.

As you direct your consciousness to be on the treasure hunt for cohesion, then your consciousness doesn't separate from you. Your witness doesn't separate from you. Your capacity to see yourself doesn't separate from you. We're saying *your consciousness*. We could use other words, yet we're choosing *consciousness* because that's what you can direct and amplify into your life from this cohesive vibration.

As we're redirecting the consciousness to be looking for cohesive vibrations, what you say to yourself will also be cohesive. It's brilliant. It's a shift into unity consciousness. You shift into unity consciousness by utilizing your consciousness, by directing your energy to see the cohesion. As you're seeing the cohesion it naturally directs you to the cohesion in any situation.

DISTORTION IS RESONANT AT ITS BASE

We know that, as we're talking about this, for some of you it's bringing up, "Wasn't it dangerous to only look for cohesion. Isn't that naive? Don't I need to protect myself? Isn't that ignoring what is?" As you know, we're staunch advocates of the ring of inclusion. We're not saying ignore your "no" or ignore the dissonance or the distortion. We're saying that you should try to see it from a place of cohesion. Be in cohesion with the "no." Include it into the wholeness. Include it into the oneness. Liberate it.

Everything at its base is energy. Everything at its base is Source consciousness. If something has gotten to a place of distortion, at its base it's resonant. As you're directing your consciousness to be focusing on cohesion, then the cohesion informs you. It informs you.

Let's say you're playing a video game and in the video game there is an obstacle course. The obstacle course comes out of nowhere. It's as if you're walking down a path and then all of a sudden a tree trunk falls in front of you. Or you're swimming across a lake and all of a sudden a net comes up to stop you from crossing the lake.

These things are happening in the moment, just in the moment. You don't know ahead of time. It's not like you studied the obstacle course and then you could say that if you take three steps and then you duck you're going to miss the tree trunk. Or if you run or swim slower or faster you're going to miss the net. This obstacle course is set up so that everything happens in the moment. It happens in the moment. It happens in the moment. It happens in the moment. As you're consciousness is tuned into the cohesive vibration, rather than being focused on avoiding the tree trunk, your system is focused on locating the cohesive path.

This is akin to maps you may have seen in the subways, in the metros, which contain different lines, different routes. The different routes are color-coded. Maybe one route's yellow, one route's green, one route's blue, one route's orange. Depending on which color route you're on, which subway track you're on, you're going to go to different destinations.

Let's posit, for a moment, that there's a cohesive vibration route and there's a noncohesive vibration route. If you're on the cohesive vibration route, you're on that color, that yellow or blue or whatever color it is. In this case, you're in a different place, you're in a different dimension from the noncohesive route. What we're speaking of here is really a paradigm shift because we know that in the past you've been conditioned and trained to look for what's not working and to try to get rid of it, to clear it or avoid it.

We're saying include it. Use it as rocket fuel. Bring it into your ring of inclusion. Recognize that it has within it the capacity to evolve from noncohesive to cohesive. By your seeing the cohesive vibration in it, it evolves. That's what we do with you. As we're with you, as we're in conversation with you, we're with you in your entirety and your totality and your multidimensionality, as your fully plugged-in Divine Source light, as our fully plugged-in Divine Source light. As such that creates an environment, it creates an atmosphere, it creates a dimensional location. When you're in that dimension of wholeness, then you're in cohesion.

Whatever you'd like in your life—greater peace, love, joy, abundance, health, purpose—all are vibrating in a cohesive state. They're vibrating in a dimensional space that's unified. As you're in the dimension of the cohesion of those, anything that's been moving more slowly or in a noncohesive state has been included into the oneness, into the wholeness. It's become one drop in the ocean of cohesion. It's gone from being active to being dormant. It's gone from being manifested to being unmanifested.

THE ALCHEMY OF INCLUSION

Let's say you have a gold necklace and you want to have a gold ring. You take the gold necklace, something that you don't want anymore, and you melt it down; you transmute it, you alchemize it, you transform it.

Then it's this liquid infinite possibility from which you forge the ring, you create the ring, you manifest the ring.

You de-manifest the necklace and you manifest the ring. It's still the same gold; it's still the same material. You don't de-manifest the necklace by saying that there's something wrong with it. You can't try to get rid of the necklace or give it away because then you don't have the *prima material* from which to create the ring.

It's why we don't encourage you to clear your system of what you perceive as negative vibrations. We say, "Be the environment of cohesion and then anything that's noncohesive will be included into the vibration of cohesion because more units of consciousness of you are in cohesion."

UNITY CONSCIOUSNESS EXERCISE
. . . .
Look for Cohesion Throughout Your Day

To complete this segment we invite you to choose to direct your consciousness to look for cohesion throughout your day, throughout your moments. We say choose, because it is your free-will choice. Would you like to direct your consciousness to be looking for cohesive Source energy? If so, then direct your consciousness. Say to your consciousness, "I direct you to be conscious of cohesive Source vibrations." Have a play with it. Notice your sensations. Notice what happens.

11
Consciousness of You

You Being You Evolves Everything

At this point of our journey you are experiencing awakenings, unfoldings, openings, and perhaps a sensation that your insatiable thirst and longing to know the Divine is being quenched, unit of consciousness by unit of consciousness. All this time it seemed as if you had to go somewhere or do something or have something in your life in order to feel that reunion with Source, with yourself. But all along it has not been a destination to get to. It has been a vibration to come from. As we spend moments together within these pages the place that you come from evolves. The delusions and disillusionment, learned helplessness, repetitive patterns—they all fall away. What is left is your unique signature energy. What is left is you being present in your life and for your life. What is left is your divinely awakened consciousness.

WHAT IS ENERGY MADE OF?

It's understood that everything is made up of energy. What is it that all energy is made up of? It's made up of consciousness. It's made of up light. It's made up of Source. We don't mean this from a religious standpoint, meaning that you have to believe in God or that you have to hold a certain belief system to evolve. These pages are not about changing your belief systems, yet reminding you of what you once experienced. In theory, an atheist could walk through these pages and unlock the inner treasure of unified consciousness.

As we say that everything at its base is consciousness, is Divine consciousness, what better approach to evolving is there than to really animate, engage, and activate your consciousness? There's nothing like attending to your consciousness from the perspective of frequency, vibration, and energy. When we say *consciousness, frequency,* and *vibration,* there are less entanglements, overlays, or projections on these words than if we were to say *God* or *enlightenment.*

Evolving your consciousness from consciousness, from frequency, from vibration, touches all aspects of your life in a way that's authentic to you, in a way that's illuminating your authentic vibration, your authentic frequency. There is only one you and being in an environment that supports you in awakening your awareness of more and more units of consciousness of your unique vibration and frequency is an extraordinary positioning of epic proportions.

Breathe into these words if you choose. Breathe into a relaxed, light state of being. Breathe into more and more units of consciousness of your evolved consciousness, your light consciousness. We simply love this word *consciousness.* As you know, we say it over and over and over again. Your consciousness is awakening, it's expanding, and it's informing you. You're in collaboration with your consciousness.

PERCEPTIONS AND TRANSCENDING OF PERCEPTIONS

You may have had the experience of something happening in your life that you then view from a variety of perspectives. You choose how you perceive what is unfolding in your life. You can perceive the same event in multiple ways. You can experience waking up in the morning in a multitude of ways. You can experience taking a shower or a bath in a multitude of ways. You can perceive your relationships in a multitude of ways. You can drive the same route over and over again, back and forth to work or to the grocery store, and perceive it in a multitude of ways.

The seemingly external experience can be the same yet your internal perception of it can vary quite dramatically from moment to moment, from day to day, from awareness to awareness. Those experiences and how you perceive them, how you're conscious of them, are the focus of this internal shift. You can have an experience, and from a partial connection to your consciousness, perceive it as something bad or something negative. You can have the same experience from a unified state of connection, of consciousness, and perceive it as the best thing that ever happened to you.

Vibrating within your authentic expression, your authentic consciousness, allows you to be in an expanded state of all that there is. This expanded state of all that there is transcends your perceptions of internal or external experiences, in order to be in communion with them all, to be with the flow of them all, to recognize the unity that exists in each and every moment and each and every thing.

Evolving your consciousness touches the way you perceive your life experiences and yet your consciousness is not the same as your perception or your interpretation of an experience. Your consciousness is illuminated light. Your consciousness is awake and aware. Your consciousness is infinite oneness. As you're plugged-in re-Sourced with your infinite oneness, your units of consciousness, vibration, and frequency enable you to live the same day from a totally different vantage point. Your life on the outside can be exactly as it is yet your experience of it can be amplified a thousandfold. Your appreciation, your bliss, your awareness as an awakened soul can transform your experience instantly.

YOUR WILLINGNESS TO STAND OUT

As you plug more and more into this heightened state of awareness, to your evolved consciousness, and you're coming from the vibration and frequency of your unique essence, your signature essence, your Source awareness, you may begin to feel as if you're living a reality that's not shared by those around you.

In some ways that is the requirement, the ante at this stage of our conversation. It is your willingness to be the difference of you, to take a stand for your awakened consciousness, to be willing to stand out, to be willing to be one of one, to be willing to let go of the false sense of security constructed by the tribal consciousness. For as you walk through this threshold of authentic expression, or authentic unification of authentic consciousness, you stop pretending in any way that you're not what you are.

We've come to a choice point in our conversation. You've already accessed and awakened so much, yet it's time to choose again. Are you choosing to continue to evolve your consciousness? Are you choosing to come from this unified Source light, this frequency of vibration and consciousness that simultaneously amplifies your awareness and also transports you into a dimensional accessing that isn't shared by anyone else but you?

For in order to be the difference that you are, to be you at this full-on level that we're speaking of, requires an embracing of what is different, what is unique. It requires a willingness to be a pioneer, to explore, to be on that leading wave of consciousness. It requires your willingness to be the snowflake, to be the unique fingerprint. To the level that we're speaking of, it means a full-on embracing, which means in some multidimensional and cosmic way, that you stand alone. You stand as you and only you. You're willing to go there, be there, and vibrate your essence.

What is your choice? Are you fully committing to be the rarefied, unique consciousness that you are, with the full awareness of what that means? You'll be vibrating in dimensional space where only you are vibrating in that space. Yes or no? Yes or no? Both are beautiful choices. Yes or no? We know what the "yes" means. We know what the "yes" means. We know that the "yes" means, among other things, that you walk through the illusion of separation, that you walk through the illusion of needing to belong by being the same as those around you. You cross the threshold of playing it safe, playing it small, hiding out, not being visible. You put down approval seeking, pleasing behaviors, masquerading as someone you're not.

Just as you put something down you also pick something up and what you pick up is your heart in its optimal, inclusionary state. For as we speak of the ring of inclusion, unity consciousness, and the vibration of love, the frequency of love, and the frequency of the heart, we're not only speaking about including what you may not prefer about yourself, we are also speaking about that 10 percent, that 15 percent, that 40 percent, that 3 percent, that 1 percent of your brilliance that you keep out because going there, embracing that brilliance, means being you.

A TRUE PARTNERSHIP WITH YOURSELF

Yes or no? You're at this choice point. Even though we say that as you choose to be the full breadth and width of frequency and vibration of your authentic expression, that's an act of singularity. That's an act of being alone. As you're there, there isn't any loneliness for as you're there, as you choose being in union with your full self, you're in communion and connection with you. You move from being separate from yourself to being with yourself. You move from being disconnected to connected. There's a shift from seeking, longing, and searching, to being in the same vibrational proximity to yourself. It's a feeling of being met in a unique way: only you can meet yourself. It's a vibration of true partnership, true equality with yourself.

There's that sense of what you think or what you thought you might experience when your external reality looked exactly the way you wanted it to. You had the body, love affair, career, health, friends, house, mission, purpose, sense of contribution, abundance, bliss, and all that you thought—the feeling that you thought would be associated with each of those states of being or with each of those experiences. Or perhaps you even experienced the essence of the purpose of this book, knowing the Divine without a doubt, being in a significant relationship with Source consciousness without a doubt.

Everything that you hoped that shifting your external environment would make you feel (but found that it didn't) *can* be felt through the actual having of and reuniting with yourself. For being in Divine Union with yourself changes your experience of all those things from separation to wholeness. As we speak about how evolving your consciousness touches every area of your life and everything in your life can seemingly stay the same, we've also spoken about how nothing stays the same because it's always changing. Everything's a new beginning. What shifts all of that from the inside out is your being so rock solid and connected to you and your authentic expression. That's what changes everything, and that's when everything shifts.

There's no longer that longing or those projections that your partner, for example, is going to fill some hole for you. Or that having a financial flow of your liking is going to create a sense of security. For example, imagine Pac-Man or a pie, a circle, with some of the pieces of the pie hollowed out like Pac-Man's mouth. There's a space there. As you're vibrating at 80 percent you or 85 percent you or whatever percentage it is, there's a sense that the external experiences are then going to complete you.

However, they don't exist in those external experiences. And yet, the person you may become in the process of being in the same vibrational proximity of those external experiences may result in you tapping into those "missing" percentages. (It's not that anything is missing. Really where they exist is in the dominion of you, in the sovereignty of you, in the equanimity of you, in the landscape of you, in the full multidimensionality of you.)

It's not that the pieces of the pie are missing; it's that they were vibrating at a faster or different vibration so when you look at the pie it seems like they weren't there. Then as you're willing to go into the brilliance of you, the extraordinariness of you, the excelling of you, you're in that vibrational space. As you're willing to go into the weirdness of you, the oddness of you, that which makes you stand out, the difference of you is what makes all the difference.

Choose to Be Connected or Disconnected

Yes or no. What are you choosing? Are you choosing the consciousness of you, which also includes the consciousness of you as Source, as the Divine, as God, Goddess, Great Spirit, all that there is? "Yes, I choose to be me. No, I choose to be in disconnection with me." We're saying this distinctly, clearly, because in each moment, that's a choice that you're making. "Yes, I choose to be me. No, I choose to be separate from me. I choose to be disconnected from me."

By me *we mean the full breadth of you. You're awakened consciousness down to the very tips of your fragmented perception of self. There is not any part of you that you're holding separate any longer. When you stop avoiding going into any aspect of your awareness or your consciousness then the interesting thing that happens is that there's an integration. There's a harmonic resonance, there's an Etch A Sketch effect where things come back into the zero-point field, where things come back into harmonic resonance, where things come back into that state of neutrality. That which had been active now becomes dormant and that which had been dormant now becomes active. There's a whole reorganization of the system because everything that's there is available to be reunited into oneness.*

Our focus in this segment is really reuniting with the full consciousness of you. We're inviting you to lean into the integration of the units of Source consciousness of you that you hadn't been willing to be vibrating from. That's our primary focus. With that there's also the awareness of what we spoke about in the ring of inclusion. When you're no longer afraid of being insecure or you're no longer resisting your fear of death or being alone or failing or whatever it is, as you're really willing to go into all the territory of you, all the spaces of you, disintegration happens. That which had a charge associated with it doesn't have a charge any longer.

INCLUDING SLOWER VIBRATIONS
INTO THE WHOLENESS

Perhaps the years or the months that have led up to us being in this conversation in this particular context also had within it moments when you felt more separate than ever, or you felt more of the slower vibrational energies of fear or anger or doubt. As you've been in those territories you've been including them into the wholeness, into the oneness, into the wholeness, into the oneness. Have the awareness of all of this as well.

All along there may have been a sense of reintegration, a sense of reclaiming the units of consciousness and energy that are you. It didn't matter what state they were in. You welcomed them all. You got to know them all. Sometimes on your journey of evolving consciousness you may have asked yourself whether or not you were getting anywhere. Had anything really changed? Had you gone backward? Why were things seeming to get worse, why were things really great, and then there were moments of feeling so separate? Everything has purpose. Everything is made up of consciousness.

It's not so much about how you're perceiving the consciousness as it is about reuniting with of all the consciousness that you are. As you do this, you do it from the vibration and frequency of unification, from the frequency and vibration of love, from the frequency and vibration of your soul's consciousness. There may have been times you felt you were scattered across the multiverse. In this scattering, it's as if you were a zillion iron filings that had been thrown into the wind or all over a room, and this lifetime has been about having that magnet so attuned to your particular type of iron filing that they all coalesce, they all come back together.

It's like a puzzle with an infinite number of pieces. You may have done puzzles of five hundred pieces or a thousand pieces or multiple thousands of pieces that take minutes, hours, days, years. Now, in this particular segment, it's as if you had most of the puzzle put together and yet there was a certain percentage of pieces that you couldn't find or you had the pieces but you didn't know where they went or you thought they were a part of a different puzzle. You thought your anger was for a different puzzle, not your unity consciousness puzzle. Or you thought that your self-doubt was for a different puzzle and not for your unity consciousness puzzle. Or you thought your brilliance was for another lifetime, not this one—perhaps telling yourself, "It's too late, I'm too old, I'm too this, I'm too that."

It's all a part of this puzzle. It's all part of the fullness of all the pieces coming together. If you look at any one piece too long without the whole perspective of the entire puzzle it makes less sense. If you have a piece of the puzzle that's just black, green, or blue, out of context you don't know what that means. But if it's part of a tapestry, texture, or landscape you can see that it's grass or sky. It's the night sky that the starlight illuminates. Nothing is wasted.

COMING BACK INTO UNION

Have a sensation of a reorganization of your system at this point, based on your choice to be willing to reunite with the fullness of you. To reunite with the fullness of you. Sense those iron filings coming back into union with your vibrational proximity, your Source light, your cosmic choice, your ring of inclusion, your oracular vision, your evolution hologram, your light sequence decoded. It's all one whole, one light, one love.

As we've mentioned, the ante at this point—to continue this evolution in consciousness, to continue our conversation at the full breadth of vibration that it's really happening from—is your choice to be willing to stand alone as the difference of you, as the uniqueness of you. We know that in the past this may have brought up that cord of separation consciousness, of the fear of being ostracized, isolated, or on your own. And yet as you're in that spaciousness of really being willing to stand alone, you're really choosing to stand as you and with you.

With that also comes the dropping away of what you thought your life should look like based on the vision that somebody else may have had for it or based on the vision that you may have even had for it at an earlier time. It's an interesting process. It's like simultaneously experiencing deconstruction and construction at the same time.

We know in linear time these things would happen separately. First you'd have the plan or the Divine design of the new building and the reason to deconstruct the old building—either it has fallen apart or it's no longer serving its purpose. There may be other, different reasons. You have the demolishing of the old building, the clearing away of all the material of it, and then the new one is constructed. Yet instead of happening sequentially, they're happening simultaneously as you evolve your consciousness. You're simultaneously deconstructing, de-identifying, and letting go, and at the same time you're experiencing a sense of growth, an excitement, an evolution, an expansion. There's a new sense of purpose, a renewed awareness.

As we're giving this example you may think, "Well, why isn't it like a renovation? That's another building project, and perhaps the structure or the core of a building is kept and then it's renovated? Things are added on or things are expanded or a wall gets taken down, something's opened up or something gets upgraded?" It's not like that. It's not a renovation. It's not a recycling of material. It is really a complete completion of the old and a resurrection of the evolved. It can get confusing at times when you're in the middle of it and occasionally you may wonder whether you are falling apart or you are evolving. The answer is it's both, and it's all beautiful.

Now bring your awareness to the units of consciousness of you, to where it is that you're coming from. Where it is that you're coming from is enriched with more and more of the units of consciousness of you. Your frequency and your vibration and feeling tone of you have shifted. They've evolved. There's a sensation of the charge that you had on some things being neutralized with the unified field of consciousness being the landscape of your origin.

CHOOSING YES AND NO
AT THE SAME TIME

Nothing's missing. Nothing needs to be cleared, rather, everything needs to be chosen. Notice what choice you are choosing. "Yes, I choose to be me. No, I choose to be disconnected from me." Even in the moments where you were living the life that somebody else envisioned for you, or going after what you thought you should have based on separation consciousness, you could still sense, "Yes, I'm choosing me. No, I'm choosing to disconnect from me."

Moving forward in the rest of your day, in the rest of this conversation, hold this as your litmus test, "Yes, I'm choosing to be me. No, I'm choosing to disconnect from me." Sometimes it may appear as both insofar as you're choosing to be you and you're also choosing to disconnect from you.

If you come to the sensation that it's a yes and a no, you may distill down the area that you're asking this question within. There may be elements of something, some experience in your life, in which you're choosing to be you and there may be elements in which you're choosing to be disconnected from you in the same area. Distilling them down may help you to notice where the area of disconnection is.

Or the opposite may be true. As you plump them up, as you get a larger perspective or a larger view, that may also resolve the discord or the dichotomy or the sensation that both are happening at the same time. If you have a yes and a no, you could also just call it a no. You could also just call it a no.

If you multiply any number by 0 you get 0. It can be 5, it can be 1,000,000, it can be 1,000,000,000. If you multiply it by 0 it's 0. The same is true when you multiply any number by 1: you arrive at that same number. If you multiply 5 by 1 or 1,000,000,000 by 1 or 1,000,000 by 1 or 100 or 1,000 or 5,000 by 1 you get the same number. It's all about 0s and 1s. Yeses and nos. Choosing to choose or choosing not to choose; being connected or disconnected.

In some ways we know that by presenting it in this way, this yes-or-no option, this 1 or 0, we're playing with duality, we're playing with the tension between connection and disconnection. Connection and disconnection are part of a whole. What if your life was lived as if you're multiplying it by one all of the time? Then the thing could just be the thing. The experience could be the experience. It could be the piece of the puzzle that's green or the piece of the puzzle that's black or the piece of the puzzle that's blue. It doesn't become the whole puzzle. It doesn't become the whole picture. It's all in right relationship. It's all integrated. It's all in oneness. It's all neutral.

Where are you multiplying something by 0? Where do you choose to disconnect from you, to separate from you? It's not right or wrong or good or bad and yet in some ways it is coming from a vibration and frequency of Source, of unity, of one of one, or it's coming from a frequency of disconnection with Source, of lack, of separation, of zero.

YOUR CONSCIOUSNESS TOUCHES EVERYTHING

The idea that your consciousness touches everything really highlights what we've been getting at in this segment. How you perceive touches everything. The vibration that you're coming from touches everything. If you're coming from Source, as you're coming from oneness, that informs your entire existence. If you're coming from separation that informs your entire existence. The way to inform your entire existence is by bringing your consciousness into a state of unification, into a state of wholeness. This unity consciousness is what then evolves and informs everything in your life.

Let's look at the multiplication, for there's an assumption even in this analogy, and we love this analogy so much. The assumption is that 0 is bad and multiplying something by 1—to be whatever the something is—is good. We understand that in the same way we understand that 0 is moving into disconnection and separation consciousness, and

1 represents unity. We understand this example it has some presumptions in it. We like it because it's as if you take everything in your life and you multiply it by 1, it's in right relationship with all that there is. It has the opportunity to vibrate in its unique vibration and frequency.

There's no overamplifying something or giving it too much power or too little power. It's in right relationship. Multiplying everything by 0 cancels it out and nullifies it, it overshadows it. The 0 then takes the place of whatever was there. In some ways that's very symbolic of the potency and the power of where it is that you come from.

As we circle back to how we began this segment, you may have the same experience, yet where you come from can make it a totally different experience. You have a lot of experience of coming from zero, lack, disconnection, of coming from separation. We're not saying this from any sense of judgment because that was what was there to be mastered in separation consciousness. That's what was there to be mastered in separation consciousness; the repetitive pattern, repetitive pattern, repetitive pattern, repetitive pattern. If you repeat the same pattern another time you're not going to garner anything more from it. There's more to be garnered from unity consciousness.

In some ways you have less experience in unity consciousness, in the cellular memory of your incarnation, of your body, yet that's why there's the full deconstruction of the old and the resurrection of the new. The new is simultaneously ancient and innovative. If you times 1 equals you, 1 times ease equals ease. One times joy equals joy. One times love equals love. One times abundance equals abundance. One times brilliance equals brilliance.

There's more we have to say about this yet we like where we've gotten to energetically. So carry this awareness. Are you multiplying everything by 1 or are you multiplying everything by 0? Or are you multiplying some things by 1 and some things by 0? "Yes, I choose to be connected to me. No, I choose to be disconnected from me." Have that in your awareness. Notice as well the reintegration, the reclaiming of these seemingly missing puzzles pieces that were in another dimensional space. Be within that anteing up, that commitment awareness. Notice where you are with that. Are you committed to embracing your full self? All of you? The brilliance as well? Or are you testing the waters with the full consciousness of you?

12
Divine Union

Occupy Your Divine Access Point

A few segments ago we spoke about the Emerald Tablets and we accessed the Emerald Tablets together. We're continuing that thread of conversation, for the ancient and innovative wisdom of the Emerald Tablets acknowledges that there's a simultaneity of the origin of consciousness, the ancient, and the evolution of consciousness, the innovative.

Some of the Emerald Tablets at their core have the same vibration, the same message, yet how they are experienced in modern day is what creates the difference as well as the evolution that they've gone through. Have an awareness that through your Source light, the consciousness of you and your Source cohesion, you're in vibrational autonomy and proximity to access the Emerald Tablets through the key of your composite of energy, your compilation of frequency and vibration. You are opening an access point to the Emerald Tablets. That's a part of your contribution to *The Tablets of Light* and to the multiverse.

As the Emerald Tablets are opening more fully, and, more importantly, you're assessing that which has been opened, you may have an awareness of your internal vibration shifting. Take a few moments to pause here to allow your sensations of being in this emerald environment. . . .

The Tablets of Light and all of the tablets within it (for each segment is a tablet), is an environment that supports you in the full remembering of being the Divine incarnate, being at ease with being the Light Being that you are, occupying that union of incarnation and divinity. By *incarnation,* we mean your life, your body, your experience of yourself through what you perceive as time. We also mean your vibrational location in what you perceive as matter. It's the Divine reunion, the Divine remembering, the Divine awakening.

RECLAIMING YOUR DIVINE ACCESS POINT

In some ways this is the ultimate shift in consciousness from the illusion that you're separate or that you're powerless or that God and heaven are above you and outside of you. To reclaim your Divine access point is a cosmic choice. The beauty of reclaiming something is that in and of itself, it denotes what's yours, it denotes that it's part of you, a part of your signature energy.

As you reclaim it there isn't any arrogance, ego, disrespect, self-centeredness in that. It's you being the you that you're designed to be in unity consciousness, neither plumping yourself up to be something that you're not, nor diminishing your presence to be not what you are. It's that sweet spot, that union with Source as a self that's exactly right for you. There is right relationship with all there is as you embrace your Divine Union.

As you're in this Emerald Tablet and in this section you may notice limiting beliefs from the collective consciousness floating in your awareness. These may be beliefs such as, "Who am I to say that I'm the Divine? Isn't that egocentric or disrespectful or saying that there is more than one God? Is that worshipping an idol, an icon, a false God?" It's natural that as you cross the threshold of ways of thinking and believing that were a part of the mass-consciousness grid, to hear slower vibrational thoughts such as these. Perhaps you hear that you were born in original sin? These are constructs that you've heard over and over again. Even if you *haven't* heard them in your direct experience of life, somehow they're in your awareness anyway.

This book is not a sermon; it's not about us choosing for you what to think or what beliefs to change or what beliefs to have. It's an invitation to be who you are. As you have that solid connection to who you are then you also have that solid connection to what you know is right for you, what you know to be true for you. This knowledge originates from deep within you. When you know something you don't have to understand it, you don't have to wrap your mind around it, you don't have to figure it out. You *know* it.

This invitation that's transmitted through these words and the frequency and vibrations of this scribed text is to be you, to take off any ways that you were viewing yourself or the world from the collective consciousness, the mass-consciousness grid, or separation consciousness. The invitation is for you to be in union with you, to unlock the oracular vision that you hold, and to share the contribution that you carry.

Another free-floating mass-consciousness thought that you may notice coming up to be included as you're within this Emerald Tablet is that of cause and effect. That you may begin to extrapolate in a way that takes you into separation. If you're the Divine incarnate, that means that others are the Divine incarnate. Then does that mean that there's more than one God or that you have all the power? Does that take away from the free will of others? Or do they have all the power? How does that all work together? Is it a co-creation? Are you the original Divine blueprint or are you an evolution; are you a facet of the Divine?

All those questions and all those wonderings—some of those being doubts—take you away from being you for that's a functionality of comparing. There's a difference between wondering, How does it all work together? What's the Divine balance of everything? How is oneness experienced? Those are different questions from the splitting off from you out of comparison or looking around or drawing a conclusion based on something, based on a part of the equation. If the part of the equation that this Emerald Tablet is providing is that you are the Divine incarnate, be with that. Don't go into the conclusion of that or what that means in relation to everything around you.

THERE'S ROOM FOR EVERYONE
AT THE DIVINE BANQUET

We're not saying don't think or explore for yourself or to take what we're saying at face value. We're not saying that at all. What we're saying is to stay first with this awareness of being the Divine incarnate and recognizing that there's space for everyone at the Divine banquet, the table of the Council of Light, just as there's space for acorns, butterflies, cats, trees, and oceans.

There's a neutrality that we would have you contemplate as you're contemplating yourself as the Divine incarnate. That doesn't cancel out anybody else's divinity. It doesn't put you up a level. It simply invites you to embody yourself, your unique characteristics, gifts, and talents and to amplify those to be the juiciest, most pineapply pineapple that can be. A quality of the embodied unity consciousness is that you're you unapologetically. There's an ease with who it is that you are. You can imagine the transformation available as each person is being his or her full authentic self.

In addition to cause and effect and comparison, another separation consciousness way to not be you was to put the direction of focus on what was wrong or what was missing or how you felt sad or afraid or angry. Separation consciousness has also evolved over the generations. What we are talking about here is the witness of the self; how's the self feeling? This all also depends on what country we're talking about. With this analogy, we're referring primarily to the Western world. In the Western world there was, over time, a shift in the generations, whether this was in your grandparents' generation, your great-grandparents' generation, or your parents' generation. Their focus was more on physical survival. Perhaps they lived during a war or during the Depression. There wasn't much time or space or the inclination to share a sense of being sad or depressed or to have that be the subject of a meeting among friends.

Then that evolved. There was this question, "How are you? How are you?" That may have developed into a talking point with friends who got together. One person would be talking about their problems and then you would talk about your problems or what you perceived as not going well. Or maybe you would go to therapy and talk about the things that were challenging to you when you were a child.

Again, initially, there was a focus on physical survival. Here we're going back several generations (as mentioned above), but you could go back even further. This then evolved to also include "the pursuit of happiness," to utilize the American words. Then not only was it about shelter and food, it was about happiness. Are you happy or not happy? All of that focused on what perhaps emotionally wasn't feeling as good. Of course this varies between individuals, between different personalities. Perhaps it varies somewhat with gender as well.

This focus on the emotional dis-ease fostered places where, if you were inclined in that direction, you could show up and talk about things that were personal and unique to you. It wasn't totally crazy to go to therapy or a support group any longer; it became more of a norm as separation consciousness evolved. We know that again we're speaking in generalities; we're speaking of a movement in consciousness. The movement of consciousness in separation consciousness also evolved. The first year in separation consciousness isn't the same as the last year in separation consciousness. We're providing a context as well.

Whether you've utilized them or not there are places where you can show up as sad, angry, fearful, or depressed and talk about what's not going right. Again, we're generalizing. Depending on who you are, yet in general in terms of the evolution of consciousness, there are fewer places in which to be the brilliance of you, fewer places that create an environment for you to display the brilliance of you.

We know that may sound funny yet a part of the trend. A part of the evolution of consciousness is the creation of those communities, the creation of those spaces, the creation of that allowing within your own system. We mean that, on a large scale, it's not just the top 3 percent of the population that's thriving, that holds the space of brilliance, or that's excelling. It's not just those who you might think of artistically: the famous artists or musicians or actors or politicians or leaders of the community that are in their Divine genius.

As consciousness evolves there's that same level of thriving on an individual basis in ways that are unique to the individual. The way we're describing it to spiral into this concept, is in cases where there is a recognition from the outside in. There's a top chef or a top model, or some hotel gets this many stars, or this restaurant has this many reviews or acknowledgments, or this book is an award-winner or a bestseller, or this actor wins the Oscar.

We're speaking of it from a perspective of some sort of recognition, from the outside in. The student is on the honor roll. This Olympic athlete wins the gold medal. Those are examples from the outside in. There are these ways of winning, of having this recognition, of having this peak experience or undergoing an important rite of passage. We're speaking about the evolution of consciousness from the recognition being from the outside in to viewing being in your Divine genius as a way of being and as a way of being for each and every person who chooses it. It may not be that the Divine genius of every person can be measured in a way that's quantifiable.

For some it is quantifiable: an Olympic athlete can have their sport measured in time or distance and that can be compared to the next person's time and distance. Or there's a certain amount of criteria in order to be a Michelin star restaurant. That same criteria applies to everyone. Yet your unique Divine genius is multidimensional and therefore goes beyond and includes that which can be quantifiable and recognized only from the outside in.

THE DIVINE GENIUS SHINING THROUGH
WITH EASE, GRACE, AND LOVE

We're not speaking about quantifiable Divine genius in a widespread way. We're speaking about ease with self to the degree that the Divine genius shines through and that Divine genius shines through in a way that is quantum and exponential yet not always quantifiable. For your Divine genius may be in grace. You may be the Olympic athlete of grace, yet how do you measure grace? Your Divine genius may be that you can create an environment, a home, a bouquet, or a meal with it being imbued with so much love and so much beauty. There's not really a beauty pageant for how you set the table or how you paint your room even though we know there are also awards in those creative arenas as well.

A part of the wide, sweeping shift that's available from the hierarchy, or the constant comparison positing that one thing is better than another, is the 100 percent thriving within each and every area of life. There's no longer this sensation of worth and value being decided upon by what the collective consciousness mandates, what the old paradigm has said has worth and value: that one career has more worth and value than another, one financial status has more worth and value than another, that one relationship has more worth and value than another, that one body type has more worth and value than another.

Your Divine genius fully occupied and vibrated transcends any of this quantifiable stuff because you're owning your gifts and talents. Isis, who is also present in the pages of this text, is the goddess of magic, the midwife. She doesn't have the sense that she's more or less valuable than Sekhmet, the lioness goddess of solar feminine fire, of fierce acceptance of self, of courage. Sekhmet doesn't have the sense that Bastet, the cat goddess of self-love, of self-adoration, of being present as things are conceived and after things are given birth to—Sekhmet doesn't feel that Bastet is better or worse than she is.

Each god and goddess, each archetypal energy, each chakra, each element—Earth and Air and Water and Fire and Akasha—have their role. It doesn't make any sense for everything on Earth to try to be the same, to try to fit, to try to model and look like what everybody else looks like.

If you're playing baseball it doesn't make sense to put all of your outfield players on second base. Instead there is a pitcher, someone at first base, second base, third base, and home base. There is somebody in the outfield. There is a more widespread field of players, each having their role, each perfecting a different level of genius, of awareness, of skill, of talent. This is the unfolding of the Divine brilliance of each and every person and each and every being occupying who it is that they are.

One of the trends of unity consciousness is having environments that pop up all over the world that really are places and spaces where you can be shining your brilliance, where you can talk about what's going well, where you don't have to feel like you have to hide your abundance, or your amazing love affair, or your joy in being a mother or a grandmother, or your talent, or your creativity.

THE FEAR OF LETTING YOUR
BRILLIANCE SHINE

This Emerald Tablet is so fascinating as we're in it because it is about Divine Union, and as more and more of that Divine Union is accessed, there are old tapes of the mass-consciousness grid that are being integrated into the wholeness. One of these is the sensation that being the same is better than being who you are. Or that if you share your absolute brilliance and what's going well that then you're a target to be persecuted, or a target to be disliked, or a target wherein the jealousy or the envy of others is projected onto you. Or you're the target for that to be coveted by somebody else, and somebody else wanting to take that away from you. We know that it's a bit like breaking the mold.

Let's say you're having tea or lunch or dinner with a friend or family member and they're talking about the things that aren't going well, all the things they don't like in their life, all the sensations of survival or of lack. Rather than empathizing with them by joining them in that vibration of being, you stay in your vibration of being.

We're exaggerating this just to show the new groove of this infrastructure that we're suggesting. In this new groove, you would start talking about what you appreciate or what's going well or what you're really great at. In some ways it may seem as if you're having two different conversations. Your friend or your family member is saying this or that, and the way of communication in the old paradigm would then be to either vibrationally join them and/or verbally join them. They say, "My house is a mess" or "My kid doesn't clean their room." And then you say, "Oh, I know exactly how you feel. My husband never picks up after himself." Then you go back and forth, back and forth, back and forth, back and forth, and back and forth.

What we're suggesting is changing the dance even if it's just vibrationally. It may seem impolite or it may seem rude or it may seem arrogant or it may seem like you're rubbing it in their face if they say, "Oh, my house is a mess" and you say, "Oh, I love where I live. I feel so good. Everything in it is exactly a representation of me."

That's a little bit like George and Jerry in *Seinfeld* where they would be having a conversation and each of them would take a turn talking, yet they are talking about two different subjects. Maybe George is talking about baseball and Jerry is talking about his last date. Even though they're friends and even though they're communicating, they have a conversation in which they're in each in their own world.

STAYING IN WHOLENESS

We're suggesting that you do this vibrationally intentionally. That's what we do with you. We stay in the vibration of wholeness, accepting all of you, including when you go into separation. We love all of you, including your brilliance, yet vibrationally we stay in the multidimensionality, we stay in the wholeness. We don't separate from Source to join you in your separation.

We know this is a bit radical yet at this level of your unity consciousness journey it's not only about how you separate within your own system, within your thoughts, within your own body, within your own mind. It's also about how you use your external environment and your relationships as a reason to separate from you. How do you do this, especially when you're nurturing, when you're empathic, when you're sensitive, when you're compassionate? The old conditioning says that compassion is to join someone in his or her misery.

Unity consciousness recognizes that all choices are valid and all choices are perfect and wherever someone chooses to be it's their right to be that. Wherever you choose to be, it's your right to be there. It's your right to be right there. It's your right to be happy, it's your right to be abundant, it's your right to be in love, it's your right to be in your Divine genius, it's your right to be unhappy, it's your right to be out of love. It's your choice.

To be conscious doesn't mean to be self-conscious of who you are. That's a distortion of the capacity to witness you. The capacity to witness yourself to be *self-conscious*, and the meaning of the word, how it's used, is to look at yourself and to somehow feel insecure, less than, or judged. The self-consciousness is often related to being around others or it can come up when you're around others.

Let's say you go to a birthday party or a swim party and you're there and you're thinking about what you're wearing or what your hair looks like or what you look like in your bathing suit. That self-consciousness is a way of utilizing the witness to look at yourself from a place of judgment, from a place of insecurity, rather than being inside of you and enjoying the water on your skin and the people that you're with at the party.

BEING WHO YOU ARE FULLY

The Tablets of Light is an environment where you can be who it is that you are and you can be in the Divine genius of you and the Divine brilliance of you. That may be what you feel when you're really engaged in something you love or when you're in nature. You're able to show up as you when you're in nature. Nature receives you. You don't have to put on a mask or get dressed up or act like you're happy if you're not. When you go into nature you can just be in nature. Nature gives and receives the fullness of you.

Or that unconditional love that you feel with animals. Your dog doesn't care if you just got out of bed. Your dog's happy to see you, your essence, your vibration.

Again, as we're within this Emerald Tablet there are old limitations or fears that are getting questioned as they're coming up. One such fear might be as follows: If you really give yourself permission to thrive and to show that you're thriving, people aren't going to like it. You're going to lose love, you're going to lose friends, you're going to be isolated, you're going to be ostracized, you're going to be thought of as being arrogant. What if that's a part of your contribution to be you? To be that beautiful rosebush that's blooming with color and lusciousness and beauty and a scent that's exquisite? You don't try to suck your roses back in when you see a rosebush next to you that didn't bloom.

You may have a sense of some of those core separation patterns being beckoned forth into the ring of inclusion through this Emerald Tablet segment. Maybe it has manifested in the past as holding back or playing invisible, playing hide-and-seek with your signature energy. Or bulldozing over or pretending to be overconfident from a place of insecurity. When you leave yourself to join someone in his or her lack or separation you've chosen to separate from yourself.

These nuances of separation consciousness and unity consciousness are being illuminated. This is not to say that you're doing it wrong, but to uncover and unwind and disengage the subtle nature of some of these ways of being that may appear cultural, they may appear loving. Yet you have a Divine design and your Divine design isn't any better or worse than anybody else's.

Imagine the world where everyone is really who they are in their totality and that they're in that quantum Divine genius that may be more qualitative than quantitative. It may be more of a state of being than something that can be measured. You've experienced that as well. Someone may have a life where they have every reason to complain or to compare what they don't have to what others have, yet they have a sparkle in their eye, their soul is shining through, and when you're with them, there's a sense of being in the presence of someone who's really hooked up.

It may be that they have a job that's not that valued or glamorous in the mass-consciousness grid yet they do it impeccably, beautifully. If everyone and everything was meant to be the same then everyone and everything would *be* the same. Life and the Beings of Light incarnate are designed to be varied. You have your Divine design, your role in the fabric of creation, your Divine areas of ascended mastery, your gifts and your talents, and you being them doesn't take away from somebody else being them because there's only you and only you will do it the way that you do it.

Let's say that one of the ways that your Divine Union gets expressed is through art. You're an artist or you're a singer or you're a chef— something creative. You're a scribe. Even if you make the same meal; let's say you're a chef and you're working with the same ingredients as eighteen other chefs. Vibrationally you're going to create something different from eighteen other chefs that have the exact same ingredients and the exact same recipe. It's about being *your* chef self. Or you can have eighteen singers sing the same song. It's not ever going to be the same and the fact that you sign the song fantastically doesn't mean that someone else can't sing the same song fantastically also.

We know that we often speak about this subject in other Divine Transmissions around abundance, around health, for there was an odd way of thinking that if you had less then it meant that somebody else who had less would have more. What's uniquely you and yours is uniquely you and yours and what's uniquely them and theirs is uniquely them and theirs. So, your having more doesn't take away from someone else. That's all based in lack consciousness. It's all based in a limited consciousness.

We're talking about you and your own atmosphere and your own vibrational autonomy. What's yours is yours, what's not is not. Your having what's you and yours doesn't take away from somebody else. If somebody else is sick, for you to get sick doesn't make them healthier. If somebody else is struggling financially, for you to struggle financially doesn't make them wealthier. You shirking your gifts and talents doesn't make somebody else more gifted and talented. You choosing to dim your brilliance and your sense that all is wellness doesn't help somebody else be more brilliant or more in the state of well-being.

This topic is usually approached from something that's quantifiable, such as a sense of health or a sense of financial well-being that we're applying to your signature energy. We know that when you amplify your signature energy—your health and your wealth and your joy—they expand as well, they amplify as well. Your experience of them amplifies, even if nothing changes on the outside.

THE MASS-CONSCIOUSNESS GRID

This is also where you get some more choice points because you can't continue your evolution of consciousness and try to keep the lid on things. You shining your signature energy full-on naturally has to acknowledge that there will be some external things in your life that will get better. If you're operating under the old collective consciousness, the old mass-consciousness grid, or past life vows or agreements that say in order to know yourself as the Divine or in order to be in union with the Divine, you have to sacrifice, you have to give up all your worldly goods, or you can't use your gifts and talents for personal gain. Well, there's going to be personal gain. There's nothing wrong with personal gain because it's not personal gain at the expense of somebody else. That's also part of the old paradigm.

We're not saying that you made these things up. Some of them are resonating more with you than with others. Some of these mass-consciousness grid beliefs apply more to you than they do to others. We're not saying that you made them up. Yes, in separation consciousness there was a sense of stepping on others to climb up the ladder.

Or there was a sense of the have-nots becoming the haves because the have-nots gave up what they had. That the power-over and power-under paradigm had been prolific and applied to many aspects of your life, so it could be natural to still have echoes of this distortion in relationships.

When all that gets put back into right relationship then there's no one better or less than. Instead, you're coming from a state of equanimity and you're coming from a state of equality and you're coming from a state of awareness, knowing that everyone has access to everything that they need, because it's within them. No one is better or less than. Everyone is who they are. Period. There's an optimal functioning and frequency in every part of your body. Your knees aren't better than your elbow. Your knees are your knees. Your elbows are your elbows. They both have important roles. Be the knee. Be the elbow. Be who you are.

Notice that as we're in this Emerald Tablet even more, it's as if a whole net that contained all of this stuff from the mass-consciousness grid is being lifted up. As it's lifted up and carried off to be brought into the oneness—brought back into the Source from which it came—you may have a sense that this net, this grid, was also a part of your grid, your net.

Imagine that you were standing in this net, and let's say for a moment that this net is an energetic net. Let's also say that the ends of the net of the mass-consciousness grid could be gathered on top of your head and the net could gently and vibrationally be pulled up from below your feet, your ankles, your shins, your knees, your legs, your pelvis, your abdomen, your chest, your throat, your head, and out the top of your head.

That net represents the mass-consciousness grid and everywhere that you were plugged into it that you've chosen to not be plugged into it any longer. When you choose to unplug from the mass-consciousness grid, you take away all the beliefs of original sin, of trying to be the same as everyone else, of dimming your light so that somebody else's light could shine brighter, all the power over and power under. You take away the hierarchy of all those illusionary beliefs that posit if you're visible in your brilliance, then you're a target.

BEING IN RIGHT RELATIONSHIP WITH THE NATURE OF YOUR DIVINE DESIGN

Again, we're not saying that you made those up or that they're crazy. You have past life experiences and you can see that they are part of the mass-consciousness grid. When somebody's visible there is a projection that can happen, yet when you're *really* visible as you, there's a neutrality so the projection doesn't stick. It's not resonating within you because there isn't the seed of that self-consciousness. You're in right relationship with the nature of your Divine design, as a Divine incarnate being.

UNITY CONSCIOUSNESS EXERCISE
· · · · · · · · · ·
Lift the Net of the Mass-Consciousness Grid

Have a sense of that net. Maybe it's been pulled all the way out and it's going back to the Source from whence it came. Or maybe it's moving more slowly than that for you. Maybe it's still at your toes or you're still gathering what it is in the mass-consciousness grid that you're unplugging from. Have the sense, in the next twenty-four hours, that that net will be lifted off from your cosmic choice to unplug from the mass-consciousness grid if you choose. We're saying it that way. You're unplugging from the mass-consciousness grid yet really what's happening is that you're plugging into your Divine Union from being in the environment of this Emerald Tablet.

As you're in coherence with your Divine Union, that automatically means that some of these things are incongruent. They get de-manifested. That's why we say you can't be on this rapid, accelerated, evolutionary, visionary, oracular vision path and stay the same. Neither can you avoid some things in your life expanding. Notice if any of that's been coming up for you as you continue to read The Tablets of Light. *Specifically, notice if you've been modulating how much you're actually willing to allow yourself to blossom. Allow your choice to be opening the way, opening the way, opening the way, opening the way, opening the way.*

Bring your awareness back to the present moment as well, to being on the oracular-vision path, to noticing what you notice. There's no rush, there's no urgency. You're not doing a whole marathon in one minute. If your system has gone into any fight-or-flight mode as we've been speaking about all this survival consciousness, allow it to come back into a state of wholeness, reconnecting to the Emerald Tablet that you're within.

AN ENERGETIC GROWTH SPURT

You may have a sense that your rosebush has been growing in a cage. Now this cage is lifted off and you can absorb the nutrients from Source consciousness within you. This time in your life may be like when you were growing physically. Maybe one summer as a teenager you experienced rapid, accelerated growth. You grew six inches. This is a bit like that.

As you thoroughly explore and, if you choose, dismantle those ways that were stunting your growth, then you may have this spurt, this blossom, this accelerated evolution. By *growth,* we simply mean taking your seat at the table as the Divine being that you are.

You may have a sense that it is the time to do this. The invitation is to revel in it, to bask in it, for you know that you don't need to go into any sense of overwhelm. The overwhelm and the tendency to modulate abundance or growth or expansion or visibility or success comes from that sensation that there's not enough, that it would be too much, that you don't have the resources, the energy, the time to be all that.

If a lot's happening right now, if you're on an accelerated path, trust it. Trust it. You may be in a prolific growth cycle as part of the developmental stage of your soul. That prolific growth cycle may manifest in a way that a lot of what you've been creating gets actualized all at once. Or maybe a lot of what you've outgrown falls away all at once. Or it may be something totally different, because it's *your* accelerated growth path.

Let's go back to our analogy of a baseball team not having every player on the same base. Similarly, the Earth's population of Beings of

Light, divinely incarnated, don't play the same role. They don't have the same gifts and talents or the same Divine light mission. What's yours is yours. What's uniquely you is uniquely you. If you haven't done so thus far and you'd like to, give yourself permission to be you: to contribute, to play your role magnificently, to unpack what you've been carrying.

As we're coming to a place of completion with this segment, have an awareness of your key, your composite of energy having unlocked within this Emerald Tablet of Divine Union, something very you. Something very you. Something very you-like. Enjoy.

13
Infinite Energy

Ride the Wave of the Impulse of Creation

ABSORBING AND ASSESSING
UNITY CONSCIOUSNESS

Our magical conversation continues from within the Emerald Tablets. You have an awareness of this ancient and innovative wisdom that resides within you. You have accessed more of the consciousness of you in connection, communion, and collaboration with your Divine Union. This Divine Union also restores your awake and aware consciousness as a creator being. Given that you are a creator being there is an illumination of the impulse of creation. You have within you everything to create worlds. You create worlds every day and in each moment.

The Emerald Tablet that's coming forward to be accessed in this segment is a continuation of the rhythm that has already been spoken about, or the cycle that's already been spoken about. This began with an awareness of your enhanced capacity to absorb. We spoke about this briefly. Your capacity to absorb and your awareness that there is more to be absorbed in each and every moment is such that as your capacity to absorb is enhanced and increased, you access the unity consciousness that exists in each moment.

It's not so much that the consciousness didn't exist before you accessed it, or that unity consciousness is new, or that the joy in each moment wasn't present all along, for it was. You can see that this capacity to absorb, this capacity to access, this capacity to take in through your consciousness more of what already exists in each moment is a pivotal skill and state of being to have. Although that isn't the focus of this particular Emerald Tablet it relates to the absorption, for the absorption and the accessing is one part of the cycle that we're getting to in this particular Emerald Tablet.

In regard to accessing and absorbing, it's not always that the first step comes first and the other step comes second in terms of the cycle that we're speaking of. You have a capacity to absorb, to receive, to access what has existed all along, because this is also the skill that you use in your oracular vision to know what it is that you carry within you. It's been there along.

In this same way, *The Tablets of Light* has been within Danielle since this incarnation and before, yet she wasn't consciously aware of it until a few years ago. That consciousness, that awareness, that which is within you is ready to be expressed. The accessing of it is part of the cycle, one part of the step. The capacity to absorb it, the consciousness of it, the embodiment of it, is another part of the step.

THE CAPACITY TO CREATE AND TRANSMIT

The Emerald Tablet that's coming forward in this moment is the capacity to be able to create, the capacity to be able to pulse something out more consciously. If we simplify all this to say that you're receiving and transmitting all the time, it's the transmission part that we're speaking about. It's the capacity to overflow and to pulse out, to transmit out, to create from your Divine Union and have the ripple effects of that.

If you look at it from the breath cycle there is the receiving of the breath, the having of the breath, the expelling of the breath, the exhale. These are often seen as separate parts of the cycle yet within the umbrella of the breath. We're talking about this in separate ways but still in all, you have the capacity to receive or access or absorb. When this is the case, then you are able to really fill up with that energy and to have the capacity to overflow, pulse out, and transmit. They're all one and the same.

In all of this, we're getting to the impulse of creation. A lot of what is talked about and thought about in terms of manifestation, in terms of actualizing, implies that you have to make something happen. Our saying that you are a creator being could be interpreted to mean that you have to create something out of thin air. What we're really getting to in this Emerald Tablet is to say that there is a rhythmic pulse of the universe, this impulse of creation that life knows how to live.

There's an infinite intelligence to each and every moment. This infinite intelligence in each and every moment is something that you access, something that you absorb, and then something that you're able to transmit, to express. You can see that as you've been carrying your unique part of the picnic of life (and this book of Thoth's tablets is helping you unpack what it is that you've been carrying), there comes a point where it's time to put it on the table. It's time to take it out of your backpack, to put it on the table, and to share it.

That's the part we're speaking about at this time. It's not a linear order. We could have this step much later or we could have this step much earlier. Yet we're speaking about it right here, right now, because when you've been carrying something for so long it doesn't necessarily occur to you to put it on the altar of life, to share it, to transmit it, to pulse it out.

There is an impulse within you that's been calling to you, it's been speaking to you, it's been saying "It's time." You have a sense that there's something there. You have a sense that there's something you're meant to do, something you're divinely designed to do.

You have a calling to explore that, to let it inform you as to what it even is and what shape it would take. This impulse is like a calling, a beckoning, a communication with your system. That's what we're speaking about. It's the way that your Divine design, your sacred architecture, your Divine blueprint interacts with you and speaks with you. It's informing you from the inside out.

EXPRESSING THE DESIRE

Then there is this impulse, this calling, this beckoning, and this desire that wants to be expressed. That wants to be expressed. There's a naturalness to that cycle. There's a naturalness to that rhythm. It's not anything that you have to force. It's not anything that you have to make happen. It's more of an overflowing. It's ready to be out. It's more of a stopping from holding it back than it is a forcing to get it out.

Within this Emerald Tablet of your rhythmic expression, your informed expression, there are divinity codes that are supporting you to simultaneously reabsorb back into the wholeness, back into the oneness, that habit of holding it back, that habit of not expressing it, then restoring the naturalness of the rhythm. It feels like that next natural step.

This doesn't mean that you don't have doubts, worries, fears, nerves, or any of that. Or that it doesn't take some kind of energy to take that next step. It does. It will. It's a pulsing, it's a transmitting. There's a trajectory of energy out that requires some level of combustion, of fuel, of activated energy. At the same time it's a natural momentum.

This is akin to having a slingshot, and pulling the sling on the slingshot shot back, back, back, back, back, back, back, back, back, back. There comes a point where this creates a very dynamic tension. All you have to do is let go and then the momentum of that slingshot will shoot whatever's in the slingshot forward with a great deal of momentum and traction.

It's like a rocket full of rocket fuel and the engines turned on. They're revved up and there's all this force underneath the rocket that propels it up and out. It's fiery, it sparks, there's a lot of energy, a lot of impulse, a lot of propelling energy. That's also *your* potency. Let's use another example: that of an airplane on the ground. Here it goes from being stopped or slowly rolling on the ground at what is not a very high speed. Then the engines are on and the plane increases in speed. There's a lot of momentum that seems to achieve the miraculous feat of lifting this weight and transcending gravity and launching the plane off the ground into the air.

You have this same potency, power, and force within you, to transcend that which seems unable to be transcended: the gravity holding you back, the procrastination, or your patterns of the comfort zone. As a creator being, there's a level of power within you, a potency within you, that can create worlds; it's *prima material,* or elemental essence. This particular Emerald Tablet is supporting you, if you choose, to get back in touch with that raw power within you. It is the instinctive capacity to create and as such, holds much momentum—so much momentum.

Your life has been leading you up to this moment. Your life has been absolutely leading you up to this moment. You're positioned in such an extraordinary place. Think back on all the times that you were in polarity, duality, or separation consciousness. Remember every time you felt lack, every time you had a desire that wasn't realized, every time you experienced something that totally lit you up and you wanted more of. It's like you kept adding, you kept adding, you kept adding, you kept adding to this rocket fuel, to this capacity to express, this capacity to be launched, this capacity to get what's been percolating inside of you out—and out in such a way that it's magical, it's incredible, it's powerful, it's extraordinary.

Have an awareness of the Emerald Tablet of your unique expression coming into the forefront of your awareness. Have an awareness of it being fully expressed. It's coming forward in that wholeness of the two parts of the cycle we've been speaking about: your capacity to access that which resides within you, and the impulse to express it, which then expresses it. Your Divine uniqueness expressed. Your Divine uniqueness expressed.

We're tapping into this momentous energy because the space has been entered into through your Divine Union and through your choice to tap into your brilliance. You are tapping into your Divine genius, which allows you to be on that breadth of the spectrum of you. This allows you to really be as joyous as you are, as abundant as you are, as creative as you are, as sassy as you are, as *you* as you are. The holding back from hiding that or putting it under the rug is not there.

TRANSCENDING THE COLLECTIVE
CONSCIOUSNESS TABOOS

We know that reading this book of Thoth's tablets is like breaking through; it's like transcending the collective consciousness taboos. Many of these taboos or no-nos are about having a Divine connection in the first place. Or they're about saying that you're the Divine and then asking you to take that next step so that not only is it internal, it is also expressed. Not that you have to scream it from the rooftops. However, it is who you really are. You're in a divine flow, and it's who you are. Then it expresses in a certain way.

That's another level of this collective consciousness taboo that we spoke about as well in the previous segment. That one posits that it's not okay to be shining really brilliantly and extraordinarily. You may stop the step before accessing what really resides within you because you're trying to stop what comes next, which is pulsing it out into the world.

Maybe that means creating something. This tablet is an infusion of life-force energy. It's a recalibration to the impulse of creation; that life knows how to live. There is an impulse, a spark, and then combustible energy. As this combustible energy builds within your system, it's natural to transmit it, to pulse it out the way that's unique to you.

We're not saying that you have to become a celebrity or be on TV in front of millions of people. It's *your* expression. There's no longer that sense that your song is within you, yet it is what you're singing. That's the threshold that this Emerald Tablet is supporting you to pivot into if you choose. You may have an awareness of your song. You may not have an awareness of your song. It may be as if your inner song, your inner voice, that which is uniquely you, that which you've been carrying, is going to come out in full force. You've been singing it in your head and now's the moment, with this Emerald Tablet, that you pivot and you express it. Then it's belted out in such a way that you can hear it, in a way that it's seen.

At this point it could be beneficial to you, if you choose, to be less focused on what it is that you're carrying. It could be beneficial to focus less on what your oracular vision is and the form of expression that it would take—these two sides of the coin. Instead, it might behoove you to be more focused on the naturalness of it taking form and to be more focused on the energy of the seed of the Divine blueprint as it goes from seedling to sprout. There's a force there. There's an energy there that is natural and yet it explodes in some ways. There's a fire to it that enables it to tap into what is within you, to recognize that you have everything within you to express your Divine design.

As you have everything within you to express your Divine design there is a natural propulsion of energy that takes you from one developmental stage of the soul and your Divine light mission into the next. Just as the seedling grows into the sprout that grows into the tree that then grows into the acorn, there's an energy there. There's a naturalness to it. You don't see the acorn tree striving, struggling, and having sweat on its brow because there's a natural flow to this impulse of creation.

In this, you see that life knows how to live. You can be in the middle of the desert or where there are temperatures that are super hot and maybe there's an asphalt road that's been paved over and there's a crack in the asphalt and there's a green sprout growing out of it. When you see it you think, "How is that possible? How is life living in the midst of this improbable location?" It's because there's that impulse within.

Maybe you've seen the same thing in a house that's become a ruin in nature. It's been abandoned for whatever reason. A tree grows from within this house, taking back a place that used to have no trees in it. A house has floors, walls, and ceilings and there's no tree growing in it, but once the house falls or loses its structure, life knows how to reoccupy it. Nature takes it back with an innate life force.

A RECONNECTION TO THE LIFE FORCE

When you had been pretending to be a diluted version of yourself, you disconnected from that life force. This Emerald Tablet is a reconnection to that life force. It becomes so compelling, so natural, you're so buoyed that the expression, the transmission, is automatic. It's divinely supported and nourished. When you're connected to the life force that naturally resides within your creations, there's an ease to them. There's a supported, nourishing energy in your life as you're connected with that life force.

We know that it's perhaps not your mind-set or your way of thinking of yourself to think that you grow like a tree grows. You may see your life as a line of time. You've had this lifetime in which you were conceived. Then you were a baby and then you were a toddler and then you were a child and a teenager and then you became an adult and how old you are now? You may not see this in the same way that you see a seed growing into a tree. You may see a tree having a vertical growth. You may perceive yourself to have a horizontal growth; you're growing in a line left to right rather than growing up, or as you tune into your quantum growth you're aware of growing in a spiral, or growing multidimensionally.

There's a reconnection to what has been informing each and every moment of your life. There's an infinite intelligence to your life. There's a life force to your life. There's an energy and a positioning to your life that's following your Divine design, especially when you stop stopping it. Especially when you stop stopping it, it's allowed to grow, it's allowed to thrive, it has the energy to cross thresholds, to go to the next developmental stage. This is where what lights your fire and following your unique rhythm come into play as very important energy vibrations and frequencies to the expression of the vision you carry.

This only happens when you're confident and connected to who it is that you are. It only happens when you're willing to give yourself permission to be who it is that you are rather than following the collective consciousness template of this is how it is.

Perhaps you have heard the saying "Follow your bliss." In this there's a sensation that as you're following your bliss, you're following your passion, you're following what lights you up, you're in touch with what we're talking about: the creative impulse. You're in touch with the *prima material.* You're in touch with the life-force energy that is unique to you. It lights you up and is what your particular cycle might be, what your particular rhythm might be—just as a sunflower is going to have a different developmental cycle than a pumpkin.

By amplifying your energy and the life force that's more fluidly feeding your Divine design, a natural momentum is created. What lights you up transcends what might be right or wrong or what you might perceive as right or wrong because right or wrong doesn't really exist in the way that you may have believed it should exist.

GOING AGAINST YOUR NATURE

One of the reasons that you may have been holding back from using this combustible energy, this force, this life-force energy to go against yourself, is out of the fear that you could do something wrong. This is especially true when you conclude that every time in the past that you did something authentically as an expression of you, it didn't look like somebody else or how they would do it. The difference of you, as you interpreted the difference of you, was deemed to be that which was wrong, or that which somebody told you was wrong.

Let's say you're left-handed and you're writing with your left hand. That's natural for you and yet you were brought up at a time and in a place where being left-handed was thought to be wrong. It was not right. It was wrong. So, you went against your nature to learn how to write with your right hand. You may have interpreted the difference of you as being wrong or doing something wrong and thus buried your connection to knowing what that difference is. Building on this, you then used the power and the potency that you naturally have as a creator being, to try to stand still, to try to not create, to try to keep everything status quo, to not rock the boat, to fit in, to go under the radar. In this is a sensation of utilizing your natural resources against yourself.

In addition to this, you may have well-meaning people in your life who love you so much that then tell you they want you to be different from you are. They want you to be more like they are. They want you to have their rhythm. They want you to do it their way. Instead, we ask you to recognize what lights you up, what's right for you. Following that will be an amplification of inner power, of life-force energy contributing to your life, and contributing to your Divine design. We ask that you continue to live your life for you, to continue to live your life as you, to be willing to be present in the face of what may be disappointment, a lack of approval, or projected ideas from those you love. In the face of this, we encourage you to not leave your Divine Union, and to not buy into the idea that there's something wrong with you because you're doing things a different way.

There is a courage that this path of the visionary requires. It requires a certain level of caring more about your inner vision than what others may think of you. The more authentically meaningful something is and the more you your life looks like, the more vulnerable you may feel. To sing your song might make you feel more vulnerable than singing a cover song and trying to mimic how somebody else sang that same song.

That's why it's so important to have a conscious connection to the life-force energy that propels you. It buoys you. It is like the inner pressure of the champagne bottle. You being you is like tilting the champagne cork to the side and then it pops out because there's an alchemy, a life-force energy, a chemistry that's propelling you forward.

We know that we're asking you to turn on aspects of yourself that you may have shut down. For example, you may have turned off and been afraid of your desire. You may have been afraid of your passion or you may have been afraid of your strength or you may have been trying to tone down your enthusiasm for a certain subject.

CONSCIOUS CHOICE EXERCISE
Choose to Reclaim Yourself

As we mentioned, there come certain places and choice points on this journey where, in order to keep going, there has to be the willingness to reclaim that which you've shut down or that which you've been trying to keep out, or that which you've been pretending that you're not really.

This is an example of one of those. This is an example of one of those thresholds, one of those cross points, where you say that you're willing to recalibrate to the inner life force that resides within you and to use it to work with you rather than against you. You're willing to awaken your brightness, your personality, that which lights you up even if somebody around you says that they don't like it. There's a commitment, a steadfastness to being you as the Divine creator, to making who you truly are your top priority.

OPEN AND AVAILABLE TO UNIVERSAL FLOW

As there is this reconnection to this impulse of creation, this life-force energy, things move, things flow, things deepen, things expand, things accelerate, things take on an even deeper and faster actualization. They come into form more quickly because you feel this life force. You feel the support of the universe as well. You're connected to more than only your personal effort. You're open and available to this universal flow and being backed by your Divine Source consciousness, having that be what animates and informs you.

We know that at times it may have made sense to you to tone things down or to dim things or to shut things down. Maybe there was a time where you hadn't done that, which then in your mind led to consequences that you didn't like—where you let your inner desires run wild and there was an interpretation that something wasn't safe to do.

Yet this type of raw, primal energy and power is in right relationship with your Divine Union. It's connected to the essence of your soul. There's a natural rhythm to it. It's not that the champagne bottle explodes into a thousand pieces and the shards of glass go everywhere. There's a certain trajectory to that type of momentum that lifts off the cork and then accesses this bubbly liquid within.

You're not depressed. You're not tired. You're not in a state of lethargy or procrastination. You're opening up to enhancing who it is that you are. As you do, in the past there might have been that tendency to pull back from that in terms of these sensations of lethargy, depression, or fatigue. You know when you're fully enjoying something; you're able to tap into an infinite source of energy, of focus, of enthusiasm.

Again, we're not saying every day is a marathon. We're talking about the infinite energy that you are, and the potency that you are, and the expanded capacity that you really have as you're turned on, as your inner fire is lit, and as you're honoring your inner authentic expression.

This Emerald Tablet is about reorienting your efficient use of energy so that you can again, if you choose, switch from using your power and your energy and this life force that thrums through you as a Divine being, as a creator being, to try to stop you, to try to slow your life down, to tone things down. You can stop trying to use it against you. We don't mean that you may even be conscious of it or that you're doing it to hurt yourself, yet that's an inefficient use of energy. Trying to keep your life the same is an inefficient use of energy. Allowing yourself to grow, to thrive, to access this life-force energy is an efficient use of energy.

VIBRATION RAISING EXERCISE
Connect with the Potency and Life Force Within

At this part of the segment we would invite you to close your eyes for a few minutes and, as your eyes are closed, connect within you to your inner power, your inner life-force energy, your Divine impulse of creation energy, and to allow it to build. Bask in it. Then continue to read the rest of this segment once you've spent a few minutes basking in, connecting to, and tapping into this resource of infinite energy within you.

Know that as you do, we're with you and we're available to support your system to turn on your access point to it even more if you choose, so it's in alignment with your free will and your conscious choice. At this time please close your eyes and take a few minutes to bask in the potency, the power, the life force, the momentum of energy that resides within you. . . .

PASSION AND A CALLING

What is it that you sensed as you were tapping into this infinite power, as your inner pilot light was getting relit, refueled? This subject corresponds with words that you have such as *passion, energy,* and other ones that we've shared: *impulse, inner drive, calling, beckoning, summoning.*

There's this momentum that is creating an amplification of energy in your system and your Divine light mission. There's a willingness to be supported by the Divine and by this infinite Source light that's also required, but it's always your choice.

We know as well that there is some collective consciousness, some old paradigm consciousness that says one of the things that you were going to shut down was your connection to the Divine. Maybe it was because you didn't believe in the Divine or that you were taught that the Divine or God was angry, was something to be feared, was something that judged you.

Or if you really allowed yourself to be in communion with Source and have clarity about what is optimal for you, this would then take your life to the next level of visibility, and you didn't want that. There is a flow in your system and to consciously open up the floodgates of this flow so that it's supporting and nourishing you and your life is the subject of this Emerald Tablet.

Again, it may be bringing up some of those sensations that it's not safe to be nourished or supported or that there are strings attached to receiving, absorbing, and taking impeccable care of yourself. It may be bringing up your trust or lack of trust sensations. It may be bringing up your skepticism that to really allow yourself and your life to be animated by your life-force energy, your spirit, your soul, it's somehow dangerous or can't be trusted. That is part of the illusion. It's part of the old paradigm.

It's always your choice. It's always your choice. What are you choosing now? What are you choosing now? What are you choosing now? What are you choosing now? What are you choosing now? What are you choosing now? What are you choosing now? What are you choosing now? What are you choosing now?

Have a sensation of being buoyed, of being even more in the flow, and a willingness to pulse out the energy. The previous segments have been about your inner connection to yourself, to your Source light. They've been about recalibration, getting plugged back in. And then there's the turning on of that plug. There's the animation of it.

You could be a brilliant light that's plugged into the wall. Everything is there: the circuits are there, the energy is there, the lightbulb is there. Without switching the switch, the light isn't turned on—it's not animated to fulfill its Divine design.

The same with a bike. A bike has everything within it to, depending on the bike, be ridden in the Tour de France, for example. Or in an Iron Man. The pedals are there, the wheels are there, the brakes are there, and the frame is there. This elite sports bike has a Divine design. What it needs to achieve that level of excelling is the athlete who partners with it, who provides the energy. It needs the athlete to provide the stability, to point the handlebars in a certain direction, and it takes energy to work the pedals, the gears, to put it in gear, and to use the brakes. It has to be animated. It can just as easily sit in the garage and do nothing.

It's not that the Divine design isn't there. The partnering, the animation, has to be there. That's what we're speaking of here. That you are like this elite bike and this athlete is your relationship with Source consciousness. You're partnering with this life-force energy, this Divine light, and this Divine consciousness. These have to be brought together and then turned on.

Allow your Divine design to be animated from within this Emerald Tablet. Allow it to be turned on. Allow it to be plugged in. Allow it to be supported. Allow it to be energized. From that flow then you can be launched, then you can pulse out, then you can transmit. Then, like the airplane, you can leave the Earth and go into the sky and transcend gravity.

We don't mean that you literally leave your body and go into the sky. We mean that you're already in one realm of life, of your Divine design. The plane is designed to also drive on the ground. It has wheels and yet it also has wings. As well, it's designed aerodynamically to travel at high speeds in the air. When it's traveling in the air at those high speeds it's accessing a part of its Divine design that it doesn't access while it's on the ground.

We know you're familiar with aspects of your Divine design and you've been living them. There are other aspects that you have within you that are now getting animated so that you can move into them, actualize them, so that which is the infinite potential within you gets pulsed out, it gets realized. This example of the plane being on the ground and being in the sky and then coming back to the ground as it lands is an example of transformation.

THE ILLUMINATION OF YOUR
DIVINE DESIGN

Just as the tadpole is in the pond, it grows legs, and then it becomes a frog, it can be on the ground and it can be in the water. It has dominion in both places. You're the same, because you're the ensouled Being of Light that you are. You're able to have adeptness and mastery in energy and in matter because it's all the same. There's also the sensation of the animation, the illumination of your Divine design.

Let's say an aspect of expressing your Divine design is dancing and you have a choreographed routine. You can go through that choreographed routine really shut down, without any light behind your eyes. You're just going through the motions. Or you can go through the routine animated, shining, exuberant, invested from the tips of your toes to the tips of your fingers. You can sleepwalk your way through it or you can be engaged with it and shine.

This is also what we're speaking about. It's re-engaging with life, being invested with your life. Not trying to get out of it or tone it down.

You are the dancer that dances every muscle, from the tip of the finger to the tip of the toe. It's all utilized. No one else can inhabit your life. Nobody else can breathe for your body. Nobody else can express your Divine mission or animate your Divine mission.

Allow yourself to be connected and have a flow of the animation of your soul, the animation of your Divine light, the support of the universe, the power that it takes to create worlds. The energy, the consciousness that resides within you is a part of your dominion, it's a part of your ascended mastery. Allow yourself permission to wield that power, to tap into it. Again, know that we're not saying that there's any forcing of it or any pretense about it or that you're puffing yourself up to be powerful. It's infusing, imbuing, empowered. It's a natural flow. There's a sensation that it's the next natural step in your evolution.

We've spoken about the momentum of the train and that it's easier to keep going at three hundred miles an hour once the train is in motion than to stop. Or if you're running it takes more energy to stop running than it does to keep going. When you're on a log flume ride at an amusement park there's a flow of the water that's pushing the log flume forward. That momentum shoots the log flume into a different destination. It would take much more energy to try to hold onto the sides of that log flume and stop it, the boat, from moving forward.

Having a life without resistance or striving is what you always have as your choice to do. Sometimes, dear one, that's what you have chosen and continue to choose. Rather than utilize this access point to Source and this flow to animate your Divine design, you've utilized it to resist it—all for well-meaning reasons.

What would your life feel like if there wasn't the resistance or the striving, yet you lived this buoyed-ness, the resourced-ness? What would it feel like to be really caught up with yourself, to be current with yourself? That's a functionality of this as well. In your evolution as a soul in this incarnation you have evolved, and the reanimation of your Divine Union and your Divine design allows you to be current with who you've become.

BEING CURRENT WITH WHO YOU ARE

Let's say you've been practicing martial arts for years and you haven't told anyone that you've gotten your black belt. Maybe you're still wearing the white or yellow belt or belts from the beginning stages. You're still presenting yourself as if you're a beginner.

Then a black belt walks into the ring with you and you start to spar. You start to do this martial art, and during that time you stop having the reflexes of the beginner or you stop having the moves of the beginner. It's natural for you to show up when you're met by an equal.

Then you start being current. You start revealing that level of being that is able to use the energy of your fellow martial arts person, your opponent, to take them to the ground. There's a sense of being current with who you are, allowing that to surprise even you . . . to surprise even you.

As an exercise to continue to amplify what you've tapped into in this Emerald Tablet, repeat this exercise of closing of your eyes and spending some minutes locating that inner fire, locating that which animates you, that potency within. Be in communion with it, allow it to fill you up, allow it to inform you, allow it to create an impulse that then overflows into an outward expression. If you'd like, continue to bask in this Emerald Tablet.

14
Quantum Consciousness
A Pivot in Consciousness

WHEN YOU CHANGE THE WAY
YOU SEE THE WORLD

Deepen your awareness around your oracular vision, deepen your awareness of what you're carrying within you, your contribution to this evolution in consciousness, deepen your awareness of the context of the consciousness in which this incarnation is unfolding. As you deepen your awareness and your connection to that which you are and that which resides within you and that which is the context of this incarnation, you are recalibrating to your Divine origin and your embodied Divine light. This process is one in which you have the possibility of pivoting the way you see yourself and the world in such a way that it then changes everything.

Our purpose together—within this book, within these sacred, scribed tablets—is such that it is your evolution in consciousness that then shifts your perception of the world that you reside within. When you change the way you see the world or your consciousness evolves into an inclusive, Divine perspective, that is the mechanism of a paradigm shift and that is the unfolding into greater multidimensionality.

These pages are filled with energetic light codes to support your system in awakening to a broader awareness and expanded state of being an embodied Being of Light. It is through the evolution of your consciousness that the accessibility you have to these divinity light codes is enhanced. Our purpose together is not one in which we're utilizing an approach that's based in separation consciousness. We're using an approach that entails you and me, Thoth—together. We, us, are using an approach that touches all aspects of your being. Applying energy and consciousness—the decoded light sequence of divinity codes to your energy and consciousness and sequence of Divine light codes—is an approach that's evolutionary.

We're not here together for incremental change, evolution, or transformation. We're here together for *quantum* evolution. Our purpose is not to increase your sense of success 10 percent. Our purpose together is one in which the entire experience of your incarnation is uplifted and expanded from a finite perspective to an infinite perspective. These tablets in *The Tablets of Light* that you are within are an environment of consciousness, of light. That environment, combined with your vibrational autonomy and your signature Source field, is one in which quantum evolution is possible.

Really allow that statement to land within your system. This environment combined with your Source light is an opening to quantum evolution. Deepen your awareness of this environment, of your Divine light codes, and of this quantum evolution. As you're deepening your awareness of your consciousness being pivotal and an exponential tool of shifting paradigms, you may begin to have some ah-ha moments, which then really changes the way you perceive your life in this incarnation.

THE CONDITIONING OF SURVIVAL CONSCIOUSNESS

Survival consciousness provided an environment of conditioning that focused on survival, and then the maintaining and securing of that survival incrementally. This way of living would be to focus on identifying potential danger or threats to survival and eliminating or diminishing them. However, due to the nature of survival consciousness, once survival was no longer an issue, once there was no longer a sense of imminent danger, the system continued to broadcast the sensation that the danger was still there or that it could come back at any second. So in the old paradigm there was a sense of always being in survival mode or being separate from security. As such, the conditioning was to survive and then incrementally secure a small surplus on top of whatever was needed to survive.

For example, if you initially created a place to live, and had food to eat, and you were in some comfort zone of temperature, of having clothing, of having relationships or a lack of threats from the external world, then life was about maintaining that level of survival and then expanding it incrementally—having it be 10 percent better. You have 10 percent more money or a home that is a nicer home by 10 percent, or a 10 percent increase in food or resources. That worked. That had its purpose.

That was also pivotal to the larger evolution in consciousness. It allowed you to create a sense of identity, a sense of individuality. However, this mechanism of looking for something that might be wrong or looking for something that could be dangerous—combined with the desire to secure and maintain whatever level of survival that you had in a linear fashion or an incremental fashion—those ways of being, that environment, won't lead to this quantum evolution that we're speaking of.

Old modes of operation and the collective consciousness, tribal consciousness, or separation consciousness informed your consciousness. It is now time to allow those outdated ways of being to fall away, to be included back into the wholeness, back into the oneness, so that your consciousness is vibrating with your Source consciousness and your Divine alchemy of unity.

An aspect of this evolution in consciousness is that you may experience adaptation sensations wherein the slower vibrations come to the surface as you come into a higher, integrated multidimensional wholeness. As you pivot from being sourced by fear, lack, hypervigilance, survival mode, as you pivot from being sourced from separation consciousness to Source consciousness, to wholeness, to knowing that all is well, to the higher vibrations of love, joy, peace, and light, the survival patterns and the survival mechanisms and the survival consciousness try to survive. They fight to survive and they get louder as they try to get your attention.

FOCUSING ON WHAT IS UNIQUELY YOU AND YOURS

You have a capacity to focus, to zero in on something. If you're in a crowd of ten thousand people and you're trying to find that one person who's wearing a yellow shirt and carrying an illuminated sparkler, you have the capacity to focus in on finding that person that you know, that person you're looking for. For in this crowd of ten thousand people, this one particular individual has a yellow shirt and a sparkler, which has a certain signature essence that you know and recognize.

This allows you to filter through to focus on what it is you're looking for to such a degree that that's what you find, that's what you see. Your system stops being in vibrational proximity to the 9,999 people that are also present. There's a vibrational recognition capacity that you have that allows you to be so zeroed in on what it is that's uniquely you and yours, so focused on what it is that's so uniquely you and yours, that you are in a state of grace.

It's not compartmentalization, denial, or blocking out everything else. It's zeroing in. It's a vibrational match. It's something that your system is actually engaged in all the time. It's a part of this resurrected consciousness of the evolved universal Source light. You call this synchronicity or the law of attraction or luck, yet this is a part your divinity. This is a part of the universal flow.

When we say, "opening up to that which is uniquely you and yours," that really is the focus of coming into a state of peace, coming into a state of right relationship with your full-on pineapple-ness. It's no longer resisting or forcing a life that's not uniquely you or yours to be and to do and to have. As you're fully vibrating with your signature energy, with your signature essence, and with your Divine light codes fully activated, there's that focus as well. Each moment in each day you're able to find that person with the yellow shirt that's holding the sparkler because that's your connection to be and to do and to have. The rest is still a part of the wholeness yet it's not in the dimensional reality that you're in.

You experience this already. It's part of the purpose that linear time and space held for you in the old paradigm. You had the experience of, if you were in Tuscany, for example, you had the experience of being in Tuscany. You know you're not in New York. Tuscany becomes that yellow shirt with the sparkler.

That experience of space, of location, allows you to have a placeholder for this evolved concept, this evolved experience of vibrational proximity, of focusing your consciousness so that it seems like everything else is in right relationship to everything else. The noise and the clutter fall away and you're zeroed in, you're plugged in. There's no longer a frenetic or chaotic sensation or interference. You know that when you're in Tuscany you're in Tuscany and that means that you're not in New York, you're not in these other places.

THE NEW PARADIGM OF TIME AND SPACE

When we say that time and space gave you somewhat of an experience of what it is we're speaking of, this quantum living that's highly focused, it's also one of the reasons why, in the new paradigm, time and space no longer exist in the way that they did in the old paradigm. It's not you physically being in Tuscany that then creates the vibrational location that you're in, which means that you're not in New York or you're not in any other place in the world. It's because in that moment what's yours to be and do and have is Tuscany. You very much know as well that while you're in Tuscany you can still be in other places at the same time, whether that's through the Internet, via a phone call, or in thinking about your home.

This artificial construct of time and space has already shifted not only among those who are choosing to awaken and evolve their consciousness, but also in a mainstream way. You're still connected to what's yours to be and do and have. You're in a state of unity, a state of union, and a state of oneness—yet in a very individualized way, in a very unique way to you. Feel this laser consolidation focus in which you also begin to recognize what is yours to be and do and have. There's a way you experience your life that's much more intuitive, it's much more in the flow. There's an ease to it.

We're pausing here to allow you to bask in the environment of what it is that we're speaking of, beyond the words, to really feel this, and to, if you choose, vibrate within the quantum multidimensionality that you are.

As you apply this opening of consciousness, this quantum field, this quantum awareness, you can see how it's not about incremental survival. It's about the application of consciousness to your divinity and your divinity to your consciousness that opens up entirely new worlds.

Let's say that you, in the old paradigm, wanted to go from Florida to California and you had to do it in an incremental and a linear way. You had to put one foot in front of the other, in front of the other, in front of the other, in front of the other. It would take you a long time to walk from Florida to California. You'd have to traverse all that was in between Florida and California. Everything that existed between Florida and California was something that you'd have to go through, you'd have to sort through, you'd have to experience. It would take a lot of time, a lot of energy, and there'd be a lot of experiences that didn't have anything to do with California.

The kind of shift we're talking about, the exponential evolution that radically changes that journey, is like taking a plane from Florida to California. You could bypass in some ways what wasn't relevant to you being in California. You could be there in five hours rather than the years that it would take you to walk from Florida to California and all the maintenance of yourself along the way would also be a part of that. You'd have to have so many more meals, changes of clothes, and nights of sleep.

A PIVOT IN CONSCIOUSNESS

This is the kind of pivoting in consciousness that we're speaking of: a paradigm shift that you can allow everything that's not uniquely you or yours to really fall away from your experience and laser in on what is uniquely you and yours. If it's uniquely you and yours to be in California, be in California. Take a plane. Then live in California. Experience what being in California is like. Be in the multidimensionality of it. Have those meals and experiences that you would have had in getting to California in California.

This incarnation, if you choose it to be, is one that is pivotal to all incarnations. What experiences are you having in your life that really feel, look, and vibrate like you? Allow yourself to zero in on those. You don't have to try to get away from or get rid of all of the states in between Florida and California. Just let them be. Let them be where they are. You're on the plane. You're flying over them. Then you're in California.

You may have already noticed things naturally falling away. Maybe relationships or old habits you used to have seemingly just fell away. You didn't try to stop being friends with somebody or you didn't try to stop having a certain thing that you did every day. Your attention went somewhere else. Or it may have seemed like your life created these shifts in a dramatic way through a breakup, job loss, health issue, a move—or something like that. What you were doing and being then is no longer what you are doing and being now.

This is another way of looking at your lifeline, your lifetime. You've had a lot of past lives in this lifetime. You're no longer a toddler. You're no longer having your first kiss. You're no longer . . . whatever you were.

Your system has that mechanism within it as well to accept the evolution. You don't try to go back to being a toddler. You may emotionally feel like you're five years old at times yet it's not a destination that you try to go back to. Allow separation consciousness to be like that. To be like a past life or a stage of your evolution that had purpose, yet it's one thing you pass through.

Sometimes there are those adaptation sensations or those awkward moments when you feel so new, perhaps when you were becoming a teenager or a young adult. You have an incredible capacity to focus your consciousness, and we mean this lovingly. You've barely scratched the surface on fully utilizing and embodying this capacity. It hasn't been time. Now that it is time, have an awareness that the active utilization of your capacity to focus your consciousness, to simply be connecting and in communion with that which is uniquely you and yours, is a game changer. It's a paradigm shifter. It's a quantum jump.

SHIFTING WHAT YOU FOCUS ON

Again, it's not that you're becoming something that you hadn't already been. You've had these experiences in tangible ways. When you're buying a car, all of a sudden you see the few cars that you're looking at on the road all the time. They were there. You passed by those same cars the day before you started looking, and you didn't even see them.

Or perhaps you're looking to buy a house and all of sudden you see a lot of For Sale signs. It's just that you've been using that capacity to focus on what's not working or what could be a potential danger or all the proof why you're *not* a Divine Light Being. Or perhaps you are scattered, unfocused, you're in resistance, you're kicking your feet, feeling like life is something to get through. Allow it to be simple to be you. Allow it to be simple to be you.

Allow your capacity to be a vibrational recognizer as well. You vibrationally recognize. You're able to pick out that one person who has the yellow shirt and the sparkler because there's a signature energy that you recognize. This can inform you as to the choices that you're making in your life. You are vibrationally recognizing what's yours to be and do and have. That informs you, that's being in the flow, being open to being surprised during your day—in a good way. You're not using your capacity to focus vibrationally, to keep maintaining the old construct of who you were and how your life was from the day before.

Each moment is new, each moment is magic. Have a sense of the peace of clicking into your vibrational proximity and your multi-dimensionality and then focusing in through your consciousness of what's uniquely you and yours. It's magic, it's synchronicity, it's delight. As you're remembering this capacity you have the sensation of having some real yeses, some real recognition, a clear sense of focus. "Yes, that's it! That's the place, that's the person, that's the thing, that's the next step." There's a real sense of recognition, of the yes, yes, yes, yes!

There may also be a real sense of recognition of no, no, no, and yet the no is not something that you have to be forceful about or be focusing on the defense of. Your system was already on the defense. The no happens, yet it happens in that universal flow. It happens from the dimensional space that you're in because you're in the dimensional space of being you full-out, of being you, your signature energy, your Source being plugged in. Then that's what you create from and that's what you create. You don't have to say no to what isn't uniquely you and yours, because it exists in a different dimension. It's still a part of the oneness, it's still a part of the wholeness. It doesn't cease to exist. It's simply that you're not focused on it and thus you're not vibrating with it.

As this is becoming second nature again there may be some things that are in your life that are yes and no at the same time, or they're close. The feeling could be, "Yeah, that's close. It looks good, it looks like it fits all the criteria," or "It looks like that would be me, and yet there's just something missing." Then you can also determine the sensations of, "Oh, yeah, that's what I'm resonating with. That's what I'm resonating with." Then you can keep moving. "Well, it's not quite that . . . that's what I'm resonating with." You are homing in on what it is that you are resonating with. Keep going. Keep going.

Let's say you're shopping for a new outfit and you're in the store and you see a shirt or pants or a dress or a sweater or a pair of shoes or whatever it is. You light up. "Yes! Yes!" Then you get closer and you realize it's not your size. It's two sizes too big or two sizes too small. There's a yes. Yes, you love that item of clothing, yet it's not a fit unless they have it in your size.

You could say, "Do you have this in my size?"

"No."

"Could you order it?"

"No."

Keep moving. Keep moving.

That's an example of what we mean when we say that there can be qualities of certain things that are a yes, yet it's not a complete fit. In the past you would try to force yourself into settling for that what wasn't a totally complete fit. You might say, "There's so much potential in this relationship." Or whatever it is. We're not saying that you have to radically change your life. There may be some aspects of your life partner, or where you live, that you love—and others that you don't, yet it's still a vibrational match, it's still a fit, it's still uniquely you and yours.

The quality or the qualifier is not that you love everything about it. We're also not talking about your preference toward it or your overlay of whether it's good or bad. We're saying that it's uniquely you or yours to be and to do and to have. It's a fit. It's a match.

It may be one that stretches you. It may be one that represents an accelerated path to bring all of what is under the surface back into the ring of inclusion. It may be that you don't know it's a match until later.

You have a capacity to focus through your consciousness in a way that creates a quantum jump in your evolution.

It's as if you're in that stadium of ten thousand people and you're looking for the person with the yellow shirt and the sparkler. Everyone's yelling and talking and there's so much chatter and you see a hundred yellow shirts and you see two hundred people carrying sparklers. When you're fully operating from your consciousness and from your signature energy, it's as if the 9,999 other people sit down and they stop talking. In this example at the stadium, it's like the camera zeroed in on your person with the yellow shirt and the sparkler and when you look out into the stadium they're the only one standing. You see their seat number from the camera.

It's that kind of laser focus that we're talking about. This has already been happening without you always being consciously aware of it. You are aware of it through your synchronicities. You notice some things and then everything gets really still and what is uniquely you and yours emerges in a clear, unmistakable way. There it is. There it is. There it is. That same sensation is what has brought you to these pages.

RECALIBRATING THE TRUE CAPACITY OF YOUR INFINITE INTELLIGENCE

Science has been documenting that only a small percentage of the brain is utilized or that only a small percentage of the DNA is utilized. This can also be expanded to include your Divine consciousness. That's what we mean when we say, in a loving way, that you haven't really scratched the surface of applying consciousness to your incarnation. There were habits that pertained to how you used your conscious awareness or your witnessing ability to actually keep the brakes on.

Let's say there was a population of people and they were living in the woods in isolation. They didn't have TV, phones, or a way to communicate. A car was dropped into this environment but they had no idea what a car was because they'd never seen one. Let's say you came back to that population five or ten years later and what they were using the car for was to fry an egg. Say it's sunny there and they were using the hot hood of the car to fry an egg on. Or let's say they were using it to put their laundry on to dry, or to put something on that they didn't want to have on the ground. They're using the car. They found ways to use the car that had nothing to do with what the car was originally designed for. Maybe that car was placed right in the middle of a path to their water supply and they have to walk around the car. The car actually slows them down. It doesn't help them.

Then let's use another example: An isolated population is given a car and they're taught how to use it; they have the instruction manual and they have gas. Then they can use the car to get to their water source and use it to bring the water back and forth. Now it enhances their life for, in this example, it accelerates their access to the water. In some ways another layer of the purpose of *The Tablets of Light* is to recalibrate the true capacity of your infinite intelligence through your consciousness . . . through your consciousness.

CONSCIOUS CHOICE EXERCISE
· · · · · · · · · ·
Choose to Be a Vibrational Recognizer

Are you choosing to awaken your quantum consciousness? If so, yes. Say, "Yes, I choose to be the awakened consciousness that I am, the quantum consciousness that I am." We know that this may create a sensation of trepidation, hesitation, anxiety, or fear. Ah, quantum consciousness! Really what happens when you're in this quantum consciousness is that things slow down, there's a stillness, a peace, a reabsorption of that chaotic, frenetic energy. Everything that's not uniquely you and yours in the stadium sits down and gets quiet and then the light shines on the person you're there to meet.

Before you go to bed tonight we would invite you to ask that you remember this mechanism of applying consciousness to your life. We would invite you to ask that this remembering happens with ease and grace for all levels of your system as you're sleeping. As you turn on this consciousness we would invite you to recognize, from a vibrational standpoint, that which is uniquely you and yours, and also that you're humming, vibrating, and living as the Source light that you are.

15
Multidimensional Wholeness

Being Buoyed by Divine Light

THE EXPERIENCE OF HAVING MORE

Awakening to your incarnated divinity is an evolution in which you move from living dimensionally to living multidimensionally. As you're experiencing this enhanced dimensionality you awaken into what had been there all along yet placed on a shelf that seemed out of reach, just a bit too high to touch or access. Or it was in a hidden chamber or compartment that you didn't have access to.

Your experience of living multidimensionally as the Divine incarnate being that you are is unique to you. It's bespoken for you, for it's your partnering with Source, which is your flavor of Divine incarnation, the signature energy of your divinity. The way you experience the embodying of more of the dimensions of your Source consciousness is going to be uniquely you and yours.

There is often an association with more, meaning that you have to accommodate the more in a way that stretches your life-force energy. *More* could mean "overwhelm." *More* could be interpreted as "chaos." If you are already surviving, we're talking about the old-paradigm perspective of how the system may have interpreted *more*. If you're already surviving and using what seems like all the energy you have, all the time you have—having more success or friends or whatever—could have been interpreted as triggering the sensation that there's not enough. You're already at the limit of your bandwidth and more is just not perceivable, it's not happening, it's not welcomed.

We're speaking of a different vantage point in terms of how your system, when it was in separation, lack, and scarcity, could interpret the experience of more dimensions of your life and then put the brakes on. As we described earlier when discussing quantum consciousness, there's actually quite a simplification vibrationally that happens from being in more dimensions, from living multidimensionally, from being re-Sourced.

There are more dimensions that you're living from and yet with the additional dimensions that you're living from there's an enhanced re-Sourced awareness. There's what you would perceive as infinite surplus overflowing. Life, actually, if you will allow it, if you choose it, can be more ease-filled, fulfilled, filled with fullness. The fulfillment is a fullness of wholeness. There's also the falling away of superfluous energies and experiences. The ones that aren't uniquely you and yours fall away. Living multidimensionally can be experienced as more because you're embodying more of your divinity codes, consciousness, and inner knowing.

EVERYTHING IS WHOLENESS

Wholeness begets wholeness. Multidimensionality begets multidimensionality. Then everything is experienced as whole—not as a fraction or not as something that's in separation. It's experienced from its wholeness. It's re-Sourced, that's always true. There's no duality or separation really at all. The things in your life also have wholeness, they have multidimensionality already. As you experience them from being less dimensional or in the fraction of separation consciousness, with the experience of them came a sensation of lack. It was always a trading around. You trade your time and energy for money. You trade your money for time. There's this moving around of fractions with other fractions, which are always separate from any totality or any wholeness.

This scribed text is also a modeling of something being created in connection with the full dimensionality. The words are Source light. The culmination, the combination of the words, are unified Source light. The words don't have to go from the infinite possibility of each and every word into separating from all words into certain words and becoming finite. Each time something is created multidimensionally and with Source consciousness it reverberates out into the universe. It plucks the guitar string of possibility, of Divine remembering of that creation, that choice. Focusing in on what's uniquely you and yours does not mean separating from you or separating from Source, or that these things are created as a fraction of consciousness.

When we say that this Divine incarnation is unique to you, it's bespoken for you, tailored to your signature essence. There's also a vibrational key in your awareness that gets unlocked so that you can lean into your life experiences, you can lean into your synchronicities, you can trust your expansion. You can reinform your system that living in more dimensional space or more dimensional vibration of you, that more-ness, actually has a component of quietness, simplicity, peace, connectedness, and of coming home. Then you're re-Sourced, you have all that you are available to you, and accessible within you. It allows you to be present with each moment, recognizing that it's whole and unto itself.

As each moment is whole and unto itself then you can be fully engaged with that moment without it triggering a sense of lack or a sense of scarcity or a sense of separation. When you live a moment as if it's fractured or a part of the whole then what you experience is not all there. Something's missing. It creates a sensation that something is missing. In order for you to plug into it you become a fraction of yourself.

AWAKENING INNER AWARENESS

What *The Tablets of Light* and this conversation is cultivating, is awakening, is that inner awareness that you already have. You can be all that

there is with all that there is in each and every moment. You can experience the individualized oneness of something in such a way that to
experience the expression of that moment in a certain way that's tangible to you, doesn't mean that it's not connected to the oneness anymore. You can create something without it feeling like the incarnation
of some creation means that then it becomes finite.

Multidimensional creation, multidimensional living, is occupying
the full unification with Source consciousness and, as such, you're accessing the full unification of Source consciousness in each and every experience. That's why in some ways your experience of life is directly related
to your consciousness. As your consciousness is vibrating from wholeness, from Source, from your full signature energy, from your multidimensionality, then you're able to also experience the multidimensionality
and the wholeness of that which is in your life already right now.

This longing that you have to know yourself and to know the Divine
is a memory of what living in total connection is like. It takes us back
to the evolution hologram in which any one part of a hologram has
the entire hologram within it. You can be in a moment, conversation,
or creation, tapped into the Divine blueprint of all there is within that
moment, within the whole hologram. In contrast, in separation consciousness, in order to experience the moment or the creation there was a
fragmenting from the wholeness that occurred. There was a fragmenting
of the self that occurred. It wasn't conceivable to be infinite and multidimensional in the experience of having a tangible incarnated life.

You may have the sense that at different times you've been shying away
from that wholeness, that infinite vibration within you, out of the sense
that you'll cease to exist. Or that you'll evaporate, disappear, disintegrate—
that you have to leave the planet, when really what we're talking about
here is nothing short of the full assimilation of all of you. All of you is
included. All of you is a part of the totality of all that there is.

Can you see how this awareness of living each moment multidimensionally and as wholeness creates an evolved experience of multidimensionality and wholeness? You're able to experience life one wholeness

after another wholeness, after another wholeness, after another wholeness, after another wholeness. Within each and every moment there
exists wholeness, which begets more wholeness. Then you have this
experience of life as wholeness, this experience of the multidimensionality of life. There's a re-Sourced experience of life. There's an infinite
energy of life. There's the conscious awareness within the codes of life.

You can trust your evolution, awakening, remembering of multidimensionality, for inherent within it is wholeness. If you look at a separation consciousness pattern such as holding back, that may be a pattern
that you're familiar with or that you've seen. There's an approach to life
that's holding back, that's not being fully engaged, and the very nature
of that separation consciousness of holding back is such that it requires
energy. As we've discussed earlier in this scribed text, it requires energy
to hold back. It's based on the false premise of not enough. You have
to hold back in order to have enough—to have enough energy to get
through the day, to have enough vitality to get through a lifetime, to
have enough creative energy to bring to each of the projects in your life,
to have enough love to give everyone in your life. There's a sense of the
holding back that comes from a space of not enough-ness or a space of
experiencing each moment as an absence of wholeness.

As you're living your Divine design and you're living your Divine
incarnation from this multidimensionality, that is your awakened state.
It energizes you and it replenishes you. There's a neutrality and a seamlessness to what you're doing, what you're spending your time and your
energy on. It's not that you spend your time and your energy and then
you're out of time and energy because as you come from Divine wholeness there's an absence of resistance. You can be engaged, fully connected, and intense at times as well. Each moment will have its own
unique presence and blend of the totality of all that there is within it.

This conversation is specifically addressing the old paradigm sensation that *more* is analogous to death, overwhelm, lack, scarcity, and
being depleted. Even the way we're speaking about more is incremental.
In actuality you're not reclaiming more for yourself, you're reclaiming

unity for yourself. You don't want more incrementally. You want the totality of you to be fully resurrected and vibrating within the Divine light of all that there is.

Claim Your Fully Resurrected Divine Light Body

At this moment, if you choose, be the one that you claim as the fullness of your fully resurrected Divine light body. You're not on and then off, plugged in and then not plugged in. You're you, that which is uniquely you and yours to experience. You may have the sensation at this point of stretching your wings, of occupying your full space, of an inner shift from having been confined to a small space to then having breathing room again. You may feel as if you're getting taller, that your vibration is pulsing brighter, louder, more clearly. Be in the vibration of your fully occupied multidimensional wholeness. Feel the aliveness, the momentum, the ease, and the clarity of that.

FOCUS YOUR CONSCIOUSNESS
TO SEE THE TOTALITY

Being in your multidimensional wholeness allows you to experience the multidimensional wholeness of your life. You have the awareness that all that there is in your life exists within all that there is in your life. As you connect to people in your life, you connect to them from your multi-dimensionality, from your fully embodied multidimensional wholeness, your fully embodied Divine light as the energy and consciousness that you are. Then you're able to connect to the units of consciousness that *they* are as the totality of all that there is. You're able to use your capacity to focus consciousness to then see their wholeness. Someone's wholeness is never compromised; it's never not there. They may be living it or not, they may be tapped into it or not, they may be vibrating it or not. Yet it's there.

This way of being is one that opens up portals of consciousness

within your life in such as a way that you then experience the rich-
ness and the wholeness of all components of your life. It unleashes your
capacity to be in a state of unified Source right now because as you're
coming from this unified Source or multidimensional wholeness and
you're experiencing or connecting to your life, you experience it as unified Source and multidimensional wholeness.

You no longer look at your finances as being separate or in a state of
lack. You see that in each and every unit of consciousness of what you
would call your finances, the wholeness exists. Money is also resurrected
as a totality, a wholeness, a multidimensional wholeness—not being separate from Source, not being used as a way to separate from Source—yet
the evolution of money has also occurred. The Divine light mission of
money has also shifted and evolved. There's a sense of really feeling the
life-enhancing relationship with money, for example, or with your soul,
your spirituality, your relationship to Source, your career, your health,
your home, or any area of your life.

We're sending vibrational pictures of wholeness, sacred geometry
light language, at this time because this multidimensional wholeness, this
multidimensional living, is like a mind meld. It's like a mind scramble. It's
the unknowing of what you know and the knowing of what you know.

We're not saying that that doesn't mean that you keep the same
external experiences in your life if they're not a fit. It's that you don't
try to change them because you're only connecting to a part of them or
to the separation of them or the lack of them. You are doing this with
the idea that when you have that next thing, or the more that you have,
is when you'll have the connection to the wholeness.

THE GOOD THAT EXISTS IN EACH
AND EVERY MOMENT

As well, we're speaking about your capacity to absorb and be present
with the good that exists in each and every moment, the wholeness
that exists in each and every moment, the hologram of creation and

Source that exists in each and every moment. As you're vibrating with that, as you're creating with that, as you're in that space with that, it doesn't matter whether you prefer an experience or not or don't prefer an experience because you're naturally connecting to the *wholeness* of the experience. Then you can let things fall away that aren't uniquely you or yours—not because they're bad or preferred or unpreferred—but because they're outdated, they're not you or yours anymore.

Here we can use the analogy of relationships. You might find that you're with someone; perhaps you're married to them, or in a long-term relationship with them. As you begin to plug into, occupy, or be your multidimensional wholeness, you may begin to see the multidimensional wholeness in them as well. New facets of your relationship may come forward. It may also be that they sit down in the stadium of ten thousand people. They're not the person. The relationship is meant to fall away. Or the relationship continues and yet there's now more to it that you are connected to. You may be in a relationship that's already going really well. It's great and yet there may be some areas in which you haven't been able to really feel it, to feel how good it is, to feel what about it *is* working.

That's why we like the example of money. You can see that the old paradigm contains the premise that you're trying to keep your survival and then incrementally create more security around it so that it keeps improving. You can see that sometimes your experience with money is that it's a fraction of an experience or that you experience not enough, whether you have enough or not.

Let's say, for example, that you have a certain amount of money in your life and whatever that money is it quadruples or it exponentiates by a million. So, if you have one hundred it's like you have one hundred million. You have a hundred million. It really, really, really, really, really, really, really expands. Whether you have a hundred or a hundred million, the way you connect to that amount may not change at all. If you're in the space of separation consciousness it may not feel any different to you whether you have a hundred dollars, a thousand dollars, or a million or a billion or a trillion dollars.

You can have the same sense of not enough-ness with any increment of money if you're connecting to and from the concept of not having enough; if you're connecting to and from scarcity. You can have the exact same amount of money that you have right now and feel more of it; you can feel more connected to it, feel more of the abundance that's already there, and feel the wholeness of it.

Multidimensional wholeness also allows you to experience the multidimensional wholeness of something that may seem like an object, such as your house, money, or a book. It may be easier for you to have the sensation that when something seems to be living, like a person or an animal, they're ensouled, that they're vibrating with Source, that they're an expression of Source. Whether something is an organic being or what seems to be an inorganic being, a physical item, an object, it still has multidimensional wholeness.

A relationship is not something that you can necessarily touch. You can't physically touch the connection you have with another person, yet there's a divinity in that, there's a multidimensional wholeness in that. By enhancing your relationship with the multidimensional wholeness of the units of finances that you have right now in this example, or the relationships that you have right now, or the activities that you're doing right now, you're tapping into more. You're tapping into the more-ness that exists without having any more; the totality and the wholeness that exists without adding any more.

THE PATTERN OF HOLDING BACK

We know that we spoke about the pattern of holding back and that some of you may be stopping yourself from having what it is that you're choosing or what it is that you want. This is derived from an illusionary fear that once you're in a state of wholeness or completion, of having everything you want, then you'll stop. You'll stop being engaged, you'll stop living, you'll stop being on Earth, you'll stop caring or that you're equating wholeness with another form of death, and this impulse of creation would cease to exist. Well, that's not the case. You'll always have the Divine design that's vibrating within, through, and around you, that's inviting you to be in the multidimensional wholeness of all that there is.

Also, what this recalibration to multidimensional wholeness illuminates is that you can be present with an individualized expression of wholeness in a way that is still very connected to wholeness. In the past that seemed impossible. How could you have something that is created and have that creation still be connected to the wholeness of all that there is?

There is another way you may stop yourself from really zeroing in or using your capacity to have quantum consciousness: If you say yes to this then you're saying no to so many other things. You didn't want to say yes to something, because the yes was perceived as a limitation. Rather than having everything wide open and all possibilities open and all the choices open you funnel in on one thing and you say, "Okay, this is the thing I'm being and doing in this moment."

Right now you're in *The Tablets of Light*. You're reading this book. You could perceive that as your having said no to all the other books that you're not reading in this *now* moment. Yet really it's that you're vibrating with the quantum consciousness that says that this is yours to be and do and have. In the example of creating and wanting to hold yourself back from really bringing forth what you're carrying, what's inside of you, in the past that oracular vision may have been perceived as meaning that you have to go into separation—you have to separate from Source and totality and all that there is in order to choose one thing.

This is the book that you're going to write or this is the person that you're going to marry or this is the place where you're going to live. Choosing was perceived as limiting or saying no and actually it's not. It's being in the yes, the multidimensional wholeness, sureness, trust, and totality—what's yours in that moment to be and do and have. If you've been experiencing a holding back from being clear, making decisions, or knowing a choice, out of that sense that if you do then you're saying no to Source or you're saying no to your wholeness, it's actually the way that you may experience your wholeness. You experience your wholeness by being connected by these expressions of Source consciousness and their wholeness.

In the old paradigm of tribal consciousness there was very much this one-size-fits-all idea, or this collective consciousness way of being. Your life should have certain ingredients in it, it should look this way, and you should be doing these things. We understand each word in this book is beckoning you to stand out and excel in your Divine genius if you choose to.

In the past you may have wondered if you could really do that or if that was somehow being irresponsible? Or don't you have to be everything to everyone and the jack-of-all-trades and spread yourself around, do things that you're less good at? It may be that you choose to continue to do things that aren't necessarily your genius. However, that doesn't matter because you're doing them and being them from the place of their wholeness.

That's where you vibrate from oneness. You vibrate from the awareness of the evolution hologram. You vibrate from the sensation that your signature energy, your unique path, using your quantum consciousness to zero in on your life, doesn't take you away from Source because you're in the multidimensional wholeness of you with the multidimensional wholeness of your life.

There are all kinds of ways that the conditioning of the collective consciousness would try to stop this from happening. You could still be using these judgments against yourself—that you're being selfish, that you could be seen as irresponsible, crazy, weird, a freak, or you will be judged—or that you're going to leave people behind. You can't leave *anybody* behind. They're where they are and you are where you are. You're in your universe and they're in their universe. You're in your multidimensional wholeness and you're with their multidimensional wholeness.

WHAT ARE YOU WAITING FOR?

What reason have you been using to not live as multidimensional Source consciousness? Have you not wanted to be perceived as you? Have you been in some pattern of camouflage, of fading into the background, going under the radar? Have you been afraid that others would perceive you as exclusive, arrogant, self-centered, or a disappointment because you weren't keeping their idea of what your life should look like?

Have you been trying to hold back from really living your Divine design out of the illusion that then you would burn out, you wouldn't have enough energy, that you'd be overwhelmed? Have you been using something in your life that you don't prefer as a reason to take yourself out of the game? Maybe it's your body that you don't like, or were judging. Or your relationships, health, finances, behaviors, family? It could be any number of things. What if those things were also in wholeness? What if you tapped into the multidimensional wholeness of the judgment of you, the judgment that you were having of yourself?

Let's say that you used your body weight as a reason to separate from yourself. Every time you thought about your body that was a reason to separate from yourself. You had a certain judgment about what your body should be like. What if your body weight did not represent separation, but it also existed in multidimensional wholeness? There's nothing wrong with it. It's not separation. It's separation only because you use it to separate from yourself. It's wholeness. It's Source. It doesn't mean that perhaps you wouldn't shift your body weight at one point if it's optimal for your system. It's that you're no longer willing to use something like that or *anything else,* for that matter, to separate from your multidimensional wholeness again.

In this moment, tap into the multidimensional wholeness in the areas, thoughtforms, patterns, beliefs, or subjects that you used in the past to separate from you or to judge you. Recognize that within them exists the hologram of evolution. Within them exists Source light. Within them exists multidimensional wholeness. All that there is exists within all that there is. Nothing is outside of Source consciousness. Everything is Source consciousness.

So what you use to separate from yourself, from Source, is actually Source consciousness. It's how you perceived it, and the premise that you built this incarnation on, which kept that mechanism in play. At this point there's clarity. You don't even try to resist, get away from, or get rid of these things. You're quantum consciousness, multidimensional wholeness, calibrated to your oracular vision, the Source light of all that there is.

· · · · · · · · · ·

Spiral Multidimensional Wholeness into Everything

Vibrate with this multidimensional wholeness. As you vibrate with this multidimensional wholeness imagine that you're spiraling this multidimensional wholeness into your relationship with your body, into your relationship with your finances, into your relationship with the people in your life, into your relationship with your career, your contribution, into your relationship with all that there is.

Let's say that this multidimensional wholeness is a color. It doesn't matter what color it is. Let's say it's a rainbow just so that there is the spectrum of color in your choice. Let's say this multidimensional wholeness is a rainbow and that you're bringing this rainbow into your awareness of each and every area of your life. As you're connecting to your finances you're this rainbow and you see the rainbow of your finances. It's like you have these rainbow glasses on and this rainbow is all that there is.

You pour the rainbow over your wallet, credit cards, bank accounts, and assets, all that you have. You spark the rainbow of multidimensional wholeness in each and every area. It's like recalibrating that which has already been in your life, which is continuing to move through and with you, yet from multidimensional wholeness. It's not only that you're imbuing the rainbow onto all areas of your life, but also it's that the rainbow is already there. You're seeing it. You're seeing it.

Spend a few minutes connecting to the multidimensional wholeness within you and within all that there is in your incarnation. Again, it may be things that you prefer or don't prefer. You may notice, as you connect to the multidimensional wholeness of these experiences, that some of them are complete. Not that they're whole and that means they're complete; they're just not yours to be and do and have any longer. Others really come to the forefront. There's an excitement you feel when you realize that multidimensional wholeness is all things. It also brings the illusion that there's a right or a wrong thing into the inclusion of all that there is. Continue to bask in the multidimensional wholeness and see it and uncover it in all areas of your life, if you choose.

16
Multidimensional Awareness

Holographic Union with Divine Knowing

BECOMING AWARE OF YOUR
NEW WAYS OF BEING

As your consciousness is evolving and has evolved multidimensionally you have access to additional ways of being that were not available before the evolution occurred. Allowing yourself space to become aware of what some of these new ways of being are is an essential part of concretizing your evolution. As you are devoted to Source consciousness, light, energy, the evolution of consciousness, realize that your connection and these areas, subjects, and topics are ones that reside in the etheric awareness.

It's different if your area of focus or adeptness or your Divine light mission is around cars. If that's your focus and your path then you see that you have this car, that car. There's a red one, a blue one, a green one. This one is from this year, that one is from that year. It's this make. It's this model. You can drive the car, you can experience the car. There's this quantifiable, seemingly factual and tangible connection with the subject matter of your passion, purpose, or mission as it relates to cars.

As your mission relates to energy, consciousness, a connection to Source and to the Divine, in the old paradigm these were perceived as the unseen realms. You can't touch your consciousness with your hand. You could touch your tongue. You could touch your ear. But how do you have your hands on your consciousness? You can see the emanation of energy and consciousness in the form of what you experience as your body or the forms of what you experience as your life. Yet in order to have a tangible experience with energy and consciousness you have to experience the evolution in your consciousness to be more multidimensional, to be in those other dimensions. In those other dimensions what had been seemingly unseen becomes visible. It becomes tangible. It becomes something that you can track, that you can see the results of, that you can measure even in your awareness.

It is always your choice to focus on the subject matter of consciousness and energy, and especially your internal relationship with consciousness and energy, for it translates into your incarnation. It happens within your life, it happens in ways that are meaningful for you. It happens in your incarnation on the Earth plane. It's not our choice or your intention either that you explore consciousness in a way that's separate from your incarnation, in a way that's separate from your body, in a way that is in a dimension that you're not connected to. Nor should it be in a way that happens later, in other words, that you live now and then you enter into heaven later. It's not that. It's the focusing and the development of adeptness with consciousness that then is experienced in your incarnation, in multidimensionally.

THE UNIQUENESS OF YOUR EVOLUTION

Because your evolution in consciousness is bespoken for you, to you, it's unique to you. We can't say that this is the way this consciousness is going to show up for you in your life, this is what you're going to experience in your incarnation. There are some umbrellas; just as a suit is bespoken or custom-made for someone, it's individualized for them, yet it's still a suit. It's still tailored. It's still made from fabric and it has the same components. It has pants and a jacket and maybe a vest. It's customized to the person and yet it's not a tortoiseshell that's being bespoken. It's an article of clothing and many different people could then choose to have their bespoken experience of that article of clothing.

We're using this example because even though your evolution in consciousness is tailor-made and customized for you and it can only be created and experienced by you, there are also some universal similarities. It's not happening in the realm of the tortoiseshell; it's happening in the realm of a suit in this example of a tailored outfit. Some of those generalities are ones that many people would experience as they evolve their consciousness, as they're living in multidimensional awareness. We're describing this as having access to states and ways of being that you hadn't previously had access to because they reside in other dimensions. We can also speak of this in ways that perhaps have more meaning, insofar as they matter to you in your everyday life.

What are some of the experiences that you're more than likely going to experience as you evolve your consciousness? That can be a way that your evolution in consciousness shows up in your life. We spoke about oracular vision. Oracular vision is also a way that this multidimensional consciousness shows up in your life. You're able to see this directory, see this direction. You're able to focus in on a possibility and then line up your *now* moments until that possibility is something that you experience in your incarnation.

We spoke about your capacity to be a focuser of consciousness and to be a recognizer of consciousness. You have the capacity more and more fluidly to recognize what's uniquely you and yours as it relates to your Divine design and how that allows the overwhelm from being connected to every possibility to create a sense of peace or create a sense of clarity, a sense of knowing. You know where it is that you are and what your next steps are and that becomes enhanced as you live multidimensionally.

Attendant to all of this is a greater sense of being centered in the signature energy, in the Divine design. Then you begin to have inner guidance, intuition, awareness, knowing. You know. You know. You begin to know that you are a star seed. You begin to know that you have a particular kind of a mission and just like a pioneer, a visionary who would get to know something on that edge of the nonknowing, you also have that experience that there's a capacity to allow yourself to see yourself with fresh eyes. You have the capacity to be open to experiencing more of who you are, so that more of who you are informs you. It informs you.

Another incarnated experience of multidimensional consciousness, of evolving your consciousness, is that you may have some sensations, in what you would consider your emotional body, that begin to resemble or look like greater states of peace, neutrality, and equanimity. You're able to stay in your center and be connected to Source regardless of what the external situations are.

MULTIDIMENSIONAL COMMUNICATION

There's also the capacity to communicate with greater awareness on the multidimensional level. This is something that you've been already doing in separation consciousness. You're aware of communications that are happening just beyond what somebody says if you're speaking about communicating with a person.

You may ask them, "Well, how are you?"

They say, "I'm great." Yet they're frowning or they're angry.

You know that the words *I'm great* don't match up with the other ways they're communicating with you.

It's not that you hadn't already been having more than one dimension in your communication. It's that now the multidimensional communication expands so that you're more conscious of what it is that you're receiving and transmitting as you connect with someone. That connection expands across time and space. You don't have to be in the same room with them to know that. You could put this under the category of heightened awareness or intuition, and also this sensation or this experience of what you might consider telepathic communication.

You can be sending communication to someone in a way that's happening in more than one dimension.

At this point you may notice some synchronicities. All of a sudden they're thinking about the same subject or they say the same sentence, reflecting thoughts that you've been thinking about. Something beyond just the words passes between you, which also creates an enhanced sense of transparency. There's really not anything that remains hidden anymore. It doesn't remain hidden to you. You know what your motivations are, you know where you leave Source, and you know where your buttons are, so to speak. Others, they're transparent; you can increasingly see where they're coming from, the source of whence they are coming.

Let's say somebody is portraying what seems to be anger. They're yelling or they're saying mean things. With a unidimensional perspective you would take these actions at face value. They're angry. As your consciousness evolves and you're communicating multidimensionally you can really see that actually, they're afraid. They're afraid they're going to lose something or they feel powerless, and the anger is the way that they're telling you that they're tired, overstretched, or they're afraid they're going to lose something. There's not this hidden-ness. Not that you're psychoanalyzing everyone, but as there is a multidimensional picture of where somebody's coming from, that sensation of taking things personally shifts to a sense of equanimity.

Your consciousness evolving doesn't mean that you don't have strong emotions. You're just able to stay in a state of greater equanimity. You're able to stay in state of being centered and connected to Source, regardless of what happens around you. In the past, in this example, when somebody would get angry, then you would separate from yourself to then enter into some kind of protection mode. If someone got angry, perhaps you would take it personally or make an assumption about why, or you might feel as if you'd done something wrong. Then it's much easier to see that it has nothing to do with you. It has absolutely nothing to do with you. It's not what you did or didn't do—and there's nothing you could have done differently. This all falls into the realm of approval seeking, over-responsibility, and people pleasing.

All of that now falls away because you realize that it's no longer possible to leave you in order to have the illusion that something in the leaving of you would create a greater connection with self and with Source.

CUTTING THROUGH THE SUPERFLUOUS

We've spoken about enhanced intuition, and multidimensional and transparent communication. There are some other considerations. There are some other ways you may have thought of that are magical ways of being, that fall in the realm of magic. As you have an adeptness with energy and consciousness it's as if the waves part and the path is clear. It's as if you're on a conveyer belt of flow. That comes from really being . . . there are so many words we could use for this.

It's being comfortable in your own skin, of having an enhanced state of authenticity. It's a state where you're really connected to your Divine design—to who it is that you are and what it is that you're here for. It cuts through. It circumvents so much inefficient use of energy. It may be that you have moments that your life experience is incredibly rich because you're connecting to the wholeness—the consciousness of wholeness in each and every experience.

There can be greater ease that you experience in your incarnation as you evolve your consciousness. That's kind of like the color of a tie or the necklace or the shoes that you would choose to put on with your customized dress or suit. That "more" depends on you. There's a possibility of greater ease, there's a possibility of greater peace, there's a possibility of feeling more fulfillment, feeling more on purpose, and being more purposeful.

As your consciousness evolves, you may have a sensation of wanting to cut through the superfluous, the unnecessary, the chaos, and just bottom-line it. There's a mindfulness, perhaps, with what it is that you

choose, which then becomes more multidimensional. You simultaneously realize that the eternal nature, the infinite nature of who is it that
you're being in this incarnation doesn't just concern the next five, ten,
or twenty years—or ten, twelve, or thirty decades of a lifetime. It also
becomes about your awareness as a multidimensional being and how the
choices that you're making now connect to what you would experience
as all time and all space. There's a multidimensional experience of your
choices.

The choices may become more automatic, more natural, more in
the flow or ease-filled, yet there is less unconsciousness. Sometimes it's
something in separation consciousness that people experience as they're
aging. They say, "Oh, okay, I probably have about twenty years left to
live, or I have about ten more years left of working." There's some kind
of time frame that then creates some heightened awareness of not wanting to just do any old thing, but to really be on point with those things
that really matter to you, that really are related to your soul's purpose,
and to your Divine light mission.

CHANGING YOUR CONSCIOUSNESS
CHANGES YOUR INCARNATION

There are other aspects of your awakened consciousness that perhaps
used to be under the umbrella of what you would consider magical. You
can utilize your consciousness as a tool for the evolution of your incarnation. As we've said before, in some ways that's the subject. It's the subject that touches everything: You change your consciousness and your
incarnation changes. It evolves. You tap into the Divine energy of all
there is and there's an incarnation of Divine energy. There's a sensation
of what you may have considered or previously called a meant-to-be-ness
of something—a destiny, a sense of fate, of inevitability in a positive
way.

If you're driving toward the ocean, then you know once you get
out of the skyscrapers you're going to arrive at the ocean. As you're

more connected to your Divine light mission, your soul's path, your raison d'être, your reason for being in this incarnation, there becomes a momentum, and an inevitability as those perfect people, places, and opportunities—what you've experienced as synchronicities—flood your life. It's like everything is like that. Your awareness of your consciousness being more awake and also being able to focus it creates what you may have believed, in the old paradigm, to be magical.

Or when you see somebody else and they're living it, you may wonder, How do they do that? How did that happen to them? For it really does seem like magic. In some instances, being adept with your consciousness can replace the unnecessary amount of action that you may previously have undertaken in order to experience what is inevitable for you to experience.

It may be that you take inspired action based on your inner knowing and that shortens the amount of time things take. That rather than there being ten million things you could do, you do that one thing, which makes all the difference. For example, you take an inspired action based on your inner knowing, which positions you in a particular place, where you meet a specific person, and a magical opportunity comes from this meeting. Your consciousness is finding that oracular vision. It's holding that oracular vision.

We know that sometimes when someone decides that they want to evolve their consciousness or they want to shift into unity consciousness there's an idea that it's going to equal nirvana, that it's going to equal paradise, that there's never going to be anything that seems to be challenging. They might believe that there will never be a problem or a pain or that there's a sense of utopia. Unity consciousness and evolving your consciousness does not equal utopia. It includes all that there is.

The way that you're being with all that there is does have increasing moments of joy and increasing moments of acceptance. There's not a resistance to what's happening even if something is unpreferred. It's approached from a place of neutrality. We know that as we speak about neutrality, as we speak about equanimity, there may be a trigger that arises based on a misidentification that neutrality equates not feeling or being a robot. That to be in unity consciousness means you have to give up one of the joys of being incarnate, which is that you can feel things intensely. That isn't what we are saying, for you can still feel things intensely in unity and in such a way that you feel what a beautiful experience it is to be incarnated as the Divine connected to wholeness.

Yet this illusion can be one of the magnets or the hooks that tries to slow down your evolution in consciousness. It's as if you then think, "Well, then, I'll just be this robot. There won't be the joy and the delight in life." It's actually not that way. You still feel and yet there is a connection to all that there is as you're feeling it. There's a re-Sourced state as you're feeling it. When you're coming from increasing units of consciousness, for example, and a re-Sourced state that, in the past, might have derailed or upset you, or might have been the reason you used to separate from Source, it's as if you're able to be with it from a larger place, a larger multidimensionality, and that larger multidimensionality creates increasing moments of grace, peace, and joy.

If you're in this awakened awareness and something happens that may be unpreferred or creates an intense emotion—like losing a loved one or having a health issue or whatever it is—it's connected with a re-Sourced state from the broader vision of who it is that you are and why it is that you're here.

FOCUSING IN ON WHAT'S UNIQUELY YOU AND YOURS

We're pointing out that this capacity to focus your consciousness and the capacity to really home in on what's uniquely you and yours is a paradigm shifter. It changes everything. It's as if you have a list of items to buy in the grocery store and you've derived them from a certain recipe. First you have the recipe, then you buy the items, then you make and serve the meal. In this case, you walk into the grocery store to buy the items in a way that's totally different from the way you would enter it if you had no idea what items you wanted to buy, what the recipe was, or what you were going to serve that night for supper.

If you're on a treasure hunt and you have no idea what the items are that you're supposed to be collecting, you could just throw everything you see in the cart. You could say, "Well, here's a tree. I'm going to put the tree in there. Here's a rock. I'm going to put the rock in. Here's the bicycle. I'm going to put the bicycle in. Oh, there are some people walking by. I'm going to put them in." There's a randomness it seems. It's as if there's no overview, guide, or reason to focus in.

But your system is *always* focusing in.

It may seem at times like it's random, that you just happen to be where you are and with the people that you're around. That's a part of the universe; that's a part of the way that the incarnation works. It's multidimensionally within Divine wholeness and within Divine order, so even that which seems to be haphazard, by accident, or chaotic, is all there with purpose and with meaning.

Just like in a movie you have some characters that you're more aware of. If you're starring in the movie, the movie of your life, and you're in a restaurant or you're in a scene where there are ten thousand people, it's not that those particular ten thousand people—the extras—are irrelevant to the story. They're a part of the story. It's just that they're more on the periphery of the story.

You can still trust that.

As you're awakened in your consciousness you have a manual, recipe, list, or capacity to know in a way that homes in. It simplifies your life experience. The Divine forgetting is replaced by the Divine remembering and the Divine remembering informs. It informs. As it informs, there is intentionality and purposefulness that floods into all areas of your life.

What we're speaking about is the deconstruction or the disentanglement of hierarchy, comparison, and filtering from a place of overwhelm, from judging what is good or bad, to recognizing that there's a greater sense of awareness as to what's yours to be and do and have. With that there's a greater acceptance of whatever is happening in each and every moment. There's an enhanced state of being re-Sourced as everything's being experienced. Then there's a full-on commitment of the fully engaged, lived moment, whatever that moment is.

It's no longer that you're living your purpose in your career or with your family or in certain compartments of your life. It's that your way of being is multidimensional consciousness and the ways of being that you have access to expand. This is a way of being that you have access to, of being so conscious, intentional, engaged with whatever it is that you are connected to. Your consciousness is informed, awake, and aware.

As you're within the realms of your multidimensional consciousness, the incarnation is connected to Source 100 percent. There's not any area of the incarnation that's disconnected from Source. The connection to Source incarnate becomes the way of being. Some of these awakened states of being that we've described, like having greater awareness or telepathic communication, are qualities that have been used to describe the Divine. There's an all-knowingness and an omnipresence. These Divine qualities, these states of being, are ones that your incarnation is fully connected to.

As we get into the customized version of the evolution in consciousness, there will be some of these Divine qualities or states of being that are your primary states of being. They are the main ways in which you are an access point of Source. In a way, you are the Divine incarnation, the incarnated Source consciousness. For you, out of all the Divine qualities that there are—joy, peace, creativity, abundance, magic, of all the different qualities—there are a few primary Divine states of being that are your bespoken ways of connecting to the Divine incarnation that you're embodying, that's connected 100 percent.

It's as if you can have a diamond and that diamond can be cut in a diamond cut to be multifaceted. Your particular facets would then be expressing the uniqueness of your multidimensionality. It's what you think of as archetypes or the awareness that you have of different pantheon gods and goddesses. There are certain areas of ascended mastery, of Divine qualities, that are particularly enhanced depending on the god or goddess. For you, to accelerate and magnify your unique go-to Divine states of being will create a quantum evolution.

THE INDIVIDUALIZED ONENESS OF YOU

This is where we really get to what we've been speaking about all along; about you being you full-out, and how important that is in the evolution in consciousness—to not just follow the herd but to really know what's important to you and what's yours to be and do and have. This focus on the individualized oneness of you gets clarified as to why—out of all the things that we could encourage you to be—are we encouraging you to be you, your unique, Divine, incarnated, beautiful self?

This is why. Because as you enhance those particular states of being that you have access to on the multidimensional level, as you're living more multidimensionally, you create quantum evolution in your life. For example, your Divine transmitter, Danielle, has a lot of access points of Source consciousness and yet creativity is one of the primary archetypes that she carries. For her to create, to be with others as they're creating, brings quantum evolution into being for her and for those around her.

Multidimensional communication is also a skill set, access point, a state of being that she is adept at, so that her creations and how those creations are connected with Source are in a state of wholeness. They are multidimensional. They transcend time and space. As you've known her or as you're just getting to know her you can see that she's been on the leading edge for a long time. She doesn't have to meet someone in order to access his or her Akashic Records; she understands that matters of time and space are not essential for communication.

For her, focusing on creativity, being a creator, creation, and multidimensional communication are keys to what unlock the quantum evolution within her. You can see how that relates to her Divine light mission. We're using her as an example for two reasons: to clarify that she already knows which areas to focus on, and also to concretize this customized way of being multidimensional. For someone else, the qualities would be different. Perhaps it would be the Divine state of being or the Divine capacity to build community or joy, or being fair.

We'd like to invite you to allow within your awareness what it is that you already know about yourself in terms of areas of consciousness and ways of being that you have and are. We'd like you to clarify and home in on what your two or three areas of consciousness are, or the adeptness that you carry, your archetypes, your ascended mastery, your Divine qualities, your states of beings. What do you carry?

You can contemplate that in a moment, but before you do, it's worth noting that, in and of itself, is a different approach. It's a different approach because the old paradigm said, "Well, you need to be the jack of all trades. For you to focus on the areas that you're really good at is irresponsible. Something bad will happen. You need to be able to do everything."

If you were meant to be like everyone else you *would* be like everyone else. You have certain Divine capacities and others have their areas of adeptness. Surrounding yourself with others who contribute to your areas of Divine genius with their own is also a part of this shift in paradigm into unity consciousness. This homing in on what your areas of ascended mastery are, and others being in theirs, fills out the other facets of the diamond. This shift is one of collaboration. Not commiserating. Collaborating. Collaborating.

UNITY CONSCIOUSNESS EXERCISE
· · · · · · · · · ·
Awareness of Your Divine Access Points

Take some time at this point to write, meditate, contemplate, or ask your soul, your team of Light Beings, what are your multidimensional consciousness access points that you now have access to? What are those states of being, those Divine qualities that you carry that are really what make you uniquely you? We don't want you to approach this from the mind, although you could figure it out that way.

You could pay attention to all that you've been interested in, all that you've focused on, what your "recipes" are, and what the items in your grocery store are that you tend to cook with. You could approach this intellectually. Allow yourself to know yourself and also the evolution of those skill sets. If you've been highly intuitive all your life, as you're tapped into the multidimensional oneness of being highly intuitive, what does that evolve into?

If this isn't coming easily to you then just let it go for now. Instead, before you go to bed, ask that when you wake up, you will know. Or ask that some synchronicities will show up in your life that will point you in the direction of knowing. Multidimensional living, multidimensional consciousness, provides access to states of being that you hadn't previously had access to. It evolves the playing field of your incarnation, of your life. That's why doing and being and what you did and were aren't the pathways for being in the state of unity consciousness.

INCREASING YOUR BANDWIDTH
FOR MULTIDIMENSIONAL CONSCIOUSNESS

There's a way of being aware of multidimensional consciousness that you could describe as occupying more space, of having a wider bandwidth. For example, if you're going to make a garden, in the beginning you may have had a hoe. You're hoeing that row, and then you're going to plant your seeds or you're going to plant your trees or whatever it is by hand, one stroke at a time, one row at a time, one dimension at a time.

Then, as you become more multidimensional, it's as if you have five hoes and that five people with hoes are helping you create the garden. It goes faster, easier. Then, as you become more multidimensional, it's as if you have a tractor that you drive and it has different sections where you can create five or six rows at a time just driving. It no longer takes the sweat and the effort it did when you used the individual hoe.

As you become more and more multidimensional, the amount of lines expand; you can do twenty lines at once! And it's as if, in some ways, time and location are transcended. You don't even have to be the one driving the tractor. As you become increasingly multidimensional, life keeps getting more and more magical like that.

When we speak about you being a multidimensional incarnated Divine being, incarnated Light Being, there is an exploration, an exploratory nature, a pioneering nature that goes a long way into then being curious. "Well, now what's possible? Now that I have access to these dimensions of being re-Sourced, what's possible? What else is possible? How has this changed? How is this evolved consciousness showing up in my life?"

We know that you understand this linearly. Let's say you've been riding horses for twenty years. As you get more adept at riding you're able to do more things. Or let's say you've been studying a martial art for years. The body coordination, memory, skill—what you can do—advances. You get to a higher state of mastery, of adeptness. You understand that linearly. It's something you've experienced; it's something that you've seen.

As you spend time with something, you're able to do it in more dimensions. You're able to have a higher skill set. You can also see that the person who is beginning to study the martial art doesn't have the same level of awareness as the person who's been doing it for twenty or thirty years. There are things that the person who is just beginning wouldn't even know that they don't know. There's an awareness of that in the old paradigm of linear mastery.

What we're speaking of is quantum and multidimensional accelerated expansion, wherein it's as if you're wielding the nunchakus and you don't even know you know how to do it and then you're able to do it. Something gets created while you're in the being of it that you didn't even know was possible. Like you had no idea that you could to a backflip and you're running across a field and you do a cartwheel and then your body just goes into this backflip afterward. It's a surprise to you. It's in the action that it happens. It's in the following of the energy of doing the cartwheel that then the recognition that you could do this backflip occurs. It happens. It's almost instinctual or what you would classify as instinctual. It's surprising. It's multidimensional.

It's the rose plant that's been growing thorns and then all of a sudden it has beautiful blossoms. That's why there is an element of the evolution in consciousness in your particular evolution in consciousness. It's when you recognize that you've already been a multidimensional being yet living it, embodying it, is realized in the being of it. It reveals itself in the moment and it requires a curiosity, it requires a pioneer spirit, a visionary spirit. The Earth that you were born onto is not the same Earth that you're sitting upon while you're reading this book. It's evolved. It's become more multidimensional.

POSSIBILITIES

We invite you to hold that question, How has all the evolution in consciousness that you've chosen showing up in your life in this incarnation? What does that make possible now that wasn't possible before? For the baby that then becomes able to walk there's a whole world that becomes possible that wasn't before while it was lying in the crib. It can cover territory. It can go into other parts of the room. There are lots of things that can now happen that weren't possible before.

When the teenager gets their driver's license and has a car, what becomes possible that wasn't possible before is they can go places that they want to go without being driven there, without asking, without having to have somebody go with them. There is something that becomes possible that wasn't possible before with each of these evolutionary stages that you're used to being aware of in a linear fashion. It makes sense to you that there's a developmental stage of a person—from a baby to a toddler to a child to a teenager to an adult. Then things become possible that weren't possible before.

You can see this with an athlete who is training their body. They're able to do things that they weren't able to do before. What does that quantum evolution look like? In a multidimensional way that you're aware of, what previously seemed to have been unseen, what does that look like? What does that feel like? What's possible from that? What's possible now that you're vibrating more in your authentic, Divine qualities? It is a bending of linear reality to an access point of quantum evolution, an access point of multidimensionality. You're also fueled by more energy and consciousness.

We'd like to pause here, not because there's not more that we could talk about. Talking about it more doesn't necessarily add to the multidimensionality of your awareness.

17
Universal Divine Design
Creating through Light and Frequency

BEING A CREATOR BEING

As you have awakened and are awakening to more of the awareness and states of being that are a part of your multidimensional consciousness, there is the awareness of how you are divinely designed in a way that spans beyond what you may have been aware of prior to having your multidimensional awareness. Your Divine design is something that you have co-created with Source consciousness. It simultaneously is your universal Divine design as Source consciousness, the Divine design of the Divine, and also your unique expression of that Divine design.

In your Divine design, which is also a hologram—a multidimensional hologram—there resides all that there is. As your consciousness evolves, you tap into more of this Divine consciousness, more of this Divine design. Then there is the experience of being the awakened creator being, the infinite nature, the all-inclusive energy.

The qualities of all that there is reside within the Divine design in this unified way, in this unified field of consciousness. A way to contemplate the Divine design is to understand that there is an aspect of the Divine design that is both transpersonal and personal. It is both unity consciousness, or unified, in that your Divine design as a Divine incarnate being has aspects to it that are universal, that are the foundation, the fabric of all that there is—every person, every stone. Every consciousness has a Divine design, it has *prima material,* and it has a blueprint.

One of the ways that you're aware of this is the sensation that there's the imprinted, or infused, consciousness of Source that resides within you and everything. You simultaneously become aware of these aspects of being the Divine and the design of divinity. One fundamental aspect of the design of divinity is to be an empowered creator being. As you are an empowered creator being, there is the conscious awareness that you are creating worlds that, through consciousness, energy, frequency, and vibration, you have the capacity to create. Being a creator being is an aspect of the universal Divine design. What you choose, which is a reflection of your signature essence and your unique Divine design, is unique to you. It's an expression of you. It takes on a shape that looks like you, feels like you, and sounds like you.

As we're describing it in this way, this universal Divine design and this unique Divine design, you can see how all that we focused on in *The Tablets of Light* thus far has been nourishing and supporting the full-on reconnection with both, with Source light and the universal Divine design, and then also with the unfolding of your unique expression of this Divine design. As you're in multidimensional awareness and you're accessing the universal Divine design light codes, there are skill sets that you hadn't previously had access to that now you do. Those aspects have to do with light, creation, frequency, and the unified field of oneness.

It's like when you are an apprentice in whatever type of trade, whether it's making shoes or being a blacksmith or being a clothing designer. While you're apprenticing, you may have access to the apprentice-level tools of the person who you are training with, which you're learning the trade from. These tools may be functional, yet not necessarily of the highest mastery. As you're learning with them, there is the potential that you're going to use a tool in a way that actually has a wear and tear on the tool that isn't there once you master the art of whatever it is that you're apprenticing in. Then once you get to that level of mastery, you're given, or you acquire, your master tool set. This master tool set is refined, it's laser light, and it has the capacity to be used at the highest possibility of adeptness for the craft.

The energy or the material that you then work with also changes. In the beginning, as you're learning how to make shoes, maybe you're learning how to make shoes from leftover scraps. As you work the material or the leather, it gets more refined, soft, and beautiful, and has more of a quality that requires a pristine approach. In and of itself it has an aspect to it of really being in that conscious awareness of all that there is.

As you become multidimensional, it's a similar process. As you were more in some dimensions and less in other dimensions, it was as if you were utilizing the apprentice's tools. You were interacting with the material at the level of which you're really able to learn your trade. This requires trial and error. It involves wiggle room, of knowing that there's going to be some clumsiness in the process of getting to a certain level of mastery.

CREATING ADEPTLY WITH LIGHT AND FREQUENCY

Now that your consciousness has evolved, and your energy, frequency, and vibration are synced up to your signature energy and to this universal Source consciousness, this universal Divine design, you're able to utilize the nuances, the higher refined aspects of the Divine design, that which is at the level of adeptness. This level of adeptness is possible because of every moment of every day of every lifetime that you have ever experienced. There is also a sense that as you are now accessing the universal Divine design, in some ways and in some cases, less is more. There is a highly refined artistry that takes less effort and more grace.

It's as if you were becoming a welder. As you're first learning how to weld, you use materials that wouldn't melt, or dissolve, with the first brush of the flame of fire. Maybe you'd work with a different kind of fuel that would provide a different trajectory of the fire. Then, as you become a master welder—and we're speaking about the universal Divine design—it's as if you have a highly concentrated laser that is being applied to something very delicate and responsive. It takes just a light touch and it's done, rather than minutes of high heat, high intensity, to create any sort of alchemy, any sort of evolution, any sort of creation.

We're looking for different analogies for this because we have the sense that it can really open your awareness up as to what is possible now in multidimensionality. This is the level of nuance that's available to you as you're in your universal Divine design, where you have access to these tools.

If you were a surgeon and, in the beginning, you were practicing surgery on a rubber surface, you did this just to practice. In this practice you used a marker to create an incision. There's not a lot of harm you can do on a rubber doll with a marker, yet that practice requires a certain skill. Then you have the butter knife and let's say you evolve and now you're working with clay and you're practicing the skills. With the clay you use the butter knife. Then there is the incision you make with the butter knife. At each stage you are developing a skill, and the matter that you're working on changes, and the tools that you have change. Next you have a scalpel and you're working on flesh, which you use the scalpel to open. Having a dull scalpel at this point would not be as efficient as having a sharp scalpel. Then you get to the point that you have a laser. Maybe it's even computerized, where you're operating the machine to create the incisions. The incisions become smaller and smaller. It's no longer necessary to open up a large space; it could be just a small, tiny place.

With this type of example you begin to see that the nuance is important. If you don't know how to draw the incision with precision, starting off with the laser robot doesn't make sense.

ECHOES OF SEPARATION
CONSCIOUSNESS UNLOCKED

We want to be very clear that the reason you didn't start out with access to these higher refined energies wasn't because you would have done harm with them. Why are we saying that? We're saying that because, as a part of the collective consciousness, as a part of some of your Akashic Records, there is a sensation, or memory, of having had access to highly refined, spiritual technologies during a time where there was a downfall of a civilization. For example, Atlantis had access to highly refined spiritual technologies and then Atlantis shifted from unity into duality. During this transition it was perceived that those refined technologies were utilized in a way that created harm; they were perceived to be contributing factors of the demise of those cultures.

That's where some of these echoes that you have, of not wanting to reclaim your spiritual gifts and your Divine birthrights, come into play. This is the sense of not wanting to be in the power of your Divine genius, of your Divine light mission, out of the sensation that you could misuse or abuse power, or that you could be responsible for the death of others, or for the downfall of a civilization. Yet all of those ways of thinking are without the full picture. Separation consciousness has had its purpose in the evolution of consciousness. There is not anything wrong with it; it's not anything to get rid of. Some people will choose to continue in separation consciousness and that is a part of the wholeness. That's perfect for them. It's not as if there is anything wrong with separation consciousness. Or when you go into a moment of separation consciousness now, or tribal consciousness now, again, there's not anything wrong with it and it's not anything to get rid of. It's inviting what resides within it to evolve into its next evolution, including it into the wholeness, into the oneness. That which was dormant becomes active. That which was inactive becomes active. That which had been active becomes inactive.

There is a vibrational component to the universal Divine design that you have as you're living multidimensionally. You, as a creator being, enjoy greater access to highly refined vibrations and energies to utilize for the purpose of creation. If you were living more unidimensionally you may not have had access to these energies, not because you didn't deserve it, or you weren't worthy, or you would have done harm with them. It's simply because they didn't exist in those dimensions. The frequencies and the vibrations that we're speaking of, of what you could call the new Earth, don't exist in the old Earth. They exist in the multidimensionality.

As you are vibrating in this multidimensional awareness and multidimensional wholeness and you have access to the universal Divine design, you're able to play with frequencies and vibrations that are natural to the dimensional environments that you're tapped into as oneness, and wholeness. You then begin to have access to all that there is through the hologram of evolution.

We want to be very clear, again, that it's all neutral. It's not that having access to more dimensions is better than having access to less dimensions. It's a choice and it's related also to the soul's Divine design, to your unique Divine expression. You're within the pages of *The Tablets of Light* because you know what it's like to live multidimensionally. You have the memory, you have the light code within you, you have the divinity code within you, and you know that's why you have come to Earth at this time. You have come here at this time to resurrect multidimensionality, to be a part of the visionary consciousness that opens that up again. This doesn't make you better than or worse than anybody else.

We hope that's landing in a way that resonates for you. That it's not a hierarchy that you have to get into, or a test that you have to pass. It's not that there is some secret society that you have to be a part of, or that this information is hidden, or that it's a secret. It's not that. It's that it exists in dimensional space that you also have to exist in to be utilizing it. You know this from your experience of linear space and time. You know that if you are a Michelin-star chef and you want to create a meal with the finest ingredients from around the world, you have to be in the same vibrational proximity to those ingredients. You can't make a meal with the most highly refined ingredients if you're not in the country that makes them, or you haven't had these ingredients brought to your pantry, or you're trying to make it with all canned foods. With your artistry you can still make a beautiful meal with whatever ingredients you have. Your Divine design and your unique expression are going to shine through when you use those more base ingredients than it would with somebody who doesn't have any skills as a chef.

Yet if you're going to use the most highly refined ingredients, the most concentrated, the ripest pineapples, then you have to have all of that in your pantry, you have to be able to be in the same location to utilize these refined ingredients. Then you also have within you the awareness of what you would know to really be able to utilize the ingredients in a way that maximizes them, and this doesn't always mean more. If you have a very strong ingredient, putting in tons of it doesn't add anything to the meal; it can actually overplay, or overpower, the other ingredients. There is a capacity that the chef has of utilizing the right amount, the right quality and quantity, combining the ingredients in a way where everything works together.

If you're working with truffles, for example, you wouldn't necessarily need to add eighty truffles to your meal. You would know that the truffle has a robust flavor, and the way that you slice it also reveals that flavor. There is an understanding if you're using garlic, for instance, that depending on whether you press it, or chop it, or slice it, the garlic will lend a different flavor to the ingredients.

YOUR VISIONARY'S PATH TO THE EVOLUTION IN CONSCIOUSNESS

As someone who has been on the path—the pioneering path, leading the awakening—you have access to the highly refined ingredients of energy and consciousness. These highly refined ingredients of energy and consciousness are also a state of being and a way that you are. It required moving beyond the recycling of the conditioned responses of separation consciousness, the embedded belief systems.

It's like having one record and you just play that one record over and over again. Every time you want to hear music you play the same record, you play the same record. Now you can play that record, and you'll play the separation consciousness record from time to time; you just will. Yet now you have access to all kinds of music, including the most highly refined music that is also related to your unique expression, your unique vibration. Again, it's not that you have to sort through the infinite possibilities of music. It's as if your jukebox has your most potent and highly refined music pieces on it.

There may be some, too, that you use for a while and then they fall away. We want to point this out because, for some of you, it's as if you've been really good at something, yet you begin to be guided to move into something where it feels like you'd be starting over or you'd be at that learning stage again, rather than at the mastery stage that you're already at with some things. Being in unity consciousness and having this multidimensional awareness and living multidimensionally and with the universal Divine design is also about moving on when it's time to move on. It's about leaving things that are already going well to explore working with these other elements and ways of being.

You can see, too, how in this universal Divine design, you're connected to everything at the base. You're connected to everything in an alchemical way. You're using the concentrated Divine consciousness that creates all that there is. In the example of glassblowing, you may be working with two-thousand-degree glass that's been melted; it's in a semiliquid form. As the creator of the glass, you can make huge pieces; you can have installations that are larger than trees. Or, as the person that works with glass, you could make a bead for a necklace. You're working with the medium of this heated glass that allows you to create; it's malleable. If you have a glass bowl and you're trying to create something new from a glass bowl, you could paint it, or you could create something to put around it to decorate it. There are ways you could decorate it yet you couldn't really change the structure of it without destroying it, melting it down, and getting it back to the malleable units of consciousness that then allows you to create a new form.

As a creator being with access to the universal Divine design, and being a glassblower at the same time, it's as if you have an infinite supply of glass. In this example, one of the ways that you create your unique expression, your personal Divine design and your Divine uniqueness is through art. It's as if you have infinite access to the form of glass that then can become anything. You have the best supplies, the best team, the colored glass, the tools, the studio—it's all there. You have access to it in its liquid form, in its form to be created. Like the elements of Earth, and Air, and Water, and Fire, and Akasha, or the letters in your DNA, of *A, T, C, G* (referenced earlier on page 40), they're always the same. The Divine consciousness is a part of all of those, yet it is you working with those base elements that then creates everything. You have access to them as you are, more and more, in your multidimensional, awakened, universal Divine design.

YOUR FULCRUM OF CREATION

With these highly refined energies of units of Divine consciousness that you have access to in your multidimensional living, there is also the awareness of utilizing touch points, or access points, in a way that then creates a lot of impact. Words like *momentum, pivoting, launching* harness these potent energies of evolution. We've spoken about the immense momentum of your soul and of your Divine light mission. As such, you can use a very small amount of effort in a highly concentrated frequency and vibration and then have a lot of results. It's like the small hinge that swings big doors, or the fulcrum point, the tipping point, the capacity to leverage something. You are no longer trying to lift something that weighs two thousand pounds with your hands; you are leveraging many dimensional points of consciousness at the same time.

Just as with a dolly, for example, when you're moving a piece of furniture. You can move that furniture using the leverage of the dolly and the wheels. A small dolly can move something quite large. If you lift up the corners of a heavy piece of furniture and you slide in a type of material that slides very easily, or you put it on rollers, when you go to push it you don't have to use ten people to push it. You push it and it rolls. You then use the momentum of the heaviness of the piece of furniture in combination with the rollers to create the movement.

There is a cohesion, a working together, of this multidimensional living of your universal Divine design that then is utilizing each dimension and each vibration in the location it resides in, in a way that maximizes all that there is from all of them, because it's all connected to oneness. You may think of something in your life that you're choosing to actualize as moving at a slower vibration, or being in the third dimension, for example. Yet as something is in the third dimension in unity consciousness and connected to this universal Divine design, it exists in all dimensions. It exists in a vibrational bandwidth, or range. It's like your piano; it has different notes. It doesn't just have one note; it has a range. It's all in the piano. You don't have one piano key in your living room and one piano key outside by your mailbox—they're all together.

At its heart, at the base, this really is our purpose together: the reunification of the Divine wholeness within all that there is. It's not the Divine discarnate; it's the Divine incarnate.

Just as it's easier for the glassblower to be working with the liquid glass in a way that's malleable than it is to try to make something new out of something that's already formed, it's like that, as well, in your life. As you're connecting to the malleable refined energies, the alchemy of the dimensions will take care of the part of what it becomes. There's really not a way for us to describe this in words. It's not linear. We invite you to tap in to it multidimensionally.

In the sequence of glassblowing, the glass initially is in a liquid state. Before that, it wasn't in a liquid state; it had to be heated. We're not saying that you couldn't use a bowl and heat it and melt it down. Yet when you go into the part of creating, when you go into the glass studio, in that moment of the creation you're tapping into the liquid glass. Then you shape it and you reheat it, and there's a whole process to shaping it into form. Then, once you have your form, it's natural for

230 THE DIVINE INCARNATE

the glass to cool. It's natural for it to move from the dimension of liquid into something that is cold. It's hard, you can touch it, it's usable, it's accessible, it exists in your life. The infinite intelligence that resides within the liquid glass, enabling it to then become the object of the glass—all of that is within it.

ACTUALIZING INFINITE INTELLIGENCE INTO INCARNATED FORM

There is also a sensation of working with the multidimensionality of the highly refined frequencies. As you are working with these highly refined frequencies, there is the understanding that within them is the infinite intelligence allowing them to show up in the incarnated form. Some of you have wanted to manifest or actualize things in the past and you've been frustrated. You haven't been able to do it, and it just seems like this light, the third dimension, has not been listening to you.

Or it's been so much effort, or you've tried everything and it hasn't worked. It's because you were trying to do it backward up, or you were trying to do it outside in, or you were trying to do it with a glass that had already been formed, rather than working with it in its malleable state. Because now you're adept with light and frequency and Divine units of consciousness, and now you're working with these highly concentrated vibrations and energies, things unfold in a way that feels more natural, more organic, more magical. Now there is a sense of ahhhh.

That is also where, at times, you have to stop yourself from trying to do it the way that somebody else is showing you how to do it. That's why we don't provide "eight steps to being the Divine, awakened being." We provide an environment that, as you're within it, sparks what you know is true for you. This is where we get into your unique, Divine design—your unique, Divine design. Having access to these high frequencies, and high vibrations, and the highly refined energies, and the concentrated units of consciousness that create all that there is, and working with these elements in their most potent state also nourishes, awakens, sparks within you your unique design. It's alchemy; it's an alchemical process.

UNITY CONSCIOUSNESS EXERCISE
• • • • • • • • • •
Awaken Universal Divine Design Codes and Connect to Your Divinity

Seeing the communion, the correlation of this universal Divine design and this personal Divine design, there is a partnership, a Source Source, a correlation, an origin origin. Staying with the universal Divine design at this point and what you have access to, and these highly refined energies, frequencies, ways of being, Divine qualities, all that there is—have an awareness of your universal Divine design as well as your brilliant system as an incarnated Divine being.

As you're focusing on your universal Divine design, have an awareness of DNA unlocking, of divinity codes sparking and awakening, of connection to these vibrational units of divinity, of remembering yourself as Source consciousness. It's not only happening in your body in this incarnation—it's happening on all levels.

As you've been spending more and more moments in unity consciousness, inclusion, Source cohesion, Source light, it's as if you've been in the liquid glass of divinity. Now this is having its natural alchemical progression or an evolution that you are able to sense in your body, or in your incarnation. It's not like you are only sensing it there; you're sensing it on all levels.

ALCHEMICAL PROCESS UNVEILING UNITY CONSCIOUSNESS

Just like with the example of glass, you have a period where, after you've created the piece and you've taken it off the pipe, you put it in an environment where it can go through a transition from having been heated to then cooling down. When you put it in the case and it's still in its heated form, you're not able to see all that it'll become. The alchemy and the chemistry of the color, for example, become visible during that cooling process, and sometimes in unanticipated ways.

You may have the experience of making a piece and you know what it is. You have an idea of what colors you put into it. Then you put it in the oven where it is slowly cooled, and a few days later you go to look at it after it's been taken out of the oven, or you go to take it out of the oven, and you may be surprised. You're able to see how the colors and the techniques that you used translated into in its full incarnation when it's fully "cooked" and actualized into form.

This sensation of it being revealed or unveiled as it's in this stage is also similar to how it is that you may be aware of yourself in this moment. There is an awakening or realization of who it is that you have become and the alchemical process of that. You are able to see this universal Divine design in ways that may be surprising even to you. It's not that they only exist in your body, or in your incarnation, but they are also simultaneously connected to the multidimensionality and are being informed by these highly refined and potent Divine unity consciousness energies.

There are so many examples in your natural world of what you see and what you don't see. You see a tree, yet most of the time you don't see the roots of the tree. You see the front of the mountain but you don't see the back of the mountain. You see the field that's been planted, yet before it sprouts, you don't see the seed that you planted. When you look at the tree before it blossoms, before it bears fruit, you don't see the figs, oranges, olives, apricots—you don't see its own unique fruit. It's not like they don't exist; it's not like they're inside of the branch.

It's analogous to a 3-D printer that you may have seen, wherein when a picture of something is put into the 3-D printer, it is transformed from being two-dimensional to three-dimensional. That's what we're describing in the multidimensionality. All that there is exists in all that there is. As you have your adept connection and awakened consciousness with your multidimensional universal Divine design, what's vibrating in your Divine unique expression is in relationship to your signature energy—and what's uniquely you and yours as you're choosing it naturally comes into visibility, into your tangible life.

There is a lot more leverage, momentum, and ease that is created by being a Being of Light, which is creating and interacting with consciousness, with Divine energy. From our perspective, this is extremely efficient. You've had moments of this, what we're describing. You've had moments where you experience this creator being-ness from the multidimensional universal Divine design. It's what you think of as synchronicities, miracles, or experiences that seem to fall into your lap, or they seem so improbable that you would meet someone that was on the other side of the planet that then would become a main player in the movie of your life. Or that you'd want to sell your house and someone who wasn't even looking to buy a house happened to be walking their dog, saw it for sale, and then, within the first day of it being on the market, they made you an offer. It's what we often speak of as positioning. It's that sense of magic.

That's also a choice, wherein you may consciously say to yourself: "This is the way. This is the way I'm choosing to live." That's where the destination, the journey, the *now* moment, is so exciting. It's like you know in some instances, for example, that a certain outcome is going to occur. Let's say you're building a house and you know that this house is going to be built. You know the outcome is going to be achieved, yet how it gets created and where you're coming from, how you experience it—that's where you get to play with these nuances, with these highly refined energies.

There are times where you have to say no. Or you may have to say, "I'm not going to do it like everyone else is telling me to do it because that isn't me or uniquely mine." There may be ways that you're doing things and you're getting results, you're building one house after another after another, yet it may feel like the process is empty. This is where you may take a stand to really emerge as your unique Divine design and to live this way—not because you couldn't create the same outcomes other ways—but because that is the particular oracular vision you hold.

The oracular vision that your Divine transmitter Danielle holds—which is a part of us connecting with her and with you—is that those Beings of Light who have come to Earth to resurrect unity consciousness through authentic expression are being and doing and living that full-out. There is right relationship once again. A bicycle is a bicycle. A strawberry is a strawberry. You are you and you're so you, at ease, without any overlays, distortions, internal push-pulls—you are fully you. Of course, that's also the full embodiment of Divine light.

CONSCIOUS CHOICE EXERCISE
· · · · · · · · · ·
Choose to Create through Universal Divine Design of Frequency and Vibration

In this moment, have an awareness of your universal Divine design and your access points and your choice—your choice to remember how to utilize these refined frequencies and energies, how to be the creator being that you are with access to the infinite pantry of highly refined ingredients.

If you're a chemistry professor, you have an understanding of how the elements work together. Let's say you're teaching your students that when they combine this and that, a certain reaction happens, a certain alchemical reaction happens. You don't give them the ingredients that are going to create an explosion—you give them the ones you know are going to create an alchemical effect or a certain alchemical reaction in a way that's in a context, it's in a larger environment.

That's the shift. You're able to work with all of the elements, all of these components, and understand that they're in right relationship. You know that the universal Divine design that you have access to multidimensionally, and now the capacity to connect to these highly refined vibrations and frequencies and to combine them together is an exquisite adventure. It's a delightful experience. It's this expanded way of being, this expanded unfolding. The choice is yours. The choice is yours. The choice is yours.

18
Divine Infusion

Being Re-Sourced in Your Divine Genius

THE STEEPING PROCESS

As you are steeping in the consciousness within these multidimensional pages, there is the enhanced potency of you—the expanded consciousness in a highly concentrated form that is you. The more the environment is conducive, nurturing, and supportive of this steeping process, the more concentrated and potent your connection to your signature energy becomes.

When you think of the word *steep* you may naturally find yourself thinking of tea. You steep a tea bag in hot water, and then depending on how long you leave the tea bag in, how hot the water is, how much water there is, and how much tea there is, the steeping will create various levels of concentration of the tea. At one point if the tea bag remains in the tea (and no one drinks it), a decrease in alchemy continues to happen after a certain point. It could even be that the tea bag begins to disintegrate.

It's the same if you look at the beginning of the process wherein the tea bag is initially introduced to the hot water. A few dunks can release and infuse a lot of essence into the water. There's a rhythm to the steeping and there's an alchemy to the steeping and there's an awareness that certain parts of the environment are more conducive to an accelerated infusion.

After a certain point there needs to be a change. You could get some more hot water and use the same tea bag and there's still more of the essence that will permeate the new water. But at some point the tea bag will be used up. It'll have given everything it can and then you must introduce a new tea bag.

We're using this analogy of tea and the infusion that's created through steeping to enumerate this process of being in *The Tablets of Light*. You may have a sense that for you, certain segments, subjects, and words that accelerate your full potential are steeping into your current consciousness. It's as if there is an accelerated concentration and potency of you that gets unlocked in the environment of *The Tablets of Light*.

THE POTENCY OF YOU

As you've been steeping in more and more of your universal Divine design, more and more of your Source light, more and more of bringing together your incarnation with Source consciousness, there's a partnering with you and you that is being created. Your divinity, your connection to Source, infuses and imbues and enhances the concentration of your life, of you, as a signature energy. It boosts the potency of you.

Sometimes it may feel as if there's this direction as to what comes first and what comes second. The Divine origin and the Divine infusion then enhance your signature energy and your incarnation. As this happens, your connection to your Source is enhanced. They go together. It's not that one happens first and then the other happens, even though that's the way we're describing it in this moment. As you steep more in connection with your Source consciousness—your signature, your signature essence, you in this incarnation—becomes amplified, becomes more potent, and becomes more concentrated.

It is your fully realized multidimensional self that gets amplified. There is the awareness that you are Source and Source is you. There is the awareness that your incarnation, your life, that which you experience in what you would call physical form, is no longer separate from your awareness of Source, consciousness, and the other dimensions that you have access to. They're all connected: multidimensional consciousness, multidimensional awareness, the consciousness of you, and universal Divine design.

These previous segments and all those leading up to them have been about a reunion with the full breadth and width and bandwidth of your soul's consciousness as the Divine incarnate. Then your incarnation is re-Sourced. It's re-Sourced multidimensionally. It's re-Sourced multidimensionally. Interesting things start to occur and your incarnation is re-Sourced multidimensionally. As this happens, your unique experience of the evolution in consciousness will be customized to you. That's why we're not saying that your experience will always be this or always be that in general terms, because it is bespoke to you.

There are some unique and interesting experiences that start to happen as the incarnation is fully re-Sourced once again, as you, as an embodied soul, as an embodied Being of Light, are fully resurrected into the Divine wholeness of all that there is. You may have a sensation of being buoyed. There is a sensation of feeling connected. There's more surface space to your being. There's an awareness that all is well and you are all. There's an awareness of equanimity, of staying in that center, in that re-Sourced space, in your internal environment as life appears to ebb and flow. There's a sense of what we speak of in terms of positioning; you're in the right place at the right time. You are a creator being so there's a sensation perhaps of greater peace, fulfillment, and ease.

What you also notice is that the particular Divine qualities that you carry as part of your Divine design will be where you hang out more completely. They'll be amplified. The genius of you starts to really flourish and be more visible, more utilized, more the space in which you are vibrating from. As you are Source consciousness, and all that there is exists within all that there is, there is the awareness that you have some Divine design geniuses in certain areas that are a part of your unique divine design. Your Divine geniuses are your areas of adeptness, where you excel and usually are comprised of what you love doing and being.

For your Divine transmitter, Danielle, her Divine genius involves creation through multidimensional communication. Vibrationally that's where the genius gets amplified. As we've explored that section pertaining to the unique qualities that you carry, you may have uncovered your Divine design genius points. As you steep in your unique Divine design geniuses you'll experience greater internal permission to be in those more and more and to utilize those naturally in a way that then accesses your entire wholeness.

INTERNAL COHESION

We also want to say that because you're evolving, your Divine design also evolves, and therefore some of the qualities of various states of being, including your Divine genius and areas of adeptness, will also evolve. It's not static. Nothing's static. Everything's always dynamic, organic, expanding, moving. You may also experience a willingness to leave behind whatever you're really great at as you have an awareness that something else is coming to the fore.

The interesting thing that happens as you're in this Source cohesion—as your incarnation is connected to Divine wholeness, as you're re-Sourced—is that your universal Divine design and your personal Divine design are steeping and amplifying one another. As you're tapping into your particular gifts and talents, your internal sensation, your internal experiences become more refined. An enhanced level of adeptness and awareness exists. As well, feelings of separation, of lack, of there being something wrong, and of things needing to be fixed, begin to dissipate. You're not withholding, resisting, or disconnected from the totality of all that there is.

There's a sense of feeling buoyed, a sense of feeling re-Sourced, or more centered, connected, that infuses and touches all areas of your life. The way you perceive your life is also more internally cohesive. The signature energy is vibrating fluidly. The connection to Source is there. The embodied divinity is experienced. That overflows into your experience of your life, into your awareness of your life. Or you're downloading a lot of frequencies at this juncture in our conversation. You may have a sense of the rich layers of consciousness within this scribed text.

This Divine infusion of light, vibrations, and frequencies is the amplification of all that there is. This Divine infusion is amplifying the potency of your signature energy and your communion with your universal Divine design. Have an awareness of the highly concentrated environment vibrationally—the potency of you exponentiated, and therefore the potency of your connection to Source amplified, and vice versa.

This infinity loop is between you as incarnated Source consciousness and the oneness of Source in wholeness, or Source in oneness or the totality of Source. This is nullifying one of the common separation consciousness illusions, which is that in order for something to come into actualized form it has to leave the totality of Source, it has to separate from Source and be a fraction of the concentration. There is the obliteration of that false truth.

As an emanation of Source you're not less concentrated than all that there is because you *are* all that there is. You are an access point in the hologram. Within you resides everything that resides within Source. You are carrying certain frequencies and vibrations of your soul, signature energy, essence, and your Divine design, which creates your individuality, which creates your uniqueness—not to the exclusion of the infinite possibilities—but for the experience of divinity to be in concentrated forms in all dimensions.

For some of you, as you've been wanting to create your life, you are faced with what seem to be decisions that, in the construct of your incarnation, you choose what it is that you want to create. As we've discussed before, if you choose one thing, it might seem that you're excluding all the other things that you don't choose. As you may remember from our earlier conversation, what's you and yours vibrates within your consciousness. There's a certain highlighting of what would be in your genre, what would be in your jukebox, what would be in your stadium—of being able to find that person with the yellow shirt.

For some of you there was a fear that to choose to bring something into form, to choose to unlock your contribution and put it on the altar of life, to share it at the communal gathering point with other hikers, would mean separating from Source again. That's a part of the collective memory that had driven so much of the shutting down of you. There was the sense as you were born in this incarnation of your having gone from being fully unified with Source consciousness to a state of forgetting that you *are* Source.

There was a shock in this—a shock in going from this sensation of all-knowing, of having the awareness of who you were and who you are and what you chose as the purpose of this incarnation to completely forgetting all of that. The sensation of incarnating equaled being separate from Source and having amnesia of all the choices you made before your conception, such as who it is that you're going to play with on the level of those Beings of Light on Earth, who you will meet, why you chose your particular parents, and what it is that you're up to in this larger Divine light mission of being incarnate during this time of great transition. You forgot what you were carrying, and now it's time to remember. Your return to Source consciousness within catalyzes this remembering.

It's like all this separation from knowing, from being re-Sourced, was a shock. It may be the shock from this lifetime; it may be the shock from the first time you incarnated. An aspect of the collective memory was driving so much after that: the muting of your potency by pretending to not be clear or to be confused or perhaps the shutting down of your power, pretending to be the most powerless powerful person, or shutting down your capacity to actualize into physical form, which then created a sensation of struggle.

There was an echo of the belief that if you powerfully choose and commit to your Divine design, then what it is that you're here for would equal more separation from Source. This is the illusion that we're talking about. It could equal all those separation consciousness patterns of feeling like you'd be kicked out of the tribe, lose love, be ridiculed, be killed, or disappear. But these attempts of trying to stop life from being lived, trying to stop the impulse of creation, to move into creation, is not possible and in fact it's exhausting.

Can you see how that might trigger the sensation that you're having to leave Source again? This illusion that you must leave Source consciousness occurs every time you specify Source consciousness, every time you move from the universal Divine design to the specific Divine design, every time you move more into the individual and the unique.

CHOICES MADE FROM THE CONNECTION TO THE WHOLENESS OF ALL THAT THERE IS

Tune into the vibration of this because the words and the clarity of the words are amplified as you tune into the vibration of what it is that we're getting at. We'll provide some examples as well. When you powerfully commit, when you choose something, when you say yes to something, there's momentum that's created. Then there's a direction, a concentrated trajectory.

As these choices are made from the unification of Source they're also imbued with wholeness. This sacred text that's been scribed is scribed with each vibration, each word, each frequency still being connected to the wholeness. It didn't have to disconnect from the wholeness in order to become a certain subject, in order to be consciousness of all that there is, in order to be this conversation about Source and with Source.

The words are one way that the multidimensional consciousness is expressed. The words are an aspect, an emanation of the environment of Divine wholeness. As you're more steeped and you have access to this Divine infusion and this higher level of concentration, the natural course will be that you'll be in more of your areas of your Divine genius. That may seem as if, as you're in those areas of Divine genius, you're separating from all the other ways of being, all the other Divine qualities. Yet moving into more of those Divine genius points connects you because you are connected to the wholeness of all that there is.

It's as if an aspect of your spiritual evolution and your journey was based on an illusion. Maybe you started meditating twenty years ago and there was this idea in your awareness or perhaps in some of the meditations that you learned that if you left your body (through meditation) you might connect more deeply with Source. Or if you gave up material things in past lives, if you renounced sexuality or remained unmarried or otherwise gave up on having a partner, or you ate or slept in certain ways, then, as a result, you would connect more strongly with Source.

All of these different falsehoods would lead you to believe that the renouncing of your incarnation, of being in the physical realm, would enhance your connection to Source. Early in your life this may have led you to not fully embody your body, or to be spacey, or to leave your body out of protection. Or for you to not having fully said yes to life at your conception, for even though you said yes to incarnating, you may not have fully said yes to incarnating in wholeness, to incarnating into Divine consciousness.

This erroneous construct that material and spiritual are separate posits that God is "out there," that heaven is above, that you have to leave your body and travel in the light body in order to connect to Source. Yet all of that is based on the illusion that Source is outside of you, that you're *not* Source and that your body *isn't* the energy location of Source. As you pay attention to your body, as you are really in your daily activities, as you're connected to your internal realm, then you access the universe inside.

We know that some of these conversations point in a direction. This happens first and this happens later. You go in and as you go in you connect to more. As above, so below; as within, so without. We are guiding you in response to your having asked to pay more attention to the internal environment and applying your consciousness there, allowing your awareness of who you are as a signature being, as a divinely incarnated being, to inform your actions, your thoughts, your choices. We are guiding you to move from there into emanating that light into your external environment.

This collective-consciousness memory—if you make a strong choice for something means you have to separate more from Source—was pervasive. It showed up in so many different ways from this desire to not be visible or not stand out or not show off or you have to tone it down or you might be considered arrogant, this idea that you also have to be and do everything yourself. There's this sense that you're alone.

CONSCIOUS CHOICE EXERCISE
· · · · · · · · · ·
Choose to Be a Fully Resurrected Being of Light

Have an awareness of you choosing to be the concentrated, divinely infused, and fully resurrected Being of Light. You are basking in your adeptness, your mastery, your Divine genius, and that's your choice. And that choice is a choice of wholeness, a choice of connection, a choice of amplified divinity. The experience of being the Divine incarnate on Earth is one in which you're able to experience something fully.

There are such a wide variety of experiences on Earth to be had. You might choose to swim in the ocean and to really experience swimming in the ocean and how that feels, or to snorkel or to dive so that you can also see what's in the ocean. To focus in at that level actually provides you an amplified awareness of one point on the hologram of all that there is. As you go deep into it, as you occupy it, there's the sensation of connecting to the full hologram. Maybe you've had that experience or you can imagine that experience.

VIBRATIONAL PROXIMITY ILLUMINATES DIVINE CONSCIOUSNESS

Let's say you've been traveling in a city and you've had a lot of impressions of that city. The trip has been filled with lots of activities and things to take in, shifts that you've experienced. In the city there is a plethora of action, noise, people, and things that you've experienced. There's an active energy to your traveling.

Then let's say you go from this city environment to snorkeling in the ocean. As you're floating on top of the water and you have your face in the water with your snorkel on, and you're swimming next to a reef, there's already a change in the sound. You're not hearing the cars, planes, people, or the hustle and bustle of what you were hearing—the auditory stimulation of what you were hearing in the city.

You experience peace and quiet and you're in another world. You're in the world of color where the fish are swimming. You're in the world of this underwater universe. For those minutes or hours you can imagine being lost in this other world, being immersed, being touched by being in this other world. Because you were in it, it was always there, yet you being in vibrational proximity to it illuminated this dimension of Divine consciousness in a way that then accesses the wholeness.

As you dive deeply into your personal Divine design and your incarnation and you immerse yourself in it, you are connected to Source consciousness. There's the microcosm and the macrocosm. How do you know Source consciousness from the vantage point of your Divine incarnation in this evolution in consciousness? It is by deeply experiencing the facets of the Divine.

Tapping into your inner awareness of the concentrated units of Source consciousness within your life then allows you to tap into the oneness, the wholeness of all that there is, which is by its very nature, done through accessing individualized oneness. Going into that which is the difference of you, your unique Divine design, your unique incarnation, makes all the difference.

This experience of your unique Divine design is one in which there is the amplification of your connection to all that there is. Allow yourself the willingness to take a deep dive into your consciousness and to what makes you uniquely you, into your areas of adeptness. Allow your life to be the oracular vision of Divine unification. This is also what creates a greater simplicity. You evolve from trying to keep everything open to being willing to choose to go deep in certain areas.

If you wake up in the morning and you're informed by your Divine design then you're in a certain rhythm, you're in a certain trajectory. The experiences that you choose on that day will be related to your Divine designs, both unique and universal. There is an infinite possibility in each and every day and yet you don't have to wake up with the sense that you're searching through *A* to *Z* of every possibility to try to find the potential of yours.

This brings us back to the example of the stadium. In it are ten thousand people and you're finding that one with the yellow shirt. It's like everything else just sits down. That is one of the interesting things that happens as you're in the concentrated Divine infusion of your embodied Divine light mission. Things get simple—simple yet potent. There's less noise, less clutter, less interference. There's not the confusion. You're informed. You're communing with your fully turned-on awareness.

You're no longer skating along the surface of all possibility, trying to keep things open so there isn't the illusion that gets tapped into that if you chose something then you're going to separate more from Source. There's the awareness that by choosing, by going deep, you are also experiencing Source here, Source now, Source in your life. It doesn't mean that you don't blend, that you're not still a creator being who uses a lot of different ingredients in living your life. That's still fun; that's still play. We're not saying to subtract things from your life. We're saying that naturally each moment is lived in wholeness from a highly concentrated Source consciousness and then that mind chatter and interference gets quiet. It's like that journey from the city to snorkeling.

STEEPING IN THE VIBRATIONS OF SOURCE CONSCIOUSNESS

Return your awareness to the amplification of this concentrated environment, the amplification of you, the amplification of this Source consciousness. Continue to steep in these vibrations. Continue to choose the individualized oneness, your unique expression of Divine consciousness, your full potency, and your awakened awareness. In each moment you create from that wholeness as a totality of you there's a nullifying effect on this separation consciousness belief that says your choosing something, your choosing to incarnate, means you have to disconnect from Source or it's going to create a deeper separation from Source.

As always, don't take our word for it. What's true for you is true for you. Try it, experience it, live it now. Now it's possible. That's also why this conversation is happening at this context at this time in the evolution of consciousness. It is possible to live a life imbued with wholeness, imbued with unity consciousness.

It's now possible to create a sacred text like this one that's imbued with wholeness. This book doesn't have to go from the infinite possibilities and separate from Source to come into this possibility. It's multidimensional. It's still connected to wholeness. It's an aspect of the hologram. It's connected to the hologram.

That's why as you reread these words you may have the sense that you're reading a different book because you're vibrating at a different place. In so doing, you access more of what's here. Every moment has everything within it. As you embody every moment fully, you're accessing all that's possible in each and every moment. This does take your choice, it does take your focus.

We would invite you to envision, imagine, bring into your conscious awareness, what a life of incarnated Divine wholeness is like for you. What gets simpler when you're really vibrating in the highly refined energies of your Divine brilliance, of your particular gifts and talents? How does that connect you to the wholeness?

19
Divine Calibration

Access Your Divine Design and
Divine Light Mission

YOUR PERSONAL DIVINE DESIGN AND
UNIQUE EXPRESSION

We've spoken about the universal Divine design that you now have access to through your multidimensional awareness. We have also opened the way through the previous Divine infusion segment, to build within you the awareness that your personal Divine design is inhabited and ensouled, occupied, by the unified Source field of consciousness. The last segment, in particular, illuminated more of your signature energy and your signature essence. As such, the echo that to embody something, to actualize something, equaled separation from Source was invited to disintegrate and be included back into the wholeness.

Now that those pieces are in place and you're continuing to unwind the energetics of what you have chosen to access and to complete from our previous segment, we are ready to speak about your personal Divine design, your unique expression, your Divine light mission, in a very specific and tangible way.

There is the awareness of what we're calling your Divine design, what you are designed in extraordinary ways for. *Divine* also means "extraordinary"; that which is natural for you, that which is a part of your Akashic Records, that which you have chosen before this incarnation. Each day of this incarnation you are allowing or disallowing that—by varying degrees—to be. It's why you have come to Earth at this time. It's what you carry within you, and the conscious unfolding of that which you carry within you allows that luminosity to reveal itself to you. Deepen into your light, deepen into that informed beingness that you have within you.

We are speaking about your extraordinary design, your brilliant design, your Source consciousness design, and we're traversing this universal awareness of it to be in your individual awareness of it—who it is that you are, what it is that you carry, your signature energy. You go from the awareness that there are all possibilities of plants, for example, or of trees, to knowing that you're a specific tree or a specific plant. You have the awareness that you're an orange tree, for example, or a tomato plant. As your evolution in consciousness continues and your awareness of this unique design of who it is that you are is deepened, you have the sensation and the consciousness of being who it is that you are. Your brilliant blueprint has everything within it to actualize what is uniquely you and yours.

In this, you become aware of the specific consciousness and oracular vision that you carry, you have an awareness of your Divine design, your Divine light mission. And when we say *Divine light mission* or *Divine design,* we know that we may be giving rise to a sensation of the old paradigm of powerlessness: "That's just how you're designed and that's just how it is." Yet know that you designed it that way. There is empowerment in that Divine design. It's what you chose to put in your package— the package that you open at various points along your journey.

The Divine light mission sometimes can be thought of as needing to—and both of them, really—of needing to be taking on a certain expression. There is the awareness of the steeping in the Divine design, steeping in that impulse of creation, steeping in the Divine light mission as you are steeping in your signature energy and your signature essence. Through that steeping there is the illumination of that which is funneling through, and in, and around you. And then the steeping builds in concentration and then it overflows.

LIVING YOUR DIVINE DESIGN IS INEVITABLE

Your Divine light mission and your brilliant design is a state of being. It is who you are. It is an awareness of your universal light, meaning you can be fully vibrating your brilliant design, and your Divine brilliance, and your Divine light mission at all points in your day. There are not certain times when you are living your Divine design and certain times when you are not. There are not certain times when you are carrying out your Divine light mission and certain times that you are not.

There isn't any longer any separation between any area of your life because you can see now that they are all an expression of your multi-dimensionality. That which you may have previously thought of as your personal life, or your professional life, or your family life, or your friends, or your home, or your hobbies, or your health, or your money—it's all one life, it's all a multidimensional expression of that one life. There isn't an on or an off when it comes to your Divine design. There may be more internalized, or ways-of-being aspects, and others that overflow when the impulse of creation reaches that point that it overflows from the impulse into the creation. It may overflow into an external form, in that you may express your Divine light mission through a certain project. That project may be personal or it may be professional.

That's also why we're using the phrase *Divine light mission*. We could say *your soul's purpose, your life purpose, your career,* yet when we say *your Divine light mission,* it really embodies who you are and what it is that you came here for. Who are you and why are you here? Or as you state it in the first person, Who am I and why am I here? These are the questions that you hold, that you carry. They are what has been a part of the consciousness of your incarnation. To be steeping in who it is that you are and why it is that you are here allows a thorough integration, acceptance, and union with that. When this happens, there are no borders, there are no boundaries, there are no separations—it is bound-less, it is infinite.

Access Your Divine Design and Divine Light Mission

To have greater awareness, consciously, of your Divine design and your Divine light mission, we will journey together into the Akashic Records, the records of all your soul's incarnations.

Have an awareness of going within with the intention to meet me, Thoth, in the Akashic Records. Your access point to the Akashic Records is within you. Have a sense of the environment of this conversation shifting to be the environment of the Akashic Records. This is where you will meet me, Thoth, in that environment, eye-to-eye, peer-to-peer, Divine-to-Divine.

Imagine that there is a table that we sit down at. As we are sitting at the table, you can see many records around you, or you can feel them, or know that they're there. They may have a certain vibrational quality that you recognize because they are about you. By being within this hall of your Akashic Records, there is also the concentration effect—you steeping in you. This particular section of the Akashic Records that we are connecting to together has to do with who you are and why you are here.

Who you are is Source, is Divine, and yet simultaneously why you incarnated on Earth has a universal, global aspect to it, in a way that is very specifically applied to you and for you. That broader stroke of your Divine light mission is to be the Divine incarnate. The process of becoming the Divine incarnate is one in which you include and transcend all illusion that you are separate from Source. Also, there is that specific mission that you carry, that unique mission that you carry—only you. You are the only one that can be you. Bask in the vibrational proximity of these Akashic Records, this nourishing environment.

Knowing that you are the key that unlocks the records of this developmental stage of your evolution, now return your focus to the table in front of you.

Notice that there are four Akashic Records before you. You may imagine them like Tarot cards or tablets or crystals or really anything—goatskin scrolls with emerald and lapis writing, sacred geometry.

Akashic Record One: The Record of Your Divine Design

Bring your attention to the first Akashic Record in particular: the record of your Divine design. Allow your sensations to emerge as you tune into the record of your Divine design. One of the global transmissions to you tuning into your Divine design and this particular Akashic Record is a reconnection to your Divine lineage. Who you are is the Divine. Take a few minutes steeping in the reconnection to your Divine lineage. . . .

Now that you've tuned into the Divine design awareness on this global scale, your Divine lineage reconnection, have an awareness of utilizing your multidimensional awareness to be informed more about your personal Divine design, your personal brilliant system, your personal Divine brilliance, your unique capacities. You may be conscious of this interaction with your Akashic Record or you may not be. It may be happening on the multidimensional levels wherein multidimensionally you are aware of what this record is transmitting to you, and your reunion with this record. You may be more unconsciously aware than consciously aware of what this record is informing you about or vice versa.

Continue to vibrate with this seed of Source consciousness. What are your areas of adeptness? What does this seed, or this blueprint, hold about the wholeness? A tomato seed becomes a tomato.

Akashic Record Two:
The Record of Your Divine Light Mission

Knowing that you are still multidimensionally connecting to this first Akashic Record of your Divine design, tune into a second record of your Divine light mission. You may have an awareness of a vibrational shift between the records; there is a different vibration that you tune into as you're connecting to the Divine light mission. What's your mission? Why are you here? What do you carry? Connect to this Akashic Record through your multidimensional awareness. *Know that you will continue to multidimensionally connect to this Akashic Record of your Divine light mission, knowing that it is also multidimensional—it is fluid, it is organic—just as your Divine design is. There are different cycles to it, there are different aspects to it, and there are evolutionary cycles within it.*

Akashic Record Three:
The Record of Your Choosing

Now bring your awareness to the third Akashic Record. This Akashic Record is unique to you, unique for you based on what you are choosing to access in this moment. What is this Akashic Record about? Connect to it through your Divine awareness, allow yourself to vibrate in proximity to it, so that it informs you. What record have you, at this time, asked to come forward? Perhaps it's your Divine genius. Perhaps it's about the merging of your Divine design and your Divine light mission, or next steps as to how to incarnate them more. Maybe it's something totally different—a past life memory of when you realized a Divine light mission, or a connection to a Being of Light, a loved one that may have transitioned out of body, or a Being of Light that is a part of your Divine team. This Akashic Record could be about the meeting of your Divine council, which is here to support you in the Divine mission and your Divine design. It may be something totally different.

Take some time to be with this Akashic Record. Allow it to inform you. What have you chosen to access from your Akashic Records?

Akashic Record Four:
Multidimensional Unity Consciousness

As you have received a download, an upload, an infusion from being within your Akashic Records, and these particular three Akashic Records, have an awareness and a sensation of the Records now shifting. That a fourth record comes forward, which is about unity consciousness. As this fourth record comes forward there may be additional Akashic records that come with it and also light up. These records are about this particular time in the evolution of Earth's consciousness. Have an awareness of these records being records pertaining to what it means to be incarnated with a Divine light mission, what it means to be a leader in this shift, to be a visionary, to be the pioneer into unity consciousness. Have an awareness of what the larger picture of that all is.

Now, in addition to the Akashic Records about unity consciousness, you may also have an awareness of what it's like to be living as you, expressing your Divine design, in a larger atmosphere of others expressing their Divine design, their light missions. Allow yourself to be informed what those practical, or tangible, experiences of living in unity consciousness are like. As the shift has been fully embodied by those who have chosen to fully embody it, what does that look like? What does that feel like for you? And also, what does that feel like on this universal level? What does it feel like on this intergalactic level? Multidimensional unity consciousness . . .

Now, taking all the time that you like to bask in these Akashic Records, slowly bring your awareness from the Akashic Records. Extend appreciation to yourself for what it is that you have chosen to access, and to the soul's incarnations, the Akashic Records, that have come forward to support you.

• • • • • • • • • •

Be in the Environment of Your Actualized Divine Design

Notice a shift in your environment once again. It is shifting from us being at this table with your Akashic Records to being in the environment of your actualized Divine design. As you come from within the Akashic Records to within your life, you're aware that these Akashic Records have now informed your life multidimensionally. They have been reconnected in alignment with your free will and conscious choice, to your Divine design, to your Divine light mission, to this awareness of living in unity consciousness. It is your choice to allow your life, to allow your incarnation, to be informed by who you are and why you are here, and the full actualization of that.

Take a few minutes to be aware of your environment as it's informed by your Divine light mission, by your Divine design, by unity consciousness. You may imagine it or sense it like a reorganization or a recalibration to that which is you, that which has meaning for you. This environment is calibrating more fully to what is uniquely you and yours. As such, some things are evolving, some things are falling away, and some things are revealing themselves to you. What are you aware of? What does your multidimensionally infused environment look like and feel like? What do you know about it? Bask, calibrate, actualize, and consecrate the divinely embodied light mission, the Divine design in its full beauty, in the larger environment of unity consciousness. Have a sense of your unique consciousness speaking to you. Breathe into it, vibrate with it, be within your illuminated consciousness within the environment of your spaciousness.

You may have the sensation of inhabiting the consciousness that you've had glimpses of. Now it's where you live. It's where you come from. That fierce longing to know the Divine that you've had for so long has now transcended into the knowing, into the embodiment of that fully calibrated connection, of that Divine Union.

There are not many words that are a part of this transmission. It is more the silent transmission, the energetic environment that also creates the actualization of what you have been leading up to for quite some time. There's the sense of being where you've wanted to be, being connected to who it is that you are, a coming home, a full embodiment, a calibration to your true north, to the Divine light within.

DIVINE MISSION HOOKUP

This Divine mission hookup calibration is one in which you may sense that what you had been seeking is now where you are living from—that you're in the vibrational proximity of that which you had been trying to get to. That gap between where you were and where you wanted to be becomes unified. You are now in union with the energies that you had associated with certain experiences in your life and the achieving of these experiences. Now you can have the experiences that are yours to be and do and have from a place of union, from a place of having the vibration within you already. Then it's for the fun of it that you experience it in a certain way.

If you thought that retiring would provide you the vibration or access to freedom, then you've embodied that freedom. You are in the same vibrational location as that freedom. Or perhaps you associated a certain goal in your life with a vibration in your awareness. As a result you are tapped into the wholeness of all that there is in this moment. You don't have to wait to experience whatever it was to have access to the vibration. You have access to the vibration now. Now your life has an openness to it—it has a pristine vibration to it. You are no longer creating to fill a void. You are no longer creating from lack or separation, or from survival.

Your creations, your choices, what you experience in your life—you're already connected to them and they're an emanation of the full calibration of your Divine Union and your Divine wholeness. The charge of what might have kept you separate, actually, from realizing what it is that you're choosing to actualize, is no longer there. You have unconditional living, multidimensional living, and multidimensional freedom. You are able to access all that there is within each and every moment of all that there is. There is a confidence, a certainty, and a joy to taking action, to creating things, to polishing your external environment. It is no longer coming from the sense that something is missing.

A full reunion with your Divine self has occurred. You will still continue to evolve, to desire, to reach new heights, yet the union, vibrationally, is calibrated. The joy of life, the brilliance of each moment, is also experienced more deeply by you and is absorbed more deeply by you.

We are choosing not to give specific examples in this moment—although there are many we could give—to allow it to stay in the calibration of unity, the calibration of infinite wholeness, the expansion and the reunion of it not being one thing. Instead it is all things. This is a demarcation point, a rite of passage, and a pivotal moment that touches everything. Divine Transmissions provides consciousness for an evolving YOUniverse—for an evolving you and an evolving universe. Continue to calibrate to this Divine Union to be in this wholeness, to own your reclaimed territory as Source in form. The form, the body, is no longer a barrier, or separate from Source. It is reintegrated; it is one and the same. Your life is no longer separate from Source; it is reintegrated, one and the same. It always was, yet the sensation of how you perceived it was as if there was a separation.

VIBRATION RAISING EXERCISE
· · · · · · · · · ·
Space to Integrate this Pivotal Experience

We would invite you to take five or ten minutes before moving on to the next segment to rest, to meditate, or to walk. Consciously give yourself space to integrate. Maybe you want to write about the Akashic Records you accessed. Then, after this break, continue on to the next segment if you are called to continue in this now moment. Or you may come back to it tonight, or in an hour, or tomorrow, or right after your break. Take the time to celebrate, integrate, and embody the vibrations that are accessed from this pivotal experience.

20
Signature Source Field
Living as the Divine Incarnate

BREATHING EXERCISE
Recalibrate Your Awareness to Being
the Divine Incarnate

Breathe your awareness into your calibrated Divine being-ness. Breathe your awareness into being the Divine incarnate, being the Being of Light that you are. As you deepen, expand, and breathe your awareness into your signature Source field, that embodiment of signature essence and Source consciousness, there is the possible sensation of recalibrating to your multidimensional awareness.

A TOOL FOR YOUR EVOLUTION
IN CONSCIOUSNESS

As you are becoming the fully remembered Divine incarnate, it is natural for there to be some sensations of adaptation. You may have moments of feeling wobbly or emotional. Bringing your awareness to your signature Source field and simultaneously into your signature energy and your connection to Source, instantly, if you allow it to, recalibrates you to your totality, to the full breadth and width of your Divine consciousness.

As you go into an emotion that creates a wobble in your system, in order to really spiral into it, you have to leave the multidimensional connection, to focus more on the dimension in which the emotional wobble resides within. All that there is exists within each and every moment. While the emotional wobble happens, there is also, still, your calibrated Divine essence—your wholeness and oneness. This is where your focus, your choice, and your experience of redirecting your consciousness come in. It's not to eliminate or get rid of the emotional wobble. It is to re-Source it into the ring of inclusion so that it's not separate from the wholeness.

It's as if you have a herd of sheep and the herd of sheep is in one field next to the river. The sheep are drinking by the river, and one sheep separates from the herd for whatever reason. That sheep is alone, and it's out of connection to the entire herd. Then the sheepdogs and the shepherd go and collect this sole sheep and bring it back into the fold, back into the oneness, back where there's the totality of all that there is.

As you go into a slower vibrational dimension you separate from the Source consciousness that you are, in its totality. It can't ever be separate, yet your experience of it is separate. Expanding the signature Source field allows you to include the wobble, reconnect the wobble, take it from the illusion that it's separate, and bring it back into the oneness.

Allow this segment and the amplification of your signature Source field to provide a reintegration of any vibrations that are in that wobble, or that are moving more slowly. As you are calibrating once again to the Divine oneness of all that there is, there is a sensation of enhanced stability, enhanced wholeness, and enhanced awareness.

Breathe into this signature Source field, if you choose. After the previous segment of Divine calibration and connecting directly to your Akashic Records of your Divine design and your Divine light mission, there is an enhanced connection that has been made, a recalibration of all that there is. As stated, sometimes after that can be this sensation of the wobble. Now that the wobble, if there was one, has been inte-grated, have an awareness of tuning back into your signature Source field, that nexus place where you are simultaneously connected to your unique Divine design and the universal Divine design. Here you are simultaneously connected to your signature essence and Source. Here is where you are simultaneously connected to your signature Source field, the field of frequency and vibration that is emanating from your fully embodied essence, re-Sourced.

Here there is an incredible elixir of potency, an incredible elixir of potency. It's like this magic consciousness, this magic awareness that is you and moves through and around you gets broadcasted through your fully re-Sourced signature Source field in a very potent way. Breathe into the universal light of this potent elixir, the emanation of your particular blended consciousness that is unique and re-Sourced. As you know, you're always broadcasting through light, through frequencies, through vibra-tions. You're always receiving through light, through frequencies, through vibrations. This potent elixir that is your signature Source field, which resides within your signature Source field, is where you are aware of the light and the frequency that you're transmitting in its rarified form.

As you bask in this rarified light that you're emanating, that you're broadcasting, that you're transmitting, have an awareness that the uni-verse is in constant communication with that signature Source field, that rarified light. You are transmitting now, based on your choice to do so, from the level of your Divine design and from the level of your Divine light mission, and from the level of your universal Divine design. You are transmitting as the Divine incarnate being. It is a clear signal now. It is a clear signal now, one in which you are aware of what is broadcasted, what is vibrated, and what is emanated.

YOU HAVE A ONE-OF-A-KIND LIFE EXPERIENCE

This is what creates the one of one, the capacity to be incarnated on the Earth with many, many, many, many, many other beings that are incarnated on the Earth, and yet you are in your own universe. You have your own unique experience. It is this signature, and now the signature Source field, that is that blueprint, or that origin, that Source, which the universe co-creates with you from. There is a sense of the illumination, the expansion, the clarity of the signal.

Then that which is a part of that signature Source field is what is a part of your life—nothing more, nothing less. You can trust what is in your life. Spend some more moments tuning into this potent, rarified vibration of your signature Source field and that which you emanate, and broadcast from it the highly concentrated elixir of you. Be in the highly concentrated elixir of you.

You have a sense, perhaps, that the universe is responding vibrationally to this signature Source field. Beautiful. That you have put out the call for the perfect people, places, and things to become part of your life. This consciousness guides your interaction with your incarnated life.

You may have had experiences where it seems that, against all odds, something extraordinary happens in your life. Maybe you meet the love of your life in a seemingly random way. Perhaps you both weren't planning to be at the location where you met, or you came from other parts of the world, or you'd been a part of each other's lives since you were kids. Or you may have other examples that illuminate what we're speaking of here. What's yours is yours and can't be anyone else's. If something leaves your life, then that time that it was yours—and by *yours* we mean it's been in vibrational proximity to you—that time that it was in vibrational proximity to you, has come to a place of completion, or it's come to a place of shifting.

Have a sense of the holographic evolutionary web that is vibrating with this signature Source light, with this potent elixir. Now tune into your multidimensional experience of what you might have thought of as the universe conspiring for your benefit, or Divine order, or that like attracts like, or that your vibrational signal sends out a broadcast and that which is a vibrational match for that broadcast comes into your life. Bring your awareness to all that falls under this category of Divine matching. Now, if you choose it to, allow your consciousness to expand beyond the people, places, and things in your life, to the multidimensionality of these people, places, and things. Now through your expanded awareness tune into your connection to a broader awareness of wholeness, to the totality of all there is.

Each cell within your body houses all that there is—the entire universe, the entire Earth. You have trillions of cells in your body that make up your body, each with a nucleus, each with a center. In the same way that there are trillions of cells in your body, you and others who have incarnated into bodies on the planet make up the global population. Earth is like a cell in the larger multiverse. Just as a widespread communication can happen, can be broadcasted from your pituitary gland to all cells in your body simultaneously, you also have this potency within your signature Source field. It's not just that you are communicating, or multidimensionally broadcasting with what is in your neighborhood, or with what is on the planet, it expands beyond that to the multiverse.

That is a part of this broader shift in consciousness that Earth has evolved to be in—that Earth has jumped dimensions to be in closer proximity to other solar systems. This transmitting and receiving goes both ways. There is also this capacity for you, now, to receive the wisdom from other galaxies and other Beings of Light. Just as this book of Thoth is happening, there are these access points as well in which a conversation like this is possible, yet the origin of all that there is, is the origin of all that there is. It's not located in what you would call physical space. It's like the pituitary gland of God, of Source, broadcasting this message to all that there is. Now it is possible to live as Source.

That is the choice that each person has. Earth has chosen to actualize that possibility. It is a part of her Divine design, just as it is a part of your Divine design. Whatever Source means to you—it could be God, it could be nature, it could be harmony, it could be peace—this grand awakening is inhabiting the light body, the fully turned-on Source light, the signature Source field, and the capacity to operate on all of those vibrational connector points to Source. It's as if a fleet of boats was coming in to dock. If you had only one dock open, all of those boats would have to wait to offload what they were carrying. There is only one access point to bring the goods from the ocean into the harbor, and it's this one dock. But if you have as many docks as you do boats, then the fleet can land all at once and bring all that there is from the ocean. It can bring its cargo to be utilized, to be shared.

This is the same with you. It's like moving from one dock—that which you would consider the physical world, or your third-dimensional awareness of being body, mind, emotions, spirit—to opening up the multidimensional access points, to connecting in, and as, and with Source consciousness. As you have more dimensions available to you, there are more of these lock and key bases. It's like that, again, with the cells. The cells in the body have this way of communicating at the level of the cellular membrane. There are thresholds that are crossed. There is an exchange that happens. Both sides of the key of that mechanism have to be healthy, or fully functioning. It's the same with an expanded awareness of living as signature Source field. As this elixir that you are invited to tap into, this highly refined residence emanates now, you can have a sense of light rushing toward you, and light rushing from you, emanating from you.

We know that it's tempting at times to go back into more unidimensional living, or less-dimensional living, because it's familiar, because it's comfortable, because you have the old codons of collective consciousness reminding you that this was the way you lived for so long. We know it can be tempting at times to go back into that familiar illusion, yet don't. Utilize this inner desire that you've had for so long to know what it's like to be fully connected to Source, and then, now that you are, allow yourself the experience of it. Allow yourself the experience of basking in it, discovering it, noticing it, and living from it.

This potent elixir is like this tractor beam of light that is broadcasting your Divine light mission, your Divine design as Source consciousness incarnate, out into the universe. Then, all the millions of facets of bringing that forward are rushing toward you in Divine order.

SEPARATION CONSCIOUSNESS EXPERIENCES

Sometimes there are things that will happen that you just scratch your head about. You may wonder, "Well, why did that happen?" Especially now that you're feeling so re-Sourced. Why would an experience of separation consciousness happen? Well, it is that choice, once again, to stay in the dimensions of all that there is, or to separate back into the illusion. Sometimes what you could perceive as separation consciousness experiences or unpreferred experiences happen. This is not a test—because we know that that's a part of the collective consciousness as well, to think that you're being tested—but it's not a test.

It's connected to what you may not be totally aware of in the moment, especially as it relates to others on their path. That may have been a part of your soul agreement before coming into this lifetime, that you were willing to play the role of some seemingly separation consciousness experience with someone else. That is where your life that is absolutely divinely designed by you has these moments that they're not about you; they are about you being in the perfect place and time for somebody else. That is what we mean by it's not always a direct indication or correlation of your consciousness, or what's going on in your consciousness.

For example, let's say you have a business deal with someone and you've signed a contract. You're providing something—a service or a building or something for the person—and then halfway through the contract or halfway through the lease, that person doesn't follow through on the contract, or they move out. If you've rented them a place, they break the lease. Now, that's probably an unpreferred experience because it appeared that you had a contract. You had the money, you had the renter, and it was a done deal.

You could interpret that as "What did I do wrong? Where in my vibration was I still in separation conscious that then I manifested this separation consciousness?" Yet sometimes the thing isn't about the thing. Sometimes this is an opportunity for you, the aspect of it that it has to do with you, to vibrate grace, to vibrate trust, to just let it move on through and not make it a big deal. That person who you had some agreement with is a part of a larger picture that you may not be tuned into. You may just respond and let the deal fizzle out. It doesn't mean that you're disempowered, or that you got taken advantage of, or any of those things. And you may choose to not let it fizzle out.

Our point in providing an example like this is that sometimes when something happens that is unpreferred, it also allows you to recognize your evolution: how you might have responded to it previously, how many days it might have spun you out in your emotions. Yet now that you have remembered and accessed your Divine Union you come back to Source much quicker and then you just keep going in unity consciousness.

Now, as you tune into your signature Source field, your Divine calibration, and the highly refined energies that you have access to, have an awareness of the signature Source field of Earth, the Being of Light that is Earth. Notice as she has resurrected her light body. Notice as she is vibrating her signature essence in its current evolutionary consciousness and reconnected to Source, that you can see or feel this, or know this beautiful, refined energy—the field of light around her, the web that she is broadcasting.

With your signature Source field and this signature Source field of Earth, have an awareness of a multidimensional communication happening, what you could call "off planet." There are some vibrations and frequencies and resonances that had not been on Earth that are now coming to Earth, that are now a part of the evolution in consciousness.

If you think about fifty years ago, one of the experiences that a child growing up fifty years ago might have had was that their immediate environment and culture was where their food would have come from. Americans would eat American food. Italians would eat Italian food. Thai people would eat Thai food. Indian people would eat Indian food. It was just that way. Now, the ingredients, the food, the exposure, what you can get in your grocery store year round, depending on where you live, is infinite. Those ingredients, they were somewhere. That cocoa bean, it existed already, but in this example it wasn't part of this child's life.

It's not that these vibrations that are now available are new. Instead it's that they were in a different atmosphere, a different vibrational location. Some people talk about this as pockets of energy, or vortices, of civilizations such as Mu and Lemuria, where this vibration of love and authenticity has been the norm. Now Earth is vibrating to be in relationship with these pockets of energy. Yet we're speaking about what has existed beyond the central sun, within other light spheres, within other Divine incarnations, within other Beings of Light.

There are also some vibrations that have been "on planet" that are also going "off planet." They are no longer necessary for the evolution of Earth's consciousness. It's what you experience sometimes when a way of thinking that you had is no longer the way that you think, or an old pattern is no longer the current pattern. Future generations can learn from separation consciousness as it goes back in the oneness, back in the wholeness, back into all that there is.

There are some flowers or plants that require a certain environment in order to thrive. You can't put an orchid in the fire and expect it to live or in the freezer and expect it to live. Some species, or plants, or flowers, or crops, or food sources, are sensitive or more particular than others. Then there are others that are hardy, more universal—places with varying climates can have them. Then there are others that are *so* sensitive that really they can only be in a particular environment.

As you may remember from our opening, that which is new and innovative is also old and ancient. Thus some of these—what we are calling new—very highly refined vibrations that had been "off planet" that are now available to come "on planet" are only able to do so because they reside in multidimensional planes. Their environment to thrive is the signature Source field. These high vibrations don't thrive in fear.

It's not only about thriving or not thriving. We use that example in nature to provide an example of a climate change, an environment change, a change in vibration on the planet, yet it's also the vibrational accessibility. When something is in a certain dimension, that's the vibration and dimension that it's related to, and that's where you have to go to connect to it.

RECOGNIZING THE FULL AND ENSOULED CONSCIOUSNESS IN ALL THINGS

We know at times that we're speaking at high levels of abstraction. However, they may not be high levels of abstraction for you; it may be exactly your language and make sense. Yet as we're talking about vibration, frequency, dimensions, multidimensionality, and signature Source field, and all of these things, there may be these moments where a dimension within you wonders, "Well, how do I relate to that?" or "What does that mean for my life right here, right now?" We're saying that this multidimensional living is why consciousness is the subject of this book, it's why Divine consciousness and the re-resurrection of Divine consciousness is what is happening on the larger scale in the shift of consciousness. This has everything to do with your life here on Earth. It has everything to do with your incarnation here on Earth. Because then you're operating wholeness-to-wholeness, multidimensionality-to-multidimensionality.

There is so much more to connect to when the full and ensouled consciousness of Divine Source light is recognized in each and every moment and each and every thing. There is then a life-force energy that you connect to on multidimensional levels. When you speak to someone, you're not only speaking to them in the words that you're exchanging, you are also receiving and transmitting on this multidimensional level. There is a connection to their soul, to their Divine design, to their Divine light mission. It's a broader perspective.

As you actualize something—like money, for example—you're not just connecting to the paper or the coins of the money. You're also tapping into the Divine design, the Divine light mission, in this new paradigm of money. There is more that you are able to connect to. There are more boats. There's a wider perspective. There's a multidimensionality in the wholeness of everything. Being in separation, being in duality, created the limited experience of connecting to things from a fraction of the totality of what was there.

It's as if your grandmother or great-grandmother could not have cooked with spices that weren't from her region, and then during her lifetime she could. If she had the proclivity, she could have access to those spices that were beyond her region. That is the same with you on Earth, now having access to what existed in other regions vibrationally. You're not only a global connector, but also a galactic being on Earth. The visionary, the pioneer, is tapping into that which had been uncharted territories in terms of your immediate vicinity, although you have always had a proclivity to that which has been out of this world. Now there is a communion beyond what was possible before. Now there are these relationships that are being formed with Beings of Light, such as me, Thoth, and such as the Council of Light. For some of you, that is the partnering that is now available, which provides that exchange of the evolution in consciousness and growth to occur.

It's as if you lived in Idaho and you wanted to learn how to be an international fashion designer or an astronaut; you may seek out the schools where you could learn that vocation. You might go to a fashion-design school in another state or another county. You might seek your astronaut schooling in a different state. There was a previous stage in consciousness where some of the energies that were on Earth were put somewhere else for safekeeping. Now you, as this incarnated Being of Light, recognize that your adeptness, and your Divine design, and your Divine light mission is requiring you in your multidimensionality to go beyond the school of Earth to tap into other resources of learning and consciousness tools. Those learning and consciousness tools are also coming back to Earth, through you, through Divine Transmissions, through this book. What had been carried to Earth and left on Earth is now awakening. What had been dormant within you, within sacred sites or physical locations, is awakening.

Breathe your awareness into your signature Source field, into this potent elixir. Have an awareness of the interchange with your multi-dimensional signature Source field and that which is a match for your Divine design and your Divine light mission. This sense of broadcasting and receiving may be beyond the beyond, which you've never experienced before. You may have a sensation of consciousness tools and spiritual technologies rushing in from "off planet," or places around the Earth that are wakening up in response to your asking, in response to your calling. You are a catalyst.

CONCLUSION

Embodied Divine

AMPLIFICATION, FLOW, LIGHTENING

Your vibration is not the same as it was when we began this conversation within the walls of this temple of *The Tablets of Light*. Your vibration is not the same as it was. Your vibration is now uniquely you and yours. Vibrational autonomy has been accessed. The amplification of your signature energy and your Divine design has been amplified. There is universal flow of consciousness. This universal flow of consciousness is in the awareness of your highly attuned vibration and orientation to your Divine autonomy, your individualized oneness.

This can feel like a lightening up of all that there is. This can feel like a lightening up of your previous vibrational set point to be flowing more in the universal light, the universal love, and the consciousness of all that there is. As *The Tablets of Light* is coming toward a place of verbal completion in that you have reached the end of these segments, these installments, the energy continues on.

This conversation has been just that: a conversation. A conversation can include many subjects. It can spiral and pivot from one to the other. There's an awareness of each word and each unit of consciousness in each block of consciousness being one that amplifies the others—whether they were read first or whether they were read last or whether they were read in the middle.

We have intentionally not followed a normal format of a clear beginning, middle, and end of a certain linear subject. For the begin-

270

ning, the middle, and end in and of itself is tied to the old paradigm of how it is that you would experience yourself in consciousness. We have been thrumming together, plucking together the Divine heartstrings of your eternal nature, of your Divine awakening. That transcends any beginning, middle, and end.

WHOLENESS

Wholeness exists within each moment. Wholeness is present in every transition from one chapter to the next, from the beginning of the book to the end of the book, from one day to the next, from one lifetime to the next. Wholeness is the constant. Wholeness is the ever present awareness of all that there is.

We have also been awakening together the memory of being fully engaged in your experience of life. As you engage in these words, and in this consciousness, and in this book, in this conversation, and then in your life in between the words and the pages, there's an enhanced level of you vibrationally showing up, of you being engaged in your life in a much more present way, a much more forward-facing way.

Bring your awareness to your capacity of your awakened Divine Union and consciously complete this book with wholeness, with the accessing of your Divine Union capacity fully turned on. Doing so allows you to access and come into union with what you may not have accessed or come into union with up until this point. This is a continuation of your having a new relationship with time and space.

You used to operate from having the sensation that something's available in a moment and then it's no longer available if it wasn't received in that moment, that you lost your chance so to speak. Because wholeness is the thread of each and every moment, you can in this moment, through the thread of wholeness, circle back if you will, to an earlier segment in this book and access more of what was there because now you have an enhanced multidimensionality.

AMPLIFICATION

As you're accessing more of what it is that you may not have accessed previously because you have more multidimensionality available to you, have the awareness as well that our purpose together has been the Divine hookup, the Divine awakening, the Divine incarnation, the Divine incarnate.

We haven't been focusing on how to implement, for example, your Divine design or how to live or express your Divine light mission. Instead we have been amplifying the energies of your Divine design, your Divine light mission, and your signature energy. From that impulse of creation, as the awakened creator being that you are, your life then overflows into creation. It overflows into the next evolution.

For example, if you have a water spigot that goes into a tub or a basin or a stone pool, and connected to it is a waterway, a long pathway of water. It's less effective to turn on the faucet for a few drops and then try to put the drops of water in the trajectory of the water. You can imagine how water was transported in previous times. You could take a few drops of water and then you could say, "Okay, here are the five steps to get these drops of water into the trajectory of water so that it goes into another place and then it becomes something."

You could do that yet it's less efficient. It's more efficient to fill up the basin, fill up the basin, fill up the basin, fill up the basin. Then as the basin is full it naturally opens this flap that then channels the water into the trajectory. Then the water circulates, the water moves, there's momentum. It doesn't just spill out the sides because there's a strong container.

That's also what you've recreated through *The Tablets of Light*—a strong container of your individuality, of your signature essence, of your life. Then it flows when there are no longer any obstructions and everything is smooth. In this, you amplify, you amplify, you amplify, you amplify, you amplify, you amplify the water. You turn on the water then it overflows, then it's that next natural step. It's not striving, struggling, or forcing.

It's almost like you can't help yourself. It's almost instinctual of this Divine knowing. You find yourself somewhere without even really having preconceived that you would be there. It is this positioning of each moment, which is also a recalibration of your relationship with time. In the past there would be a sensation of anticipating where you might be in five years or trying to make a plan in advance. Then your life would feel so scheduled or so dry. Or there wouldn't be this space, this luxuriousness for life to surprise you. Or there wouldn't be an interaction between you and the universe, which is bringing to you, in reflection, your unique Divine design and your access to the universal Divine design—your Divine light mission bringing to you those perfect people, places, and opportunities.

Now that there is this space and this flowing, as the water is flowing and it's flowing and it's flowing, it's in the channel. Then at one point it may be that the channel turns or it goes in a different direction. Or it builds up in another pool somewhere else and that pool builds and builds and builds and builds and builds and builds. It includes more and it includes more and it includes more until then it's on again. There's another launch, there's another trajectory, there's another buildup of momentum. Then it pulses out. It pulses out.

THE NATURAL RHYTHM OF CYCLES

There's also the restoration of your Divine nature in relationship to cycles. Let's take the example of an orange tree. When it's barely grown it doesn't try to force out the oranges. It's not overflowing into that next step. If it were to have oranges when it was barely sprouting it would fall over. There wouldn't be enough energy. It just wouldn't be the next natural evolution of the cycle. As you're in each moment of that next evolution of your soul's remembering, and your actualization of being the Divine incarnate, then you're also informed in the moment. You're informed in the moment.

We know that you'll continue to plan. It's not that you don't plan things or you don't schedule things in advance. It's that you're fresh in the moment. When you arrive you're clear, you're paying attention, you're noticing the synchronicities, you're seeing what would feel like that next natural step. There is then the quantum evolution that occurs through this positioning of living as the Divine incarnate and as the creator being in that you're creating moment to moment to moment to moment to moment.

If you were going to have your family come visit you or a group of friends come visit you and they were going to stay for a month you wouldn't cook all the meals a month in advance. You wouldn't do all of the shopping a month in advance. You wouldn't sleep for the whole month a month in advance. It doesn't work that way. It's not unfolding that way.

There's also a rhythm reflected in your brilliant system. In your brilliant system there is one moment of wholeness to the next moment of wholeness to the next moment of wholeness to the next moment of wholeness to the next moment of wholeness. Then there's a next natural step, the next part of the cycle. Something begins, something grows, and something ends. Even in this cycle it is never outside of the wholeness. The wholeness resides through each of those aspects of the cycle.

In addition to your vibration not being the same as it was when we began this journey together, there is also the recalibration to your Divine being-ness, and therefore the infusion of that divinity and that calibration of your Divine design, your Divine light mission. Then it naturally unfolds into action, into action. There's the impulse for the inspired action. There's the knowing of the inspired action. It's not hollow. It's replenished, rejuvenated, fulfilled. It's a strong pulsing; it's a strong pulsing.

You're buoyed; you're riding the current of Divine love. You're riding the current of your Divine currency, being current with the Divine. Then you're in what appear to be the parts of your life that are not segmented any longer or not separate anymore. For the common denominator in all aspects of your life is Divine Union, is your signature Source field. It is wholeness.

As we're speaking, there's an invitation of your fully turned-on capacity to access through Divine Union anything that you haven't accessed from this book. Now you're choosing to access it on a multi-dimensional level. Now you're able to access it on a multidimensional level. You may find moving forward that you're drawn to open this book again. To, as it completes, start it again. If you were to do that, if you were to do that, you would realize the difference of who it is that you are now as you're going through the pages again, as you're walking through the tablets again, as you're journeying through the multidimensional consciousness again.

If you were a key and *The Tablets of Light* has been fine-tuning this key, if you go through it again you would open up more dimensions. You could also have this book by your bedside table or on your reading table or somewhere where you go frequently and open it up. Open it up and read a few words. As you open it up and read a few words it's like pulling a Tarot card for the day. It's like going into the hologram of wholeness with a few vibrational drops of consciousness, a few words.

We invite you to celebrate your Divine awakening, for we are celebrating with you. It has been something that has been led up to by you and through you for many lifetimes.

All is well and you are all.

Divine Transmissions
Offerings

This is Thoth, the Council of Light, and the Divine Light Activation Sequence that are moving more into the forefront of this Divine Transmission. The purpose of this transmission is to place energies, consciousness, and offerings onto the altar of the heart for you to vibe into to see if they are yours to be, do, and have or not.

We at Divine Transmissions are available to continue our multidimensional conversation in a variety of ways. We know that these offerings are in response to your asking, in response to your calling, and as such they are like treasures that you have been looking for on your treasure hunt of evolution. Sometimes you are clear about what is on your treasure-hunt list and sometimes you aren't clear on what it is that you are looking for until you find it. We would invite you to tune into vibrationally recognizing if these are gifts you have left for yourself to find at this time.

We are choosing to mention three ways of engaging more deeply with me, Thoth, and the Divine Transmissions Council of Light. You can find out more about how we can support you in being your multidimensional, fully embodied Divine self below and by visiting our website, **www.divinetransmissions.com**.

THOTH'S MAGIC ACADEMY

Be You Full-Out Anchored in Unity
Consciousness Video Program

This year-and-a-day journey is one in which we have daily contact through video transmissions, the purpose of which is multidimensional. Firstly, to gift yourself with an environment that fosters your connection to Source as a top priority in your life. Secondly, to include all slower vibrational and separation consciousness energies—such as playing small, seeking approval, and fear of visibility—into the wholeness as rocket fuel for your evolution in consciousness. Thirdly, to amplify who you are and what you are here to be, do, and have in this incarnation. There is more to be garnered from being in unity consciousness (joy, abundance, and unity) than repeating another repetitive pattern of separation consciousness (fear, doubt, and lack). Thoth's Magic Academy is a pathway to shift out of separation and into unity permanently.

DIVINE LIGHT ACTIVATION

An Evolutionary Sequence of 22 Light Activations to Actualize
the Vision that You Carry as a Being of Light Incarnate—
Reunited with Multidimensional Cosmic Consciousness

The Divine Light Activation is a 22-light activation sequence that we, Thoth and the Council of Light, are transmitting for the purpose of initiating the return of the Divine wholeness on Earth. Those that are called to partner with us in this initiation sequence will have been on a journey of evolution and devotion that spans across this lifetime to past and future lifetimes. Being you as the Being of Light incarnate is an awakening of your origin Source codes, a preparing of your system and your incarnation to embody your Divine design, and it is a *choice*. We are placing the Divine Light Activation on the altar of the heart for you to choose or not.

IN-DEPTH 1:1 DIVINE PARTNERSHIP

Co-create with Thoth and the Council of Light

This in-depth partnership with us is a potent environment of being matched Being of Light to Being of Light. Our focus together is bespoken to you as the creator being you are based on the oracular vision you carry. We will serve as midwife in supporting you in birthing your unique contribution into the world. This partnership opens up the areas of ascended mastery of the lineage of Thoth: scribe, Akashic Records, merchant priestess, magic, alignment (healing), divination, and sacred architecture.

We would also place our other books *The Temples of Light* and *The Council of Light* on the altar. You are invited to connect deeper with us on a journey of evolution in consciousness through joining the mission of Divine Transmissions to resurrect the living Divine incarnate.

ALL IS WELL AND YOU ARE ALL,

THOTH, THE COUNCIL OF LIGHT,

AND THE DIVINE LIGHT ACTIVATION SEQUENCE

To explore the treasures listed above and to find out about new offerings please contact me, Danielle Rama Hoffman, and my team, care of our website:

www.divinetransmissions.com

Or e-mail us at:

Danielle@divinetransmissions.com

Index

About the Author

Danielle Rama Hoffman is an innovator, scribe, and creator of Divine Transmissions. Through her direct connection with Thoth and the Council of Light she transmits energy and consciousness for the purpose of shifting from separation consciousness (fear, lack, and disconnection) into unity consciousness (love, abundance, and connection). Danielle specializes in helping light workers, change agents, coaches, and spiritual-growth enthusiasts bring in bodies of work (books, businesses, and creations) direct from Source. The author of *The Council of Light* and *The Temples of Light* and creator of life-enhancing programs such as Thoth's Magic Academy and Scribe It in southern France, she has more than twenty-four years of experience in the healing arts. Danielle lives in France with her husband, Dr. Friedemann Schaub, five cats, and three horses, and enjoys hiking, being in nature, and communing with Beings of Light from across the multiverse.

BOOKS OF RELATED INTEREST

The Council of Light
Divine Transmissions for Manifesting the Deepest Desires of the Soul
by Danielle Rama Hoffman

The Temples of Light
An Initiatory Journey into the Heart Teachings
of the Egyptian Mystery Schools
by Danielle Rama Hoffman
Foreword by Nicki Scully

The Anubis Oracle
A Journey into the Shamanic Mysteries of Egypt
by Nicki Scully and Linda Star Wolf, Ph.D.
Illustrated by Kris Waldherr

Bringers of the Dawn
Teachings from the Pleiadians
by Barbara Marciniak

Earth
Pleiadian Keys to the Living Library
by Barbara Marciniak

The Pleiadian Workbook
Awakening Your Divine Ka
by Amorah Quan Yin

The Pleiadian Agenda
A New Cosmology for the Age of Light
by Barbara Hand Clow

The Pleiadian House of Initiation
A Journey through the Rooms of the Wisdomkeepers
by Mary T. Beben
Foreword by Barbara Hand Clow

INNER TRADITIONS • BEAR & COMPANY
P.O. Box 388 • Rochester, VT 05767
1-800-246-8648 • www.InnerTraditions.com

Or contact your local bookseller